Basic Facts of Digital Library

Basic Facts of Digital Library

M. Ram

RANDOM

RANDOM PUBLICATIONS

NEW DELHI (INDIA)

Basic Facts of Digital Library

ISBN 978-93-5111-849-7

Published in 2016 in India by
RANDOM PUBLICATIONS

4376-A/4B, Gali Murari Lal, Ansari Road
New Delhi-110 002
Phone : +9111-43580356, 011-23289044, 011-43142548
e-mail: sales@randompublications.com,
info@randompublications.com, randomexports@gmail.com

Reprint 2021

Type Setting by : Friends Media, Delhi-110089
Digitally Printed at: Replika Press Pvt. Ltd.

Preface

A Digital Library is a special library with a focused collection of digital objects that can include text, visual material, audio material, video material, stored as electronic media formats, along with means for organizing, storing, and retrieving the files and media contained in the library collection. Digital libraries can vary immensely in size and scope, and can be maintained by individuals, organizations, or affiliated with established physical library buildings or institutions, or with academic institutions.

The electronic content may be stored locally, or accessed remotely via computer networks. An electronic library is a type of information retrieval system. The technology used to create digital libraries is even more revolutionary for archives since it breaks down the second and third of these general rules. In other words, "digital archives" or "online archives" will still generally contain primary sources, but they are likely to be described individually rather than in groups or collections. Further, because they are digital, their contents are easily reproducible and may indeed have been reproduced from elsewhere. The Oxford Text Archive is generally considered to be the oldest digital archive of academic physical primary source materials.

– Author

Contents

1

The Role of Libraries in Modern Society

First, the general development of the information society is pushing to re-evaluation of all the institutions which work with information, data, and knowledge-indirectly also with culture. In this connection the roles of education and media have been discussed already quite largely also in the European Union.

But libraries-as well as other memory institutions like archives and museums-have not been considered. Still, there is a clear need in the information society to maintain an institution which is concentrating in collecting and organizing information and offering general access to it. Until now, this work has been underestimated, but I argue the situation will change! Libraries are especially important now when the whole idea of education is stressing more and more independent learning and acting.

All citizens must be able to find and use information. It is the key raw material-but it is a zero resource, if there are no access points to it and if documents are in chaotic order.

Here we can see libraries enter the stage:

- The unique function of libraries is to acquire, organize, offer for use and preserve publicly available material irrespective of the form in which it is packaged in such a way that, when it is needed, it can be found and put to use. No other institution carries out this long-term, systematic work. Culture must be nominated especially: it has an important and unique role in mobilizing resources of human beings. It has been described: To some extent, culture makes its influence felt more indirectly than knowledge, but it is impossible to imagine how people's creative powers could be fully activated without the impact of culture, which extends into the depths of the mind.

The challenge to modern societies is that the basic resource, knowledge, is developing from information in very individual, capricious and unpredictable process. It cannot be commanded. Still, societies can support this development, *e.g.* by offering access to cultural and knowledge treasures.

This can even be translated into economic language: to get out the best from the human resources in Europe, this resource must be feeded up with rich and various cultural and infor-mation contents! I would like to stress especially the idea of organizing information by libraries. It is often shadowed by the second important side of library work: offering access. But in the life-long learning and new technology context just all forms of organizing documents are getting more to the focus. This is clear to anybody who has tried to find something from not-so-often-used Internet websites.

NEW LINES IN THE EU-AND IN THE UNITED STATES

In accordance with these phenomenons, there are new political lines in the European Union: The Maastricht Treaty in 1992 launched the cultural aspects. This was only after a long discussion, which made it clear that we have to remember to separate the national view and the European view. The Amsterdam Treaty in 1997 declared citizenship as an important theme. A significant part of this are a.o. granting information skills and access to information to every European.

In addition to this, the European future strategies need to meet the democratic aspects of the information society development. One of the crucial points is again general access to information. Libraries, especially public libraries, are a good tool in all of these new areas.

But the European union does not support whichever cultural or citizen concentrated projects in Europe.In the interests of the European Union there is always to find the European element. So, what can be done in library policy on the European level, taking in account that libraries are primarily a part of national education and cultural policies? *The own-initiative report "The role of libraries in modern societies," adopted by the European Parliament in October 1998, is the first effort to answer these questions.*

The same topics have been discussed in the United States. They have reached the point where especially the problems of those lacking access to digital resources have been studied. The report Falling Through the Net: Defining the Digital Divide by the U.S. Department of Commerce was released earlier in July 1999.

The report finds that minorities, low-income persons, the less educated, and children of single parent households, particularly when they reside in rural areas or central cities, are risk groups. The report calls for public policies and private initiatives to expand affordable access to critical information resources. But it also shows,, for the first time as far as I know, that libraries and community centres really can diminish the information gap between haves and not-haves.

The 1998 data from the U.S. demonstrates very clearly that community access centers, primarily public libraries, are particularly well used by those groups who lack access at home or at work: *e.g.* unemployed groups used Internet in libraries three times as often as an average citizen.

EARLIER ACTIONS IN EU

In the European Union, there have been some efforts to mobilize "the treasures of the European libraries" since the mid-80'ies. These discussions and resolutions led to two special library programmes under the 3rd and 4th Framework programmes of research and development. The later programme has been known as "Telematics for Libraries".

They have been strongly concentrated in IT, because it has been seen as a good tool to produce better access to the existing, underused library resources. These programmes have had a clear impact in the European library co-operation and development. Benefits of this work come to public libraries indirectly: common standards and working methods help in the end all kind of libraries.

But a fact is, that nearly all the libraries active in these EU projects are national libraries or big research and university libraries. Two main exceptions are Publican, a network of European public libraries, and ECUP, which was a copyright awareness raising project, and reached public libraries as well. A new beginning was the so called Morgan report in 1997. In this report libraries were for the first time put clearly onto the place where they belong in the information society. As one result of the Morgan report, the European Commission informed that it will produce a Green Paper about the role of libraries in the information society. For one or another reason, this was made quite ready but was never published. In this situation the Committee on Culture, Youth, Education and the Media in the European Parliament decided to produce an own-initiative report about libraries.

The main reason was that they wanted to influence the big issues under work in the EU, first of all the copyright directive and the 5th framework programme, which will have a direct impact to libraries. I was nominated the rapporteur of the own-initiative report. The report was adopted almost unanimously and with a very encouraging discussion in the Plenary session of the Parliament in October 1998.

DECISIONS OF THE EP CONCERNING LIBRARY POLICY

In short, when adopting the own-initiative report, the EP was calling the Commission and/or the member states to following actions:

- Libraries must be taken in account in national and EU information society strategies and in the respective budgets.
- Libraries need more resources for acquiring expensive books.
- The Green Paper on libraries by the Commission must be completed.
- The users position must be taken in account in the copyright directive process, the balance must be maintained-this was politically the most important decision in short run.
- Support to libraries was demanded from the 5th Framework programme of research and development, *e.g.* for networking,

drafting standards, preserving, and transferring information; there is no more named library programme under the 5th framework programme

- A clearing-house to solve problems of long-term conservation should be founded.
- Studies concerning permanent paper should be done on European level.
- The member states should take care of digitizing their cultural heritage for future.
- There should be studies and concrete support to libraries in licensing matters, which are–will be the next big issue in library work.
- The EU cultural and information budget should be opened to libraries as well, libraries and their co-operation should be taken in account in planning new programmes.
- Problems of legal deposit in international and multinational materials, especially in electronic materials should be solved.
- The member states should provide all types of libraries with modern equipment, particularly with Internet connections.
- Free of charge use of public libraries, in the spirit of the UNESCO Public Library Manifest, was demanded.
- Free and easy access via libraries to material produced with the aid of tax revenues was demanded.
- The members states should organize for their library professionals up-dating education and training.
- A European Union focal point for libraries should be set up
- The member states should found European information points at libraries in countries where they do not yet exist.
- Library statistics should be better and more comparable both on national and European level.
- The national Parliament libraries should be opened to the MEP's in countries where this is not yet the practice.

In addition to these, the report strongly stresses that the library financing must be re-thought in the information society. Without new resources libraries are unable to do everything they are expected to do! After the EP adoption of this report, the European Commission informed that it will next prepare a communication about actions to do.

It was stated that the report had already served as a discussion paper, and so the need for the Green Paper had disappeared. The communication is in summer 1999 still under work in the Commission DGXIII/2.

TRADITIONS AND NEW FORMS OF WORK IN THE SAME HOUSE

The European Commission R&D framework programmes have concentrated in IT matters. The three cultural programmes, Caledoskope,

Ariane and Raphael, have not been very useful for libraries, because their scope has been quite narrow. *E.g.* the books and reading programme Ariane has concentrated in translations. In the coming framework programme Culture 2000 libraries will have more possibilities to get support also for their cultural actions.

What then will be the fate of the traditional tasks of libraries in general? Will the information society wipe out book loaning and poems?

THE PUBLIC LIBRARIES IN THE KNOWLEDGE SOCIETY

THE LIBRARIES IN A STATE OF FLUX

The municipal reform in 2007 had major consequences for the library service. The number of libraries decreased and the remaining libraries grew in size. The reform thus underlined and intensified various tendencies in library development over the past many years.

The public library is in a state of flux. *Library service to children* from 2008 that chose as its point of reference the changes in children's use of the library. Thus this report had a strong focus on one target group and on how the library can develop new services to that group. The present report also focuses on the target group, but slightly more on the institution–the public library.

Based on a number of societal needs and new opportunities the report also considers how the library can be developed as an institution.

The library offer is changing rapidly, but it continues to be much sought after. Two out of three Danes use the public library, and 29% of the adult population visit the library at least once a month. In 2008 the public libraries registered more than 34 mil. visits.

This makes the library one of our most popular, public cultural offers, and this has been the case for many years. But the way we use the library is undergoing a change. On the one hand the loan of physical materials–books, CDs etc.–is falling. In the period 2000-2008 the public libraries' loan of physical materials has thus fallen by 22%, from ca. 62 mil. to app. 48 mil. materials.

On the other hand the use of digital offers is growing, an offer that spans from downloads of music and e-books to renewals of loans via the library's homepage. Bibliotekernes Netmusik, where as a library user you can via your municipality download music for free, experienced over 2,5 mil. downloads in 2008–an increase of 48% compared with 2007.

One explanation of the change in borrowing patterns could be that the technology and media development has resulted in new media habits on behalf of the library users. At the same time the libraries' consistently high visiting show that they have succeeded in reorganizing and revitalizing themselves and continue to be attractive.

This happens by developing new library services, particularly digital services, but also by turning the library into something more than just a collection of materials, so that the physical library maintains its desirability.

Today the library is also a place for being and meeting, where one for example gets instruction, uses the Internet or gets help in the local citizen service centre.

However, borrowing books remains the main reason why Danes visit the library. The latest cultural habits survey from 2004 shows that 85% of adult library users visit the library to borrow books and journals. The same tendency becomes apparent in more recent studies. In a Gallup poll conducted on behalf of the Danish Library Association, the Union of Danish Librarians and HK Kommunal (white collar workers' union (municipal) in 2009, "borrowing books" is the most frequent reason for visiting the library, followed by "borrowing electronic media", "taking the children to the library" and "watching events".

There is in fact also a growing interest in the library's non-users, as can be seen from the large number of new initiatives, which the libraries participate in at municipal level. In many cases these have a social aspect, and the library is here used as a partner in a targeted initiative towards certain target groups.

This effort is particularly relevant in the light of the challenges that globalization presents to less resourceful citizens. The focusing on non-users also has another angle, which is i.a. clearly expressed in former minister for culture, Carina Christensen's strategy Culture for everybody from 2009. Here the emphasis is on the value of participating in a cultural community and the individual citizen's benefit from cultural offers.

The strategy suggests that all citizens should be able to take advantage of the cultural offers and consequently–that the cultural institutions focus more purposefully on non-users.

THE POLITICAL BASIS FOR THE COMMITTEE'S WORK

The appointment of the Committee on the Public Libraries in the Knowledge Society was decided by the minister for culture in connection with several consultations in Folketingets Kulturudvalg (parliamentary cultural committee), which took place in the wake of a large number of public library branches being closed down during the first year of the municipal reform.

The discussion fuelled by this naturally included the media and technology development. A suggestion for a more extensive, interdepartmental committee work was rejected by the minister, who referred to the work that had already been done by the Globalisation Council. The committee's work builds on the report *Future library service to children* from 2008.

The report contains a number of recommendations as to how to make sure that a strong library offer continues to be available to all Danish children. In 2008 the Danish Agency for Libraries and Media also published the report *The public libraries after the municipal reform*, which analysed the development within the public library area with particular focus on any consequences due to the municipal reform. The report concluded that the closure of the branches in 2006-2007 was a natural adaptation of the library service, and that at the same time it demonstrated a prioritisation in order to deliver a more up-to-date and value-enhancing library offer. With the report from the Committee on the Public Libraries in the Knowledge Society we now have a number of recommendations as to how this prioritisation can be made so that the public libraries also in future will be able to meet the public's need for enlightenment, education and cultural activity.

The committee presents its recommendations within an expenditure-neutral framework with the perspective that it may be both necessary and correct with local changes of priorities within the library field in order to support and strengthen the public library in the knowledge society.

THE COMMISSION'S ASSIGNMENT: MANDATE FOR THE COMMITTEE ON THE PUBLIC LIBRARIES IN THE KNOWLEDGE SOCIETY

The committee must focus on continuous development of the public libraries in Denmark. This includes the public libraries' interaction with other libraries and relevant institutions. Focus must be on the libraries as an easily accessible offer to everybody.

The committee must build on the report *Future library service to children* and pay particular attention to service to youngsters and adults. The committee must assess the public libraries' role in relation to the challenges facing the knowledge society, the globalisation strategy's focus on education, lifelong learning and societal cohesive force.

The committee must assess to which extent there is basis for establishing new concepts for a library service that meets the public's needs in terms of enlightenment, education and cultural activity, and close to the citizens. Likewise the committee must asses the possibilities for continuous development of traditional core services such as literature dissemination.

In particular, the committee must asses the need for further development of the libraries' digital infrastructure and the interaction between digital and traditional services. The committee must furthermore describe models for the mediation of digital cultural heritage and licensed digital media and models for various forms of learning and inspiration activities (*e.g.* in relation to citizens with poor reading and IT skills).

The committee must likewise give examples of new partnerships, including inter-institutional cooperations and binding networking commitments. Finally the committee must assess the need for competence development of library staff.

On the basis of its analyses the committee must put forward recommendations and suggestions as to how the strategy's objectives can be realised within the present legislation and existing division of labour between state and municipalities. The committee's suggestions must be expenditure-neutral. The committee is composed upon appointment, so that the minister for culture appoints three members, while Local Government (KL), Danish Library Association, Association of Library Directors, Danish Research Library Association, the Regional Libraries, Union of Danish Librarians and Børne-og Kulturchefforeningen each appoints a member.

The Danish Agency for Library and Media's director general is chairman of the committee, and the Agency is the committee's secretariat. The committee must have completed its work primo 2010.

DIGITAL LIBRARIES AND SOCIETY

Digital libraries are large, organized collections of information objects. Whereas standard library automation systems provide a computerized version of the catalog—a gateway into the treasure-house of information stored in the library—digital libraries incorporate the treasure itself, namely the information objects that constitute the library's collection.

Whereas standard libraries are, of necessity, ponderous and substantial institutions, with large buildings and significant funding requirements, even large digital libraries can be lightweight. Whereas standard libraries, whose mandate includes preservation as well as access, are "conservative" by definition, with institutional infrastructure to match, digital libraries are nimble: they emphasize access and evolve rapidly.

The five stages in this part provide an excellent illustration of the huge variety of interesting issues in digital library research that impacts the Asia Pacific region. Unlike the New World, where most of the research on technological aspects of digital libraries originates, Asia has an exceptionally rich cultural heritage.

This manifests itself in a huge legacy of documents, in various forms—from paper to palm leaves—and in various different conditions. The need to preserve this legacy is particularly pressing in today's world, where political instability is rife and climate change is beginning to have an effect. As recent events have shown, disasters, both manmade and natural, can have a devastating effect on fragile cultural artifacts. S.M. Shafi from the University of Kashmir, India, surveys the many issues involved with digital archiving of medieval manuscripts in Asia. Libraries are pillars of education, and it is natural to expect that digital libraries will provide new opportunities for innovative educational practices.

These will be particularly relevant to the Asia Pacific region because of the huge disparities in access to education between the different communities there. Peer-to-peer learning has always been a crucial factor in personal development, although it is frequently ignored in educational studies.

Natalie Lee-San from Nanyang Technological University, Singapore, describes her studies of how digital libraries can provide an innovative, perhaps revolutionary, environment for peer-to-peer learning amongst youths. She touches on many practical issues: gender differences, different learning styles, different levels of media and computer literacy, and age-related differences. Many economies in the Asia Pacific region are agricul-turally-based.

Modern agriculture is a knowledge-based activity that can benefit greatly from digital libraries. Mila Ramos from the International Rice Research Institute in the Philippines describes a large-scale digital library system designed to support the growth, nurturing, harvesting, and distribution of that most Asian of staples, rice.

This digital library supports an institute whose goal is to improve the well-being of present and future generations of rice farmers and consumers, particularly those with low incomes. The institute's library houses the world's most comprehensive collection of technical literature on rice, and provides a widely-used international reference service.

As in many specialized libraries, digital library technology is seen to have special advantages in a world of shrinking library budgets. Intellectual property issues are a central driving force behind the market in information of which libraries are a part. And the questions become more complex as the nature of today's information shifts from a primarily book-based culture to one that embraces all types of multimedia objects, and large, carefully-curated, collections of such objects.

The stage on *"Multimedia digital library as intellectual property"* by Hideyasu Sasaki and Yasujshi Kiyoki at Keio University in Japan clarify the copyright situation as it affects multimedia collections and compilations. They go on to discuss the patentability of particular retrieval mechanisms, an essential component of digital libraries.

The fifth stage in this part on how digital library research impacts the Asia Pacific region is the present one, on digital libraries in society. Most existing digital library projects, being research-oriented, are predicated on state-of-the-art equipment and interfaces, academic and research institutions, special collections.

In contrast: digital library technology can and should be available to everyone, on all platforms, in all countries; and it can and should enable ordinary people to exercise their creative powers to conceive, assemble, build, and disseminate new information collections that are designed not just for western academics but for a wide diversity of different audiences throughout the world.

Though less glamorous, this may, in the end, be a more important goal for society. Digital libraries pose an inherent tension between the technologist's desire for advanced solutions that use the latest and greatest hardware and software, and the librarian's desire for wide, crossplatform availability and long-term preser-vation—as epitomized by the sustained success of paper as a delivery medium.

To achieve universal access for both information consumers and collection-builders is really a problem for HCI. We examine the social need for digital libraries, particularly in developing countries, by briefly sketching some trends in commercial publishing and contrasting them with a growing international perspective of information as a public good.

We draw out the implications for the user interface, which is the principal bottleneck in allowing non-specialist people to make public information available in focused collections that are universally usable. Then we introduce digital library technology and illustrate it with a particular example, the Greenstone digital library software, which is designed for a broad user base and is in widespread use in many corners of the world—from Uganda to the US, Kazakhstan to Canada, Nepal to New Zealand. Following that, we review a project that is applying digital library technology to the distribution of humanitarian information in the developing world, a context that is both innovative and socially motivated.

Next we discuss issues of universal access and illustrate them with reference to the Greenstone software. We include a brief demonstration of a prototype system that is intended to allow anyone to build and disseminate information collections, and illustrates some human interface challenges that arise when providing necessarily complex functionality to a non-computer-oriented user base.

We close with the hope that future digital libraries will find a new role to play in helping to reduce the social inequity that haunts today's world, both within our own countries and between nations.

BOOKS, LIBRARIES, AND THE SOCIALLY DISADVANTAGED

Today, the long-standing three-way tension between the commercial interests of publishers, the needs of society and information users, and the social mandate of public libraries, is being pulled and stretched as never before.

First, the very notion of a "book" is evolving in many different directions: books become more interactive; publishers rent content; books are distributed under restrictive conditions that mechanically prohibit sharing. While it would be premature to make specific predictions, it seems likely that these trends will further disadvantage the disadvantaged—particularly those in poorer countries who have yet to benefit from ready access to ordinary books.

Second, a huge body of information is becoming freely available on the Internet. Much is of questionable quality, but some is very good indeed. In many cases the information is provided for the "public good" rather than for commercial profit, and the redistribution of such information is likely to be encouraged, rather than prohibited, by those who make it available.

Initiatives like UNESCO's "Information for all" programme and the upcoming World Summit on the Information Society highlight the importance of public information; they are founded on the belief that information literacy will help alleviate many of the problems confronting human societies. Third, the implications for libraries are mixed.

Whereas new controls by publishers over how the content they own may be used presents libraries with significant problems, the ready availability of "public good" information meshes well with library philosophy. A new role is emerging for information professionals who can select material, index it, add appropriate metadata, and redistribute it in added-value form for the good of society.

Suitable technological infrastructure is being provided by the open source movement, which is making available high-quality software for repackaging and distribution of information (and not just on computer networks).

What future has the book in the digital world? The question is a complex one that is being widely aired. Authors and publishers ask how many copies of a work will be sold if networked digital libraries enable worldwide access to an electronic copy of it.

Their nightmare is that the answer is *one*: how many books will be published online if the entire market can be extinguished by the sale of one electronic copy to a public library? To counter this threat, the entertainment industry is promoting new *"digital rights management"* (DRM) schemes that permit a degree of control over what users can do that goes far beyond the traditional legal bounds of copyright. ndeed, the acronym is more aptly expanded as "digital restrictions management" because it is concerned solely with content owners rights and not at all with user's rights.

It is, in effect, a "private governance system in which computer systems regulate which acts users are and are not authorized to perform". nticircumvention rules are sanctioned by the *Digital Millennium Copyright Act* (DMCA) in the US.

The DMCA has been used, for example, to prosecute a Norwegian teenager for writing software to play a DVD that he had purchased on a computer for which no commercial playback systems exist. an DRM be applied to books? The motion picture industry can compel manufacturers to incorporate encryption into their products because it holds key patents on DVD players. Commercial book publishers are promoting e-book readers that, if adopted on a wide scale, would allow the same kind of control to be exerted over reading material. asic rights that we take for granted—such as the ability to lend a book to a friend, resell it on the second-hand market, keep it indefinitely, continue to use it when your e-book reader breaks down, donate it to charity, preserve it for your grandchildren, copy excerpts without resorting to a handwritten transcription—are in jeopardy. DRM allows such rights to be controlled, monitored, and withdrawn instantly, and DMCA legislation makes it illegal for users to seek redress by taking matters into their own hands.

Fortunately, perhaps, lack of standardization and compatibility issues are delaying consumer adoption of e-books. n the realm of scholarly publishing, digital rights management is more advanced. Academic libraries license access to content in electronic form, often in tandem with purchase of print versions too. They have been able to negotiate reasonable conditions with publishers—probably because they represent the lion's share of the scholarly market. owever, the extent of libraries' power in the consumer book market is moot. One can envisage a scenario where publishers establish a system of commercial, pay-per-view, libraries for e-books and refuse public libraries access to books in a form that can be circulated. These new directions present our society with puzzling challenges, and it would be rash to predict what society's response will be. But one thing is certain: they will surely increase the degree of disenfranchisement of those who do not have access to the technology.

In parallel with publishers' moves to reposition books as technological artifacts with refined and flexible control over how they can be used, an opposing trend has emerged: the ready availability of free information on the Internet.

Of course, the world-wide web is an unreliable source of enlightenment, and undiscriminating use is dangerous—and widespread. As early as 1996 complaints arose that the Web's contents are largely unattributed, undated, unannotated, unreliable; information about author and publisher is unavailable or incomplete; far too many resource catalogues are chasing far too few original or non-trivial documents—complaints that are very familiar today.

But one thing has changed: search engines and other portals have enormously increased our ability to locate information that is at least ostensibly relevant to any given question. Teachers complain bitterly that students view the Web as a replacement for the library, harvesting information indiscriminately to provide answers to assignments that are at best shallow and at worst incoherent and incorrect. One consolation is that the very same search facilities can be used to detect plagiarism.

Nevertheless, the Web abounds with accessible, high-quality information. Many social groups, non-profit societies and charities make it their business to create sites and collect and organize information there. To take a single example at random, a Google search for *diabetes* returns three national diabetes associations in the top ten hits, and of course many more exist. ach of these sites offers a cornucopia of valuable information on the disease, which is not commercial and provided for the public good.

Widespread use is strongly encouraged, and it seems likely that arrangements could be made for re-distribution of the material presented there, particularly it was intended as a not-for-profit service and appropriate acknowledgement was made. ne of the key problems with information distribution via the Web is that it disenfranchises developing countries.

Although the Web does not extend into the homes of the socially disadvantaged in developed countries either, various national programmes are working to provide access. ut network access varies enormously across the world. Whereas in 1998 more than a quarter of the US population were surfing the Internet, the figures for Latin America and the Caribbean was 0.8%, for Sub-Saharan Africa 0.1%, and for South Asia 0.04%. Schools and hospitals in developing countries are poorly connected. ven in South Africa, the bestconnected African country, many hospitals and 75% of schools have no telephone line.

Universities are better equipped, but even there up to 1,000 people can depend on just one terminal. The Internet "is failing the developing world". Prompted by this inequity, the importance of information, and particularly public information, is today being highlighted by prominent international bodies.

For example, UNESCO's "Information for all" programme was established in 2001 to foster debate on the political, ethical and societal challenges of the emerging global knowledge society and to carry out projects promoting equitable access to information.

It reflects a growing awareness that information is playing an increasing role in generating wealth and human capital, and that participation in the "global knowledge society" is essential for social and individual development. Information literacy is described as "a new frontier" by the Director of UNESCO's Information Society Division. The Inter-national Telecommunications Union has established a World Summit on the Information Society, held in Geneva in December 2003 and Tunis in 2005, to promote a global discussion of the fundamental changes that are being brought about in our lives by the transformation from an industrial to an information society, and to confront the extreme disparities of access to information between the industrialized countries and the developing world.

What is the librarian to make of all this? The mandate of today's public libraries, in sharp contrast to that of publishers, is to facilitate the open distribution of knowledge.

Librarians strive to enable the free flow of information. Their traditions are liberal, founded on the belief that libraries should serve democracy. To help fulfill their mission as resource centers for citizens, public libraries maintain collections of records, policy statements, government documents, and so on.

A recent promotional video from the American Librarian's Association exults that "the library is democracy's place of worship". learly, the impending redefinition of the book as a digital artifact that is licensed rather than sold, tied to a particular replay device, with restrictions that are clearly laid out and mechanically enforced, is an innovation that goes right to the heart of libraries. he changing nature of the book may make it hard, or even impossible, for libraries to fulfill their mandate by providing quality information to readers.

And on the other hand, the emergence of a vast storehouse of information on the Internet poses a different kind of conundrum. Librarians, the traditional gatekeepers of knowledge, are in danger of being bypassed, their skills ignored, their advice unsought. earch engines send users straight to the information they require—or so users think—without any need for an inter-mediary to classify, catalogue, cross-reference, advise on sources. The ready availability of information on the Internet, and its widespread use, really presents librarians with an opportunity, not a threat. avvy users realise they need help, which librarians can provide. A good example is Infomine, a cooperative project of the University of California and California State University. Infomine contains descriptions and links to a wealth of scholarly and educational Internet resources, each of which has been selected and described by a professional academic librarian who is a specialist in the subject and in resource description generally.

Participating librarians see this as an important expenditure of effort for their users, a natural evolution of their traditional task of collecting and organizing information in print. What kind of technical infrastructure is needed to support and promote this kind of work? Open source software is a powerful ally for librarians who wish to extend liberal traditions of information access.

These systems make the source code freely available for others to view, modify, and adapt; and the very nature of the licensing agreement prevents the software from being appropriated by proprietary vendors. But the open-source movement is more than just a vehicle for librarians to use: its link with library traditions goes much deeper.

Public libraries and open source software both enshrine the same philosophy: to promote learning and understanding through the dissemination of knowledge. Both are pervaded by a sense of community, on the one hand the kind of inter-institutional cooperation exemplified by interlibrary loan and on the other teams of designers and programmers that frequently cross national boundaries. ew trends in information access present librarians in developed countries with difficult and conflicting challenges.

Meanwhile, however, the situation in the developing world is dire. Here, traditional publishing and distribution mechanisms have failed tragically. or example, whereas a US medical library subscribes to about 5,000 journals, the Nairobi University Medical School Library, long regarded as a flagship center in East Africa, last year received just 20 journals. In Brazzaville, Congo, the university has only 40 medical books and a dozen journals, all from before 1993, and the library in a large district hospital consisted of a single bookshelf filled mostly with novels.

Traditional libraries are substantial institutions that occupy physical space, present a physical appearance, and exhibit tangible physical organization. When standing on the threshold of a large bricks-and-mortar library you gain a sense of presence and permanence that reflects the care taken in building and maintaining the collection inside. Digital libraries, in contrast, are lightweight.

But they provide potentially far greater accessibility, which means that they will have even greater social effects. Once created, they can, without significant institutional support, continue to serve users.

They can be distributed throughout most of the developed world over the Internet. In developing countries and remote corners of the developed world they can be circulated on removable media—CD-ROM, DVD, or 100 Gb disk units the size of videocassettes—and updated over radio. Issues of copyright pose difficult problems, but they are manageable. or example, there is plenty of non-copyright material, or material whose owners are prepared to donate copyright for socially useful purposes, and trends towards more open access to academic and humanitarian information are visible.

Not everyone sees digital rights management and the DMCA as the way forward, and in the longer term publishers, to remain viable, will have to investigate alternative revenue models for the information they own. No wonder international organizations such as the United Nations, along with many smaller *non-government organizations* (NGOs), are keenly interested in digital library technology. Advances in digital library technology are radically lowering the bar for the design and production of richly-organized, coherent, focused collections of information.

Now, anyone with access to sufficient source material can use public-domain software to build large, fullysearchable, collections the size of traditional personal or institutional libraries—in minutes. Let the minutes stretch to hours and the collection can be polished, organized, branded, distributed.

It can include fully-illustrated text, images, video, music. t can present attractively-designed pages with consistent use of icons. Keywords, key phrases, even acronyms and their definitions, can be extracted—automatically—and used to underpin novel means of access. Let the hours stretch to days and metadata can be manually added that permits further levels of organization. Given access to programming skills, creative new facilities that stretch the imagination can be rapidly integrated into the system.

All this, one might say, can be done with ordinary Web sites: there is no need for digital library technology. owever, bitter experience has shown that all but the most rudimentary sites do require significant institutional support—for organization and maintenance.

The Web is littered with incomplete, unfinished, unmaintained, out-dated, inconsistently-organized, useless information collections. ust as traditional library cataloging procedures integrate new works into existing collections with minimal overhead so that they immediately become first-class members of the collection, so digital libraries allow new documents to be added completely automatically.

In the case of traditional libraries this is done through the small but nonnegligible overhead of generating a new catalog entry. With ordinary Web sites it requires inserting links manually into index pages and the like, and may involve adding links not only into the new document but also into existing ones that ought to reference it—it's like rewriting the book, and maybe revising all other books in the library too! In contrast, digital libraries bring access structures instantly and effortlessly up to date whenever new documents are added. The challenge for HCI is to design and build digital library systems that fulfill the potential of digital libraries as a "killer app" for computers in developing countries, which will bring concomitant benefits in almost every other sphere of application. or the information consumer we need access to information that is guaranteed across space, time, and culture.

We need flexible distribution mechanisms for documents, and for information objects of all types, that can be accessed on all computer platforms—including the lowliest. We need a choice of distribution over the Web or on removable media such as CD-ROM or DVD. igital libraries can incorporate flexible presentation that caters to individual differences, such as large-font displays or spoken output for the visually impaired.

Libraries are places where information is preserved, not rendered obsolete, and digital libraries must instill confidence that information prepared today can be accessed next week, next decade, next century—regardless of technological changes. An important aspect of digital libraries is their ability to work in local languages, promoting pluralism and reducing the risks of homogeneity. Because language is the vehicle of thought, communication, and cultural identity, this will encourage diversity and strengthen individual cultures. But there is a long way to go: even Unicode is woefully incomplete in certain areas, such as African languages.

Naturally, today's digital library systems focus principally on the reader: the consumer of the material stored in the library's treasure-house. But digital libraries make a more radical, and perhaps ultimately more important, contribution by empowering ordinary users to conceive, assemble, build, and disseminate new information collections themselves and principle, modest computing resources are quite sufficient to enable users to build new collections by gathering together material in local files or on the Web; augmenting it with appropriate metadata that supports convenient search and browsing operations; incorporating advanced features like key-phrase extraction, document summarization, and metadata extraction; designing an attractive and functional interface; and publishing the collection on a variety of different media that are suitable for the intended readership.

The HCI challenge is to realise this potential for users—such as most librarians—who have a strong understanding of information and its organization, but no more interest in computers than they have in papermaking technology, last millennium's vehicle for information dissemination.

UNIVERSAL ACCESS

Universal access to digital libraries presents huge challenges to software engineers and HCI practitioners. The Greenstone digital library software allows us to glimpse some of the issues, although it certainly does not yet effectively address them all.

Most digital libraries are accessed over the web, using any web browser. However, in many environments, particularly in developing countries, web access is insufficient and the system must run locally.

And if people are to build and control their own libraries, a centralized solution is inadequate: the software must run on their own computers. Thus digital library systems intended for broad access should run on a wide variety of computer systems, particularly low-end ones. Developed under Linux, the Greenstone server runs on any Windows, Unix, or MacOS/X system. All versions of Windows are supported, from 3.1 up.

Supporting primitive platforms poses substantial challenges of a rather mundane nature: for example, Microsoft compilers no longer support Windows 3.1 and it is necessary to acquire obsolete versions. Under Windows, pre-built collections can be viewed on any system with at least 8 Mb RAM, but collections cannot be built under Windows 3.1/3.11—for this at least a Pentium processor is generally required, except for very small collections.

The fact that Greenstone does not run on early Macintosh systems is a serious drawback in certain environments. In an international cooperative effort established in August 2000 with UNESCO and the Belgium-based Human Info NGO, Greenstone is being distributed widely in developing countries with the aim of empowering users, particularly in universities, libraries, and other public service institutions, to build their own digital libraries.

UNESCO recognizes that digital libraries are radically reforming how information is acquired and disseminated in its partner communities and institutions in the fields of education, science and culture around the world, and particularly in developing countries.

Their hope is that this software will encourage the effective deployment of digital libraries to share information and place it in the public domain. he UNESCO distribution of Greenstone is a CD-ROM that contains the full source code and executable binaries for Windows and Linux, along with all necessary associated software.

Full documentation and five demonstration collections are included. he current CD-ROM is trilingual, with complete interfaces, instructions, and documentation in English, French and Spanish. For those with Web access, the same package is also available for download from the Greenstone Web site, often in a form that is slightly ahead of the CD-ROM version—for example, many other language interfaces are included and full documentation is available in Russian and Kazakh too. Providing accessibility in different languages is more difficult than one might at first realise. As well as the manuals, installation instructions and installation prompts, the licensing agreement, and the readme files have to be translated too. Greenstone collections like the Humanity

Development Library can be published as standalone collections on removable media such as CD-ROM, or presented on the Web. CD-ROM is a very practical format in developing countries.

Any Greenstone collection can be converted into a self-contained Windows CD-ROM that includes the Greenstone server software itself and an integrated installation package. The installation procedure has been thoroughly honed to ensure that only the most basic of computer skills are needed to install and run a collection under Windows.

Even standalone Greenstone users interact through a Web browser: Netscape is supplied on each CD-ROM for those who do not already have a browser. In standalone mode the software runs locally but incorporates a Web server so that if the system happens to be connected to a network—say a hospital or school intranet—information is available to other machines that may not possess CD drives.

This happens automatically: no special configuration is necessary. Another difficult engineering challenge is checking for the existence of a network. While installed network software is easily detected, it is hard to determine non-intrusively whether it is operational.

Incorrectly installed or configured software is endemic in developing countries, because computers there are often cast-offs whose software is inappropriate to their present environment, yet system support to rectify the problems is unavailable.

It is essential for universal access that such problems are addressed properly and solved satisfactorily without involving the user, even though they are mundane and timeconsuming. Greenstone provides some support for the visually impaired by incorporating a "textual" mode of access that replaces all images by textual prompts.

This output is suitable for users with speech synthesizers or other specialized access devices. However, the facility is not well advanced: in particular, we have not yet refined it through usability testing and interface improvement.

2

Framework, Construction and Evaluation for Digital Library

FRAMEWORK FOR BUILDING DIGITAL LIBRARY

The Greenstone digital library software provides a wide range of tools for building digital library collections. Based on our own extensive and varied experience, and that of others, we have designed a new framework for building digital library collections. We call it "Greenstone 3" to distinguish it from the earlier system, "Greenstone 2". The new framework is supported by a fresh implementation that is completely independent of the existing one.

It capitalizes on the best ideas from the existing system, which we have further refined and developed to open new avenues through which users can tailor their digital library collections.

Several pertinent new open standards have emerged since the original design many years ago, and a key objective is to incorporate them into the new design. The trend towards increasingly open, flexible architectures can be traced in the development of digital library protocols.

The Open Archives Protocol for Metadata Harvesting has provided a simple base-line for metadata access, and subsequent work strives to base component-based, modular protocols upon it. The METS document framework provides an open, extensible system for representing documents in digital repositories. Greenstone 3 adopts the same approach for a range of digital library functions, as this paper demonstrates.

Set against the move towards standard protocols, today's digital library systems must confront an increasing range of document formats and media, architectural designs for browsing and classification, indexing requirements, and user interface techniques. This drives the demand for open architectures, but makes it hard to provide well-formed and supportive infrastructures that maximise reuse of individual components and the reliability of the system as a whole. This paper proceeds as follows.

First we introduce and describe the configuration structure and document representation used through our new building architecture. The second section describes the building process itself.

This is followed by the model that we have adopted to ensure that the new architecture is extensible. Fourth, we compare this with the previous Greenstone 2 design and present an example use-case scenario, identifying the key advantages of the new open collection-building architecture. We conclude by relating the new architecture to existing collection-building systems.

COLLECTION CONFIGURATION AND DOCUMENT REPRESENTATION

Before describing the process by which collections are built, we will show how the collection-building process is configured, and how documents are represented internally within the system. In we described our "plugin" mechanism and showed how it provides great flexibility for such varied tasks as ingesting both document files and metadata files, extracting text and metadata from different file formats, and expanding compressed files.

It has proved so successful that we have adopted it in the new framework. However, we depart radically from our earlier system by using the METS framework (which postdates that system) throughout for internal document representation.

Configuration

Collections are designed individually, and the structure of a collection is encapsulated in an XML file called the "collection configuration file." Its contents include build-time configuration options such as:

- The document types that the collection should recognise
- The metadata access structures or "classifiers" that are to be provided for users to browse the collection, such as by Titles A–Z
- The full-text indexes to build for searching the collection. The configuration file also contains run-time information about the collections, for example display options.

The bulk of an example configuration file can be seen in Figure—all that is omitted is the part concerning the purely runtime configuration. It defines a simple collection of HTML pages and plain text files, along with XML files that define metadata that is to be associated with these documents.

A document may consist of several separate files—for example, in this collection any images associated with the HTML pages will be contained within the HTML document rather than being identified as documents in their own right. Or a document may comprise complementary pairs of files—like a Word file and matching PDF version.

A collection configuration file

```
<documenttypes>
<document type="HTML">
<document type="Text">
<document type="MetadataXML">
</doctypes>
<search type="mg">
<index name="dtx" level="document" field="text">
<displayItem name="name" lang="en">entire documents</
displayItem>
<displayItem name="name" lang="fr">documents entiers</
displayItem>
<displayItem name="name" lang="es">documentos enteros</
displayItem>
</index>
<index name="stx" level="section" field="text">
<displayItem name="name" lang="en">chapters</displayItem>
<displayItem name="name" lang="fr">chapitres</displayItem>
<displayItem name="name" lang="es">cap?tulos</displayItem>
</index>
<index name="stt" level="section" field="title">
<displayItem name="name" lang="en">section titles</displayItem>
<displayItem name="name" lang="fr">titres des sections</
displayItem>
<displayItem name="name" lang="es">t?tulos de las secciones</
displayItem>
</index>
<format>
<gsf:template match="documentNode"><td
valign="top"><gsf:link><gsf:icon/></gsf:link>
</td><td><gsf:metadata name="Title"/></td></gsf:template>
</format>
</search>
<browse>
<classifier name="CLSubject" type="Hierarchy" file="subject.xml"
field="Subject"/>
<classifier name="CLTitle" type="AZList" />
<classifier name="CLOrganization" type="Hierarchy"
file="organization.xml"
field="Organization"/>
<classifier name="CLKeyword" type="List" file="howto.xml"
field="HowTo">
```

```
<displayItem name="name" lang="en">HowTo</displayItem>
</classifier>
</browse>
```

The search block in Figure defines the full-text-searchable indexes that will be built. In this case the MG indexer will be used to build document-level and section-level indexes of the main text, and a section-level index of Title metadata. The browse block defines the metadata-based browsing mechanisms through which users can access the collection. This configuration file specifies a hierarchical subject browser by defining a Hierarchy-type classifier of each document's Subject metadata, and the file that defines that hierarchy is named.

Other browsing classifiers are also defined. Run-time configuration items can be seen in both the classification and indexation parts of the file. For example. the "displayItem" nodes give names for the indexes (in English, French and Spanish) and for one of the browsers.

The Greenstone 3 building programme reads this file and configures the components to be used by the collection-building process. Many default options are implied. For instance, this collection would automatically expand Zip files—because the Zip expansion plugin is enabled by default. The process followed during building will be described later.

METS and Document Representation

We were eager to adopt an open, standard form for modelling the content and metadata of a document. The METS framework supports a free selection of metadata formats and avoids duplicating data that is already stored in constituent files. Using this standard, open framework should facilitate interoperation with other digital library systems. These are the METS Header, Administrative Metadata, Descriptive Metadata, File lists and Structural lists.

The structural content is the only required section, and the content of the remaining sections is mapped onto the encoded structure. For the sake of clarity, this example shows only the connections between sections and the descriptive metadata and files.

A document is encoded into METS form by a plugin that corresponds to the type of the document. Each such plugin extracts any appropriate metadata from the document files (e.g. title), catalogues the files that comprise the document, and extracts the document text in subsequent phases.

In other words, it encapsulates the document content and acts as a standard gateway to its METS representation. This means that other phases of the building process are able to access data without having to understand the particulars of each file format—even if the data is stored as a binary object.

Document text can be provided in one of three ways, as the processing component requires. Plain Unicode is a simple baseline recognized throughout the system. At a higher level of sophistication, an XML representation is supported.

Finally, indexers can use the underlying binary files if they so desire. A complete document plugin provides all these formats, though the XML representation is optional. In any case, a document may have no textual content whatsoever (in which case all forms are empty).

For example, a PostScript file can be translated into an XML format. The PostScript plugin allows a plain-text reduction of this, but if an indexer wishes to treat PostScript files in a special way, it can access the original files directly. METS documents are partitioned into several components, the most common elements being structure, files, administrative metadata and descriptive metadata. A given document may form part of a single file, or be an agglomeration of individual files and parts of files. Metadata can be associated with a document as a whole or with any part of its structure. A document may also have more than one structural form.

For instance, it may have both a page based structure and a logical chapter-and-section based structure. Metadata may be provided in several different formats and standards, and this allows for the native coding of metadata on the document in different formats—for instance RFC1807 and Dublin Core.

When a document first enters the library, it is given a unique identifier. That identifier will remain with the document throughout any subsequent revisions, and is recorded within the METS framework. Having described the configuration controls and document representation that underpin the new collection-building architecture, we now describe the building process itself.

Building Digital Library Collections

In our new architecture, collections are built in several distinct phases, which occur in sequence.

- *Expansion*: Compressed files such as Zip archives are expanded, and links to web sites are expanded into lists of constituent web pages.
- *Recognition*: All files are sent to the Recognition Manager, which identifies groups of files as documents.
- *Encoding*: All the recognised documents are catalogued for the subsequent phases of building.
- *Extraction*: Every document is passed through extractors, which use special processing algorithms to extract information from the document (e.g. title, keyphrases) or add metadata stored in special files.
- *Classification*: Documents are assigned to classifiers (e.g. topical classifiers, ordered list classifiers) depending on their inherent and extracted metadata.
- *Indexation*: Documents are sent to indexers to build indexes that support later searching.
- *Validation*: Post-building checks are carried out on the collection as a whole, and on its constituent documents.

Expansion

Before any individual documents are identified, any files that are compressed, or refer to external sources, are expanded. The case of a Zip archive has already been mentioned; other cases include OAI repositories, and links to web sites via a file of URLs.

The purpose of this phase is to create a complete list of all files that are available for building the collection. These raw files are then passed to the next phase for grouping into documents.

Recognition

The relationship between files and documents is complex. A file of emails may be seen as one file that contains many documents. Conversely, a JPEG image and a plain text file that describes it may constitute a two-file document. Our architecture uses special "recogniser" plugins to address the problem of distinguishing documents from files. When the building process is initialised, all plugins listed in the collection configuration file are registered by a "Recogniser Manager." When the Expansion phase terminates, this Manager is handed each file in the collection in turn. It sends these files to each plugin.

For some simple cases—like a plain text document comprising a single file—the plugins are trivial. However, in other circumstances conflicts can emerge, and the Recogniser Manager includes a scheme for resolving these. For example, suppose a collection includes both web pages and digital photographs. A single JPEG file may be a document in its own right, or form part of a web page. By default, JPEG files that are referred to by web pages, being constituent parts of a larger whole, are not treated as documents in their own right, while JPEGs that do not appear in the web pages are identified as separate, discrete documents. This default behaviour can be adjusted, if desired, to allow all JPEG files to be treated as documents, even ones that also appear in a web document.

The same issue arises with any image file on a web page. Furthermore, such a file (for instance a logo) could well be part of more than one document. In this case it is treated as a subcomponent of all the documents in which it appears. A web page and associated files cannot form a strict subset of another web page, because the.html files must necessarily differ. The same strategy is used in other cases.

Once the Recogniser Manager has taken a pass through the entire inventory of files and identified the documents, it resolves any conflicts that occur and hands the output on to the Encoding phase.

At this stage all that is known of a document is the list of files that constitute its content. No metadata has yet been assigned—even that found within the document itself. The content and representation of any metadata internal to the document is identified in the next phase.

Encoding

Documents appear in a wide variety of forms, textual encodings and file formats. The Encoding phase creates the document framework that is used throughout the remainder of the building process.

This framework supports the retrieval of the full text of the document. It contains metadata defined within the document, and will also contain any metadata added to it. Finally, it binds the document, with its representation, into the classification and indexation structures.

The METS document framework is used to encapsulate the files, metadata and structure of each document. At the end of the Encoding phase, documents are ready to be processed by extracting further metadata, indexation and storage.

Extraction

The Extraction phase is controlled by the Extraction Manager, which filters the documents through a series of extraction plugins. These can have one of two origins:

- Metadata-only files identified in the recognition phase above
- Explicit mention in the collection configuration file

The former method is typically used for files of descriptive metadata that are provided with the documents. The latter is used to invoke automatic extraction tools such as the KEA Keyphrase Extractor.

At the conclusion of the Extraction phase, all metadata has been collected and stored in the METS document representation. The next two phases place the documents into the context of the collection as a whole.

Classification

The Classification phase uses each document's metadata to site it within the browsing structures, or "classifiers," that are supplied by the collection to access the documents it contains. Each classification is represented by a plugin specified in the collection configuration file.

There may be more than one instance of any given classification type, achieved by initiating a separate copy of the plugin for each classification. Classifications are stored in a database, and when a document is matched to a node in a classification, this fact is recorded in both the document and the classification node.

Indexation

Indexing follows classification. To support the widest range of indexing systems, indexers are also treated as plugins. Again, the indexer—or indexers—used when building a collection are determined by the collection configuration file. For each indexer, parameters can be supplied that control its behaviour.

Indexers can build several different indexes, each with its own parameters. In the case of MG, for example, the structure level (e.g. document, section) and field (full text, title, etc.) can be controlled.

Validation

Validation plugins are used to control the quality of the collection by checking the final form of each document, and the collection as a whole. For example, a collection may insist on a complete metadata set—that is, all compulsory fields must be present.

Or the databases may be checked for empty classification nodes, which may be suppressed. Validation could be done in earlier phases, but we separate it into a final phase for architectural clarity.

Summary

Greenstone 3 uses a seven-phase build architecture. The first three phases identify and store each document. The next three phases enrich and index those documents. The final phase provides for quality control.

The phases support different behaviours and activities that are required by different types of software, and a set of distinct functions that should assist programmers in extending any given implementation of the architecture.

Individual documents are recorded in the METS framework, which provides a standard form that gives access to different metadata formats, file formats and document structures. The document plugins give the indexation and classification components access to content without having to decode or transcribe documents.

EXTENDIBILITY: MANAGERS AND PLUGINS

The central role of plugins in each phase should now be apparent. However, we have made little mention of the structure of plugins themselves, or how they connect to the core system. The architecture achieves extensibility through Plugins and Managers. Each phase of the building process is controlled by a Manager— e.g. the Recogniser Manager, the Indexer Manager.

Managers are configured through the collection configuration file when the building process starts; and in some cases further configuration occurs when special files—like metadata-only files—are found when building.

Each manager coordinates the plugins for its phase of the build cycle. Each manager works in the same way. It initialises and configures its plugins. Then, when its phase runs, it takes each plugin in turn and tells it to do any necessary preparatory work. Next it passes each document or file in turn to that plugin. Finally it sends the plugin a termination message. Document plugins are unique in that they apply to several different phases of the building operation, whereas other plugins appear only within one phase. Managers accept a list of plugins from the configuration file.

New plugins are readily installed into the system by placing them into the plugin directory corresponding to their type, and adding them to the configuration file of one or more collections.

There is a standardised interface for all extraction, indexation and classification plugins.

This includes:

- GetNumberOfPasses Return the number of passes required by the plugin
- StartPass(int) Begin a pass for this plugin
- ProcessDocument(Document) Process the given document
- EndPass(int) Terminate a given pass
- Tidyup Close the plugin
- Configure(Node)

Pass configuration information to the plugin. The configuration information mentioned in the last method is taken from the collection configuration file, where it is specified as an XML node. It is particular to each plugin. The get Number Of Passes method allows plugins to request multiple passes over the documents.

The MG indexation plugin, for example, requires a minimum of two passes plus a further two passes for each index it builds. Running each plugin separately and serially keeps memory overheads down.

ADVANCE OVER EARLIER WORK

The architecture that we have described capitalizes on lessons learned from the existing Greenstone digital library system, and incorporates some very significant improvements. At the time the earlier system was designed several important open standards did not exist, or were available only in draft form.

For example, the METS Document Framework, a key component of the new architecture, was unborn. The original Greenstone design adopted ad hoc file formats that became inconsistent with emerging norms.

Collection configuration was viewed as a compilation process directed by a configuration file whose format was similar to the Makefile format rather than by directives couched in a structured markup language. It used an HTML-like structure, the Greenstone Archive format, to store documents and metadata, which is less structured than modern XML.

The internal formats were also inconsistent with each other—configuration files being flat files whereas document files were derived from HTML. These simple and apparently cosmetic differences magnified into large-scale divergence.

Architecture

In Greenstone 2, collections are constructed in two phases: importing and building. The first parallels the Expansion, Recognition and Encoding phases of Greenstone 3, while the second mirrors the Extraction, Classification and Indexation phases. Both phases use the same set of plugins, which are listed in the collection's configuration file and loaded separately in each phase—despite the fact that some plugins only pertain to one phase.

Document plugins, like HTMLPlug, played a rather different role from that described above. Documents were identified by a single key file—e.g. an HTML file—and complex document structures were poorly supported.

A special generic plugin was later developed that recognized multi-component documents such as a Word file and its corresponding PDF version. However, the plugins had to be carefully ordered in the configuration file to recognize this compound document.

Once a file was captured by a plugin, subsequent plugins could not see it. The Recognition phase described above facilitates complex document forms and arbitrates competing claims for a file by different document types.

Plugin Details

Document plugins handle Encoding very differently in the new design. Originally, all documents were encoded into the standard Greenstone Archive Format as soon as they were encountered. This duplicated content, and could lose, or render inaccessible, some information in the original file.

The benefit was that all documents were presented to subsequent phases in a standardised format. In the new architecture, plugins convert document content to either plain text or well-formed XML, which allows formats such as TEI to be retained verbatim.

The METS Framework provides a standard container for metadata and structural information. This open public standard retains the benefits of the original Greenstone Archive Format, and goes further by allowing multiple structures within the same document. Plugins in Greenstone 2 could be of three types—Expansion (then called "structural"), Document, and Extraction (called "metadata").

All were placed in the same pipeline. The new architecture makes a clearer distinction between phases and allows a richer variety of documents. For most tasks, it supports clearer, more compact, interfaces. In addition, monolithic parts of the old design, such as indexation, are now readily adjusted and extended in the flexible manner exhibited by other phases (such as Expansion).

Example: The Kids Digital Library

We briefly present an actual digital libraries that was difficult to accommodate within the earlier design, and show how it benefits from the new architecture. In the Kids Digital Library each document can belong to several collections. Some collections are private (e.g. a child's own documents), others public. Some documents are unchanging (accepted final essays); others are under continually revision by a restricted group of users.

Students can annotate the work of others, and teachers provide feedback too. All collections support full-text searching and metadata-based browsing; some have additional browsing facilities. Collections sometimes change rapidly over a short period—e.g. during a scheduled class. Using the new architecture, many of these requirements can be delivered far more easily.

Consistent document identifiers and explicit change history allows revisions of a document, and comments made between changes, to be tracked. Incremental indexing is supported by recording accession and revision data as METS administrative metadata. The METS framework allows files to be duplicated between collections yet reside in only one location.

The Kids Digital Library featured some unusual browsing classifiers such as the "Top ten" and "Latest ten" stories. These require simple support for feature extraction. In the earlier design, this could only be done by altering the building scripts—which caused portability problems, and made it difficult to install new versions of the software. The new architecture circumvents the problem by modularizing feature extraction.

Comparison with other Digital Library Systems

Cheshire II emphasises the construction of digital libraries from original scanned documents. The process described for collection building reveals a system of fixed metadata fields and a strict control of the format in which documents are presented to the system.

Nowhere is support for feature extraction, expansion of compressed files, or novel indexes described. The CORR 2 is built on the NCSTRL software. The CORR documentation reports that the system requires documents to be submitted in a standard source format. No documentation on CORR or NCSTRL describes the parameters for collection configuration.

Conclusion

In the new collection building architecture we have described, the building process is segmented into a number of distinct phases. Once documents are identified, they are encoded into a flexible, open framework (METS) and are passed in that form to the succeeding phases of the build process. Within each phase, the elements are componentised to support greater portability and simpler development.

The build process is configured through a simple XML format file which is readily extensible for future components. We have implemented this architecture in a practical digital library system.

The use of a document framework rather than standardised document encoding has not created any obstacle to providing existing features. Rather, it supports our move to more complex document file structures and permits any processing of the document (e.g. by an indexer) to either refer to the original binary or to extracted content as it chooses.

We believe that the challenge of providing effective, portable solutions to building digital library collections is an important one. As file formats diversify, the issue of digital preservation grows. Similarly, if extraction and indexation technologies are not made more portable their adoption will slow. Our new architecture provides a step forward in meeting these challenges.

CONSTRUCTION OF DYNAMIC DIGITAL LIBRARY

This paper describes a digital library architecture and implementation that is configurable, extensible and dynamic in the way it presents content and in the services it provides. The design manifests itself as a network of modules that communicate in terms of XML messages.

All modules characterize the functionality they implement in response to a "describe yourself" message, and can transform messages using XSLT to support different levels of configurability.

Traditional library values such as backwards compatibility and multiplatform operation are combined with the ability to add new collections and services adaptively. The paper describes the new design and shows how it can be used to build four different digital library systems.

We conclude by showing how the design fits existing interoperability frameworks. This paper describes a digital library design that improves upon the Greenstone toolkit. First, it provides more flexible ways of dynamically configuring the run-time system and adding new services to it.

Second, it lowers the overhead incurred by collection developers when accessing this flexibility to organize and present their content. Third, it modularizes the internal structure and simplifies the addition of new modules.

The design is based on widely-accepted standards such as XML, current software practices such as simple protocols (like SOAP), cross-platform development strategies (Java), and contemporary schemes for software modularization and dynamic updates.

Most important of all, it is informed by our experience with the current Greenstone system and the problems and challenges faced by real users, international collection developers, and practicing librarians.

The structure of the paper is as follows. First we give some background out of which the requirements for the digital library software arose. Next we describe the new design, called Greenstone, and discuss how it meets the identified needs. Fundamental to the approach is the use of XML throughout for data representation, combined with XSL Transforms to provide a flexible mechanism for adjusting the functionality of the runtime system without having to modify and recompile the source code.

To promote cross-platform independence (which has consumed inordinate human resources in the present Greenstone system) and facilitate the dynamic loading of services and other modules, the implementation uses Java. Following this we describe four very different examples built using the new design.

The first demonstrates backwards compatibility, and, in addition, operates within a distributed environment. The second augments text at display time, using an established software tool for text mining developed elsewhere, to show how functionality can be enriched through the introduction of a new service.

The third is a map-based digital library that introduces two new services to support geographic functionality and, while still accessed through a web-based interface, is highly tailored to the specific domain of its source documents.

The fourth is a radically different interface for the interactive viewing of search results as a hierarchically organized cluster of documents, and illustrates the versatility of the design in coping with fine-grained interaction. We conclude with a commentary on how the design fits existing interoperability frameworks, from which many valuable lessons have been learned.

Background

Over the years the Greenstone digital library software has been employed by many users internationally to develop a wide variety of digital libraries. In addition to operation over the Web, an early application, and still a major one, is collections of humanitarian information in the form of CD-ROMs that run on any Windows computer (including Windows 3.1).

There are now over two dozen of these collections, and they have been distributed widely by the United Nations and other non government agencies. Many other styles of collection have been developed under Greenstone.

They range from numerous personal collections based around common document formats such as E-mail, photographs, Word, and PDF documents through to largescale bibliographic catalogs such as the BBC radio and TV archives.

There are mixed media collections involving text, images and audio drawn from data such as historic newspapers and oral history. Several demonstration music collections support direct content-based retrieval through "query by humming." Many customized and branded user interfaces exist, such as the New York Botanical Gardens, and many international collections in local languages created by institutions in China, India, Croatia, Russia and Israel.

The software is distributed in source form, and for convenience binaries are available for Windows, Linux and MacOS X. The user interface is available in 30 languages. A recent addition is a graphical interface for collection design and construction which is also multilingual.

A portfolio of demonstration collections is available at www.nzdl.org, and selected example collections built internationally can be found at www.greenstone.org.

Weaknesses

Many experimental interfaces have been built for Greenstone, some of which make use of a CORBA-based protocol to support distributed client-server interaction. These include a Venn diagram tool for formulating Boolean queries graphically, and a bibliographic visualization tool that plots matching citations on an x-y grid based on publication year and ranked relevance score to the query terms.

However, while perfectly functional, some of these variants are implemented inelegantly, exposing limitations caused by certain aspects of the design. For instance, the immutable nature of the index files generated during the building process makes incremental adjustments to a collection expensive. Another hindrance is the low level of functional customization supported by the runtime system. Although minor presentation tweaks are easy, more extensive changes involve modifying and recompiling the source code. The strongly typed nature of the CORBA protocol was also found to be overly restrictive in many practical situations.

Requirements

From these and other considerations arose the following requirements for an improved design.

- *Backwards compatibility:* Naturally we wish to retain the existing system's strengths. This is accomplished by ensuring that the new design is backward compatible, which has the added benefit of providing existing developers and users with an easy migration path.
- *Levels of customization:* To match the different categories of people involved in constructing digital libraries, different levels of customization are required. For instance, a content developer may wish to include source documents in a new format; a collection editor may seek influence over diverse issues of presentation.
- *Software modularity:* To facilitate development and long-term management of the software, code modularization—a mantra of any software engineering approach—is essential. This is promoted by adopting off-the-shelf technology such as a database system, indexing tools, and page rendering software; and by the use of standards.
- *Service based:* Basing a digital library around a set of services is another way to accomplish modularity—in this case, modularity of function.
- *Distributed architecture:* A rich digital library infrastructure can only be supported by a distributed architecture, and the addition of an open protocol helps to foster interoperability.
- *Future compatibility*: Libraries are long-term institutions with a mandate for preservation, and it is essential that old collections can be presented by future versions of the system. This is a more ambitious requirement than mere extensibility which, although an admirable quality in any design, does not necessarily ensure that future versions can safely interact with current ones.

- *Dynamic:* Many aspects of the library should be dynamic, for example content, whereby documents and metadata can be added, revised and removed while a repository remains on-line, and configuration, where presentational issues can be adjusted and services added at runtime.
- *Integrated documentation:* Large-scale software systems such as digital libraries benefit immensely from the use of an integrated documentation system.
- *Self-describing modules:* This goes a stage further than the previous item: modules describe themselves in a machine-readable format so that other modules can interact with them without the need for explicit control. Computer environment integration. A digital library should mesh well into a user's existing computer environment. Full integration makes a digital library become a seamless component of each user's work environment.

SOFTWARE DESIGN

The new software design has evolved from the requirements articulated above, our own experience of developing digital library systems, and studies of other open source software and research projects.

This section provides an overview of modularity and inter-module communication, and then works through a simple, stand-alone example. The next section describes four very different examples built using the new design, to illustrate the general applicability of the approach.

Modularity

We decided that the best way to meet the challenges posed by the list of requirements was to reimplement Greenstone using a modular topology. In the design, a digital library manifests itself as a network of modules, and communication between them is expressed through an instantiation of XML.

A mandatory requirement for a module—enforced through its base class definition—is that it handles "describe yourself" messages. What kinds of messages follow typically depend on the outcome of an initial "describe yourself".

Modules have the ability to transform messages by applying an XSL Transform. This is a particularly useful mechanism for dynamically controlling levels of configurability—one of our requirements. Within the network of modules comprising a digital library, a set of services are defined that prescribe the functionality supported by that particular digital library configuration.

Communication

Modules communicate using synchronous request-response pairs. Figure shows an example XML exchange, where the Text Query module in a collection called "demo" is asked to describe itself. It does this, providing information about the structure of the service as well as fragments of text to be used for display.

These are returned in the language specified in the request. While the language used is structured and typed, it has been crafted in such a way that the information it contains can be open-ended.

For example the paramList structure allows other items to be included, such as whether stemming is on or off. In addition to supporting optional parameters, extensions can be introduced without having to update the protocol's API, thereby avoiding the need to propagate code changes to the entire distributed network (which may require taking it off-line while the changes are made).

Programming for a sample XML exchange as a request/response pair.

```
<request to='demo/TextQuery' lang='en' type='describe' uid='21'/>
<response from='demo/TextQuery' lang='en' type='describe'>
<service name='TextQuery' type='query'>
<displayItem name='name'>Search</displayItem>
<displayItem name='description'>Full text search</displayItem>
<displayItem name='submit'>Search</displayItem>
<paramList>
<param name='index' type='enum_single' default='stx'>
<displayItem name="name">Index to search in</displayItem>
<option name="dtx">
<displayItem name="name">entire documents</displayItem>
</option>
<option name="stx">
<displayItem name="name">chapters</displayItem>
</option>
</param>
<param name='maxDocs' type='integer' default='10'>
<displayItem name="name">Maximum hits to return</displayItem>
</param>
<param name="query" type="string">
<displayItem name="name">Query string</displayItem>
</param>
</paramList>
</service>
</response>
```

A Simple Stand-alone Example

The simple stand-alone example shown in Figure encapsulates many of the design's key features. It comprises a "back end" server, termed a digital library site in our design, coupled to a "front end" that provides the user interface. The modules' names were chosen to emphasize the roles they play.

The Receptionist's point of contact with the server is the Message Router (MR) module—all communication with the site occurs through this module. The configuration is designed to generalize to a distributed environment. The digital library back end in Figure contains two collections, demo and fao, and a cluster of collection-formation services.

Add Document is a service that adds a document to a collection. Import Collection imports into the system all documents associated with a collection, converting them where necessary from their original form. Build Collection builds all indexes and browsing structures that are associated with a collection. Activate Collection makes a newly-built collection active, so that it can be seen by digital library users.

These services are all concerned with creating a digital library collection. Being related, they are grouped together into a "service cluster." In Figure the services just listed are accessed through the Collection Formation service cluster module.

As far as the digital library user is concerned, a "collection" is a focused group of documents with a uniform means of access. For the system, it is a service cluster that groups a set of services that are related by the data they work on.

For example, the demo collection towards the lower left of Figure contains three modules providing four services to the user.

The modules are called "Search," which provides a Text Query service, "Retrieve," which provides a document retrieval service Resource Retrieve and a metadata retrieval service Metadata Retrieve, and "Browse," which provides a metadata browsing service Classifier Browse. The Web-based front end at the upper left of Figure centers around the Receptionist, which is the point of contact for the interface generator. A servlet (labeled "Library Servlet") takes HTTP commands in the form of URLs and arguments and translates them into XML for the Receptionist.

The Receptionist is capable of executing various different actions, each of which involves (usually) many calls to the digital library's Message Router. The builtin ability for Receptionist modules to transform XML messages using XSLT is used—in conjunction with a style sheet—to generate the HTML that is finally presented to the user.

Examples

For pedagogical purposes, the example configuration in Figure is rudimentary. The front and back ends (receptionist and site server) are compiled together into a single executable process with a single Message Router handling all communication between them. However, the design supports a far richer infrastructure than this. Message Routers have the capability to communicate across a distributed network with other Message Routers and with Receptionists.

Different implementations of the same service can be switched in and out to give a digital library site different algorithmic behaviour (such as incremental building); and new services can be introduced and brought on-line, dynamically if necessary. The library can also have many different user interfaces. We now describe four more interesting scenarios.

The first emulates "classic" Greenstone to demonstrate backwards compatibility, with a distributed configuration a straightforward addition. The second augments text at display time, to show how functionality can be enriched through the introduction of a new service.

The third and fourth utilize novel interfaces to enrich the interaction: the former is specialized for geographic maps, and the latter for text based collections.

Classic Greenstone, with collections on remote sites

To provide backwards compatibility, a set of Greenstone services have been implemented that access index and database files generated by a Greenstone system. Indeed we have already seen these in Figure.

Moreover, using Cascading Style Sheets (CSS), the look and feel of the traditional interface has been matched one-for-one, so that the user's experience of the digital library remains the same.

Of course with the more versatile design, more sophisticated internal structures can be built within the digital libary.

For instance, because of the design decision that all communication be XML based, it is straightforward to arrange for the XML messages sent between modules to be seamlessly streamed across remote machines.

For this we employ the Simple Object Access Protocol (SOAP), but any protocol that can process text can be used.

To the user there is no disernable difference accessing collections this way. Backwards compatability is not the sole aim, however, and the structure allows increasingly interesting digital library designs—ones that do provide a distinctly different expierence for the user. We discuss three such examples next.

Dynamic Text Mining

The next example shows how a new Greenstone service can be provided that enhances documents for the reader, based upon the open source GATE system for text mining. The motivation is that highlighting selected items in documents can make it easier for users to scan them for particular pieces of information.

In this implementation, digital library documents, once located, are mined on the fly marking up entities such as keywords and place names before presenting them to the user. Figure shows a section of a book on Butterfly Farming in Papua New Guinea (from the Humanity Development Library at www.nzdl.org) that the user is reading.

The Annotate document menu at the top right calls the display time text mining feature. When items on this menu are selected, text of the selected type is highlighted in the document displayed. In this case the user has selected Places and Organizations, and these are highlighted wherever they occur, in different colors (simulated by white-on-grey and black-on grey in the illustration).

The selectable items in Figure were identified and extracted by ANNIE, GATE's information extraction system. Whenever an annotation type is selected from the menu, Greenstone calls the information extraction module dynamically to identify items of that type.

This incurs a delay that depends on the document's size but is usually short: the system processes text at the average rate of 15 Kb/sec on a typical workstation. In order to achieve this the software is loaded when the Greenstone server is executed and remains resident in memory thereafter, to avoid a start-up delay (of about 10 seconds) in which all the text processors are initialized and prepared for use.

In Greenstone3, GATE is encapsulated in a module as just another service. It takes messages with two parameters, the type of annotation and a document, and returns the document with relevant items marked up with XML tags.

A style sheet in the server module chooses the colors in which the items are displayed. In order to generate the menu in the figure, a "describe yourself" message is sent to the GATE module, which returns a list of the annotations that are available. Apart from this one module, the rest of the digital library system knows nothing of GATE.

However, it does know about a general class of services, Enrich, that take a document and return the same document with some elements marked up. To add this text-mining ability to an existing Greenstone site dynamically the Java class files for the new service need to added to the correct folder on the DL site's file system, the site's configuration file updated to name the new service, and a "reconfigure" signal sent (which can be initiated through a web browser) to the DL site server.

Geographical map based interface Figure is taken from a site configured to support map searching based on a small collection of New Zealand maps drawn between 1770 and 1953, part of our university library's special collections.

It shows the result of searching for "Rangiriri"—a township in the North Island of New Zealand and, on a hill nearby of the same name, the scene of a battle in 1863 between Maori and British soldiers. Two crosses (colored red when viewed online) have been overlaid on the map showing the position of the township and hill. This new functionality is provided by adding two new services, including geographic metadata with the collection's source documents (the maps), and a gazetteer of over 40,000 entries from Land Information New Zealand (LINZ). Searching is handled by the Map Query service. For each place name query term that is located in the gazetteer, its longitude and latitude are checked against each map to see if it falls within its boundaries.

Once all cross-referencing is complete, the list of maps with matching entries is sorted by the number of query terms on each map. Image manipulation and the results display are handled by the Map Retrieve service, which makes use of the open source Image Magick toolkit for copying, annotating (such as placing a cross at an x, y location) and resizing images.

Cluster Visualizations

Figure shows a web-based interface, but there may be other forms, ranging from standalone applications and applets that display documents in different ways to alert services that recognize when new information becomes available in one of the collections and formulate appropriate E-mail to users. Figure is one such instance: a Java applet that supports browsing result sets as document clusters through a multi-viewed, interactive interface.

To function it needs the addition of a new build-time service, Vis Construct, which is responsible for computing additional statistics about the collection necessary to perform subsequent document clustering operations, and a sub-classing of the Applet service, tailored for the HTML necessary to embed the visualization applet within a web page.

Besides this, the visualization can interact with any text-based Greenstone collection that defines keyword metadata. The distinctly different interface behaviour is achieved through fine-grained interaction with the existing Text Query and Metadata Retrieve services using SOAP. Derived from the query term entered, there are four views in the visualization.

The first is the standard result list format; the other three are based around a shared model of hierarchically clustered documents.

In Figure the user has entered the query term "recession" to a collection based on the Wall Street Journal and is viewing the result as a Dendro map—the circular arranged tree displayed in the main panel—which contains words like slowing, slowdown and inflationary around the circumference. The size of nodes in the tree represents the number of documents clustered at that point in the hierarchy, and for reasons of space only 5 levels of the tree are shown at a time. Clicking on a node shows a popup menu with the precise number of documents in the cluster and the option of "drilling down" as shown in the figure. The consequence of choosing this option is for the tree to be redrawn with the selected node at the centre of the map, thereby exposing more of the detail in that part of the hierarchy.

While all this is going on, the left-panel displays the keywords relevant to the selected cluster, and the bottom panel lists the documents involved. Within the left panel, keywords can be activated or deactivated and the bottom panel dynamically filtered to reflect the changes.

INTEROPERABILITY FRAMEWORKS

This modular, service-based and dynamically configurable approach to digital library architecture can be found in other designs and systems. Two key examples are the Extended Open Archives Initiative protocol (XOAI) proposed by Suleman and Fox and the Open DLib system of Castelli and Pagano.

The XOAI protocol, based upon XML and related technologies, builds upon the basic OAI Protocol for Metadata Harvesting. It is a modular protocol which represents each service as a different type of OAI request. This service-based approach is readily seen in Greenstone's protocol, where each service has its own request and response format.

Like OAI and XOAI, Greenstone uses XML for representing requests and responses; providing a gateway between Greenstone and XOAI servers and clients should be readily achievable. The Open DLib system also takes a modular approach to service communication and library construction.

Many of its features are similar to those of XOAI and Greenstone, and the handling of requests to the library map as readily as for XOAI. However, Open DLib is centered upon a "manager" service that coordinates services, responding to the introduction of new services and alterations to existing ones.

Coordination is achieved through a communication protocol between the manager and each service. Individual services, including each library in a federation, acquire data from the manager.

The manager does not itself control or direct requests for searches, documents, and so on but instead coordinates between services to ensure consistency. Greenstone provides many of these features—for instance, service description requests—without requiring a centralized manager.

The similarity of protocols between Greenstone, XOAI and OpenDLib echoes experience with the previous generation of DL protocols and augers well for interoperability. Greenstone's widespread adoption and free availability allows others to adopt it as a platform for experimenting with the service-centered design approach.

It facilitates the addition of new digital library features which would have been hampered by the less open structures of Greenstone and its contemporaries. Greenstone retains and extends the lightweight configurability of its predecessor without requiring centralized management processes.

This paper has presented a new digital library design which is significantly different from the present Greenstone, but strongly rooted in past success. To meet a broad range of requirements a modular based topology is utilized to provide a flexible infrastructure. Written in Java to promote portability, dynamic loading of objects and internationalization, modules communicate by streaming XML messages between each other. Using SOAP this communication can be distributed across a network. All modules have the ability to describe themselves in a machine readable form, and to apply an XSLT to transform messages. The latter is instrumental in providing different levels of configurability, an important ability given the different types of people involved in the life-cycle of a digital library. Several working examples have been given to convey the general applicability of the design. The first example demonstrated backwards compatibility to collections built with Greenstone, and satisfies another of the identified requirements: to help minimize the migration path of existing developers and users. It also demonstrated the design functioning in a distributed environment.

The second example augmented an existing DL site with text mining capabilities with the introduction of a new service. The third and fourth examples illustrated substantially different user interfaces: one specialized for maps that required two extra services to provide the necessary geographical functionality; the other provided an interactive visualization to search results through a Java applet that was applicable to a wider realm of text-based collections.

Numerous aspects of the design contribute to its dynamic configurability. The "describe yourself" feature allows receptionists to adapt to the facilities that a server presents. Through XSLT a corpus editor can exert significant control over the function and appearance of a digital library such as modifying the structure of a generated page, for example adding a transform that sorts the query results alphabetically by title rather than ranked score. Alternatively they may reformat the results according to OAI syntax in preparation for exporting.

Previously such changes required editing the source code and restarting the digital library software after recompilation. Implementing the design in Java has promoted dynamic attributes in the system, particularly through the ease in which modules can be loaded at runtime.

The re-reading of configuration files is also straightforward to arrange and adds dynamic abilities that a digital library administrator can take advantage of. In addition to integrating the documentation with the software using JavaDoc and other techniques, usability of the software also benefits from the development of self-documenting collections that both demonstrate and describe particular aspects of design.

The list of requirements is ambitious, however, and not all of them have been proven yet. For example, while none of the sample implementations demonstrate computer environment integration, the design is capable of supporting the idea through specialized receptionists. For future compatibility, more time is needed to establish if the design successfully meets such a criteria.

EVALUATION

When an animal bred in captivity runs, flaps or slithers into the wilderness for the first time, scientists do not simply wave goodbye, wish it well and move on to the next project. Usually the animal is tracked and observed for a long time thereafter—the point of release is where the research really begins.

However, this has been less true for grant-funded digital library projects. Administrative and institutional barriers tend to confine evaluation to the funding period when the system is being designed, and when its uses and effects can only be guessed at.

In this short paper I will discuss a digital library project in environmental science where some of these evaluation issues arose, the value of eliciting narrative data from users, and some ways to take better advantage of existing but underused mechanisms for long-term evaluation of digital libraries.

Viewing information technologies and society as inextricably co-determined makes it necessary to gather data both on the design process and on how the finished systems are used by people—often in quite unexpected ways.

Iterative design and formative evaluation are ways to introduce user feedback into ongoing design, but while these strategies can serve as an effective translation layer between users, designers and builders, the focus is on how an evolving system *might* be used.

How it is *actually* used can be more accurately determined when the system is in the wild, when the designers and their formal evaluation instruments have gone away.

Digital libraries are social entities. They tell stories about a culture, a science, a place or a time, through the items represented and organized in the collection, and in use, they help generate new stories as well.

Manovich has advanced the idea of database and narrative as two ends of same continuum; both structure information, but where a database aims for access, a narrative aims for psychological immersion in the story. From an institutional standpoint, digital libraries are rarely ends in themselves.

The social missions of the funding organizations—the stories they wish to tell— often drive the creation of digital libraries, but how well a finished system supports the mission can't be fully evaluated until the digital library has had some time to develop a user base.

This line of research began with a participant observation of the design of a digital library of environmental science collections. Funded by an Library Services and Technology Act (LSTA) grant, the project involved diverse designers, content, metadata and institutional participants.

As one of the participants in the environmental science digital library noted, "Part of the art of grant writing is interpreting vague language in a way that lets you do what you want to do," or in other words, making project proposals and achievements dovetail with the mission and goals of the funding agency.

These goals included outreach and evaluation, so a usability component was included in the grant proposal. My initial role in the project was to develop the instruments and conduct the evaluation.

Understandably, digital library designers tend to create evaluation instruments that demonstrate in a measurable way the work they've done, a tacit statement of the value produced for the grant funds received. For example, the design of the interface, the appropriateness of descriptive metadata, and user success at canned search tasks are classic evaluative measures.

However, in an analysis of the Perseus Digital Library (PDL), Marchionini writes: "Operational data are powerful components in a chain of inferences that address impact but the PDL evaluation illustrates the value of anecdotes and "stories" that illustrate new effects, i.e., how DLs augment existing capabilities with new ones. These augmentations garner public support for a DL and should not be underestimated in assessing impact.

Integrating multiple views is more naturally done with narratives than summary statistics and integrating these forms of evidence can aid in assessing complex change." In the evaluation, statistical and demographic data were not hard to come by.

Observation, interviews, document analysis, narrative analysis and social network analysis were effective ways to construct as complete a picture as possible about the interactions of the designers. But the usability component needed to be completed at the same time as the digital library, in time for the results to be included in the final LSTA grant report (though the exact LSTA grant regulations vary by state, most LSTA grantees must submit a final grant report within 15-30 days of project completion).

Participants in the usability study were evaluating a still evolving system, and had to project potential uses into their responses to open-ended interview questions. By the time they might integrate the collections into their professional lives, and perhaps surprise themselves with unexpected dimensions of usefulness, the evaluation would be long over. This is certainly not to say that there is no such thing as continuing evaluation of grant-funded digital libraries.

But the mechanisms for long-term evaluation are usually little more than Web forms or e-mail links, not organic components of the digital library. In practice, designers are more concerned with present and future digital library projects than with continuing evaluation of those of the past.

Digital library researchers have an opportunity to conduct this longer-term research, to question and reveal the impacts of digital libraries as social entities, and to apply the resulting knowledge to future projects.

The good news is that in some situations, a mechanism for longer term evaluation already exists. For example, the State Library of Ohio's LSTA grant process makes use of a "year-after" evaluation form (http://winslo.state.oh.us/

publib/lstayraft.html), which includes questions such as "Did the project produce any unexpected results?" and encourages narrative ("Please provide a success story of how your project has impacted someone's life or had a positive impact on the community.").

This is precisely the sort of openended data collection instrument that can reveal how a digital library is actually being used—but even this document is only the length of a one-page questionnaire. Subsequent research will attempt to evaluate the usefulness of this and other longer-term evaluation instruments, and how they might be expanded.

While longer-term evaluation should include quantitative data such as transaction logs and perhaps a list of external sites that link to collection content, evaluation instruments should also be open-ended, designed to encourage narrative expressions of unexpected use, the kind of data that reveal to funding agencies the real impact of their grants.

Iterative digital library design philosophies have always had at their core the sense that user input should feed back into ongoing system design. I propose here simply a wider iterative design circle, one that allows for more naturalistic data about longer-term use to be fed back into future systems.

In sum, lessons learned that will be explored in future research include an increased emphasis on:

- Long-term evaluation of digital libraries
- Narrative data; allowing users to tell stories
- Unexpected uses
- Evaluating social outcomes, not just the design process or product
- Linking findings more directly to the higherlevel goals of funding agencies

DIGITAL LIBRARY INFORMATION APPLIANCES

Although digital libraries are intended to support education and knowledge work, current digital library interfaces are narrowly focused on retrieval. Furthermore, they are designed for desktop computers with keyboards, mice, and high-speed network connections. Desktop computers fail to support many key aspects of knowledge work, including active reading, free form ink annotation, fluid movement among document activities, and physical mobility.

This paper proposes portable computers specialized for knowledge work, or *digital library information appliances*, as a new platform for accessing digital libraries. We present a number of ways that knowledge work can be augmented and transformed by the use of such appliances.

These insights are based on our implementation of two research prototype systems: XLibris, an "active reading machine," and Tele- Web, a mobile World Wide Web browser. The standard platform for accessing today's digital libraries is a desktop computer with a keyboard, a mouse, information retrieval software, and a network connection. Unfortunately, desktop computers are not suitable for many types of knowledge work.

Studies of people using electronic and paper documents show that desktop systems fail to support four important activities:

- Active reading
- Free form ink annotation
- Fluid movement among document activities
- Physical mobility

As a result of focusing on the desktop, today's interfaces for accessing digital libraries support retrieval in isolation, without addressing these broader work practices. We propose a new platform for accessing digital libraries: specialized portable computers designed for knowledge work, or *digital library information appliances.*

In this paper, we draw on our experience designing and building two research prototype information appliances— the XLibris "active reading machine" and the TeleWeb mobile Web browser— to show how these devices can support a broad range of activities in the digital library.

READING AND DIGITAL LIBRARIES

The first and most fundamental document activity is reading. "Reading" encompasses a broad range of complex and poorly understood practices involving documents, including skimming, searching, browsing, speed-reading, surfing, reviewing, and rereading. Although we often take it for granted, reading can be hard work. We use the term *active reading* to distinguish this rich collection of activities from simply looking at words on a page.

Desktop computers do not support active reading. Once expected to create a paperless office, computers have instead produced ever-increasing quantities of paper documents. Dataquest predicts printers and copiers will generate over 1012 pages in the U.S. in 1997.

This statistic suggests that people do not use computers to read. The reason for this is obvious: paper supports extended, focused, deep reading practices better. Current research on digital libraries does not address a broad range of reading activities. Instead, as David Levy points out, digital libraries support shallower, more fragmented, and less concentrated reading.

The research focus in this field is on tools for search, selection, and distillation, tools that promote identification and extraction of information fragments. Because digital library interfaces do not support active reading, people search online and then print documents to read them. This "search and print" reality contrasts with the "search and read" ideal held by researchers.

Although a dual online/paper system is not *a priori* undesirable, we will show the many advantages of an online system that enables a variety of reading practices. The XLibris active reading machine supports a broad class of reading activities by employing a "paper document metaphor" (as opposed to the desktop metaphor) that imitates the physical experience of reading and marking on paper.

The paper document metaphor follows lessons learned from a number of studies comparing reading online to reading on paper, summarized below.

TANGIBILITY

Readers often move paper documents to avoid glare, to speed up handwriting, or to adjust their perspective of a text. In contrast, most computer displays are stationary while in use, so that readers must move themselves—their heads, their bodies, and their arms— rather than their display. XLibris supports paper document-like tangibility by running on tablet displays. Although XLibris has not been deployed for real use, people say that holding a page-sized display in their lap and being able to easily reposition it changes their online reading experience. The tangibility of paper documents also supports navigation. Turning paper pages seems easy and natural, and the weight and thickness of a paper document convey length and location.

In XLibris, pressure strips on the case of the device provide a tangible interface for page turning: pressing on one side of a sensor moves to the next or previous page, and holding down initiates riffling through pages. The harder you press, the faster you move. A quick animated transition indicates the direction of turning. Finally, "location guides" of varying thickness drawn in the top cor- ners of each page provide feedback about the length of the document and the reader's current location.

Page Orientation & Fixed Layout

Paper documents are laid out on fixed-size pages. The page layout often communicates the type of the document (e.g., business letter versus technical article) and where to find important information (e.g., a return address). The fixed layout also supports spatial memory and helps readers find old information.

In these and other ways, paper pages give readers an excellent "sense of the document." This sense of the document is often lost online.

Most CRT monitors cannot display a full page of text legibly, leading to awkward scrolling and zooming. Word processors and Web browsers commonly re-flow the text on a "page." And hypertext versions of paper documents can lead to disorientation and a sense of being lost. XLibris respects pages by displaying the image of a single page at a time.

Because the LCD panels we use are designed for landscape viewing, XLibris rotates the image 90° to approximate the portrait orientation of a typical printed page. XLibris stores the image of each page and the underlying text; this "image + text" file format is compatible with printed and with scanned documents.

Multiple Displays

People often work with multiple pieces of paper simultaneously, either with several pages from one document or with several documents. Most of today's computers provide multiple virtual displays through use of a windowing system. Unfortunately, the effort of managing window layout and switching among windows can interfere with reading.

Therefore XLibris displays a single page image and does not support windows. Since limiting the digital library information appliance to a single page image is problematic, we have considered a number of ways to address the need for collateral displays. Presenting two full-page images side by side, as in Book Emulator, makes text unreadable on current tablet displays, but may be feasible as LCD technology evolves. A form factor with multiple physical displays is another approach.

(Bush's vision of a Memex desk included multiple displays). In our case, to maintain mobility, a book (instead of a tablet or desk) with two opposable LCD panels may be appropriate. Weiser presents an enticing vision of ubiquitous computing with devices so cheap they can be scattered and used as paper.

In the near term, however, a small number of pen computers in conjunction with nearby desktop displays or even paper may provide the most practical solution to the problem of collateral document work. In summary, XLibris employs tangibility, page orientation, and fixed layout to provide an online reading experience comparable, in many ways, to reading from paper.

FREE FORM INK ANNOTATION

"Until we provide support for smooth integration of annotation with reading, it is likely that people will continue to annotate paper materials, even as they read materials in a digital library." – Cathy Marshall The second key document activity is annotation.

Knowledge work involves reading combined with categorizing, speculating, remembering, judging, or, more broadly, critical thinking.

This active reading process is facilitated by underlining, highlighting and making notes on the text or in a separate notebook. Marking on paper helps readers "make the text their own" and is a common practice associated with deep understanding of written information. In a nutshell, readers write.

Unfortunately, annotation online is quite different from its paper-based cousin. Interfaces for annotating often involve selecting a command, pointing with a mouse, and typing on a keyboard. They generally require much more effort than scribbling with a pen.

Text annotations are not as visually distinct as ink marks, and online annotations often cause changes in the layout of the document.

We believe that the ability to make unstructured, free-form, idiosyncratic ink marks is a crucial feature of any interface to digital libraries.

Although such marks may not have explicit meaning to the computer, they have rich semantic meaning, supporting visual and episodic memory. An essential aspect of ink on paper is its lack of modality: users can write anything they want, anywhere on the page. In XLibris, we followed this principle by letting users scribble notes, draw figures, highlight, or annotate text, all without switching modes or applications. Readers highlight and mark-up document page images as they read or flip to a blank page in a lined notebook for more space. XLibris provides several colors of ink, several highlighter pens, and a stroke-based eraser.

FLUID MOVEMENT AMONG DOCUMENT ACTIVITIES

The third key aspect of knowledge work is fluid movement among different styles of reading and different document activities. As an example, consider the process of "information triage" where an analyst skims through a pile of search results and reduces them to a manageable set.

The current practice is to fire off a query to a search engine, retrieve the 100 top-ranked documents, print them out, mark them up with highlighters, and put them into piles. Analysts then read the most relevant passages to answer the original question. Consider an alternative scenario where the analyst owns a digital library information appliance.

After conducting a search, the analyst skims the documents online. The appliance enhances skimming by emphasizing important material. As on paper, the analyst marks up important information as it is found. Instead of reviewing the collected information by thumbing through piles of paper, the analyst views a concise collection of his or her text annotations.

If any of the annotated material is worth reading in greater depth, the analyst can do so comfortably online. If the analyst needs more information, the text that has already been highlighted can be used to generate the next query.

At a high level, this scenario demonstrates fluid movement among document activities. The analyst quickly moves among searching, skimming, annotating, reviewing, and deep reading.

There is no waiting for a printer. Because skimming and deep reading are tightly integrated with retrieval, analysts can determine if the information they are collecting is useful before they invest much effort. This scenario also demonstrates how computation can enhance skimming, reviewing, and searching.

Because the interface is based on a paper document metaphor, the reading and annotation activities remain much the same as on paper. In our design, the "computer" remains in the background and, when requested, rises to the surface to assist the reader with the tasks of skimming, reviewing, and searching. Below we describe how XLibris supports and augments these three activities.

Skimming Mode

Skimming is one way readers gain a quick impression of a text. When skimming, the reader's eyes typically search for and alight on key words or sentences and take in short passages before moving on. Sometimes the reader becomes engaged and shifts into deep reading, or is distracted and moves into quicker skimming or into riffling. XLibris' "skimming mode" highlights phrases and sentences that are characteristic of the document being skimmed. We call out key phrases because they can be read at a glance and tend to reflect the topic of the nearby text.

This assists with the activity of scanning the text for relevant portions to read. The *Wall Street Journal* and *People Magazine* use a similar technique of boldfacing company names and Hollywood celebrities' name to help readers find information. We also highlight summary sentences to support a speedreading– like activity. Skimming mode uses a commercial text summarizer to identify summary sentences that are emphasized. Skimming through a document of highlighted summary sentences provides a narrative overview that is not available by just reading key phrases.

Both of these highlighting techniques permit a smooth transition from skimming to deep reading: key terms and sentences can help readers decide whether a passage is worth reading and are likely to be appropriate places to transition to deep reading. Skimming mode uses shades from gray to black to indicate term importance. Meaningful terms are identified by heuristics that select noun phrases.

The shade for each term is then based on a statistical information retrieval measure: terms that occur frequently in the document but occur rarely in other documents are colored black, while terms common to many documents are colored light gray. For example, the term "digital library information appliance" would be colored black when it appears in this document. Skimming is a common practice: a study of college students' reading habits reported that skimming occupied 32% of their reading time, and that "86% of the descriptions of skimming strategies mentioned a selection process based on key words and/or particular sentences and paragraphs in certain text locations".

Although our design requires empirical evaluation to confirm its utility, from our experiences thus far, we are optimistic that computers can improve the skimming activity and that augmented skimming is a useful function for a digital library information appliance.

Reviewing the Reader's Notebook

Reviewing paper documents is facilitated by the marks made during reading: marks not only record information but are also used to organize it for later review. There are three common venues for marking: annotating on the page, taking notes in a notebook, and writing on loose-leaf paper. Annotations on the page highlight key information but tend to be lost in piles of paper. Notebooks are compact and can be reviewed quickly, but taking notes can be tedious and error-prone.

Unbound notes can be reorganized flexibly, but require even more effort by the note taker. XLibris' Reader's Notebook combines the best features of annotating directly on the page, of taking notes in a separate notebook, and of organizing index cards. As with paper documents, readers mark on the page in the context of the document, yet without the laborious and imprecise step of copying.

As with a bound notebook, readers can review concise annotations by time. Finally, as with note cards, flexible filtering and sorting of the view allow readers to reorganize their information as needs change. The Reader's Notebook extracts "clippings" of annotated text and lays them end to end in a separate, multipage view.

Each clipping is linked to the corresponding annotated page, so readers can move fluidly between notes and documents. Each clipping includes some surrounding text, and is labeled with document title and page number to help readers understand the meaning of the marks. In designing clippings, we had to decide how much of the document should be shown for each annotation.

Starting with the bounding rectangle of each ink stroke, we expand it horizontally to the width of the page and vertically to include complete words. Snippets that overlap are merged together resulting in reasonably sized clippings of annotated text.

The Reader's Notebook can display, sort, and filter clippings from one document or from all documents. By default, clippings are sorted by document page number, which is analogous to rummaging through a pile of paper, but should be faster because readers do not see the less important (i.e., un-annotated) information. Clippings can also be sorted by time so that new information appears at the end, as in a paper notebook.

Finally, readers can filter the clippings by ink colour to search for different kinds of marks or to group related items together. Many readers already use different pens to mark different types of information. For example, some lawyers highlight "pro" information in green and "con" information in red.

Finding Information Related to Readers' Annotations

Readers often search for related material and move from one text to another. For example, an ecology student studying the effects of acid rain in the Appalachian Mountains decides to search the Internet for information on the economy of West Virginia. A doctor reading up on a drug she has never prescribed decides to follow a reference to a study of its side effects.

Unfortunately, in both online and offline situations, finding related materials and reading are not well integrated. Typical information retrieval interfaces force users to stop reading, to identify related documents, and then to print them.

References found in paper documents are even more timeconsuming to track down. Although hypertext was designed to address some of these problems, authors cannot anticipate the information needs of all readers. Ironically, despite the fact that readers' interests may change rapidly, interfaces for moving from reading to finding and back to reading again are time consuming and disruptive.

Clearly this is another example where fluid movement across document activities is desirable. XLibris facilitates fluid transitions among reading, searching and browsing by creating a dynamic hypertext from readers' marks.

The system observes readers' annotations and the text of the underlying document and generates hypertext links (margin links) to related documents: no additional effort from readers or authors is required. Because XLibris suggests links of interest to particular readers at particular times— based on the passages they are marking— people can discover useful information *serendipitously*. This type of serendipitous retrieval is a benefit of paper libraries: as people walk to the shelf for a particular book, walls of related books surround them, making it possible to find interesting material accidentally.

MARGIN LINKS

Margin links provide serendipitous access to related documents *during* the active reading process. As readers mark up passages, the system finds related documents and presents links unobtrusively in the margin; our intent is to provide a modeless link suggestion mechanism. Because margin links persist, readers can follow links at their leisure.

We use thumbnail images of the target page as anchors. The reader taps on an anchor to move to that page. For the most part, link creation does not disrupt the reading process since the reader is free to disregard the suggestion and to continue reading. In the current design, however, margin links intrude on the reading process more than we would like.

One problem is that XLibris computes a separate query for each stroke (although strokes often do not result in margin links because of a similarity threshold).

We have begun to address this by adding a button to turn links off and by designing ways to manage the frequency with which margin links appear.

FURTHER READING LISTS

When readers reach the end of a document, they often want to know more. The document may not emphasize the topic they are most interested in, or it may spark an interest in a new topic without providing enough depth or detail. Sometimes this need is addressed.

For example, articles in *Scientific American* typically describe an area of research at a high level, without providing much technical detail. The *Scientific American* example illustrates the limitations of authored reading lists. The article describes a technological vision for protecting digital copyrights. Consider a reader with a narrower interest, such as "how digital copyright affects librarians." The reference to a six-page article on digital copyright law may help track down this information, but the reference is unlikely to answer the question directly. Furthermore, by the time the reader scans the further reading list, more appropriate articles may have been written. XLibris augments this traditional editorial practice by automatically generating further reading lists for each document.

Unlike static references, these lists reflect the interests of a specific reader at a specific point in time. As with margin links, the reader's interests are inferred from annotations, and no additional intervention from the reader is required. Of course, the more annotations the user has made, the more focused the resulting list is on the reader's interest as opposed to the document as a whole. Visually, the further reading list looks like a Reader's Notebook of annotations except that each clipping is a segment of a related document obtained from a search engine.

These clippings, with matching terms underlined, help readers understand the destination of the link and also make the target passage more recognizable if they choose to follow the link.

Query-mediated Links

Both margin links and further reading lists use a technique called *query-mediated links*. Query-mediated links derive a query from a user's interaction with a document and use that query to identify related documents. Golovchinsky has shown that query-mediated links based on explicitly selected words and passages are effective in supporting information exploration tasks.

XLibris computes margin links from the words, phrases and passages that are implicitly selected by the reader's marks. (We do not expect readers to make marks for querying explicitly, but rather as part of their existing annotation practice.)

Marks are converted into text selections, which are then expressed as full-text queries that yield a best-matching passage. The system adds a margin link to the best match if its similarity value (or belief score) is above a threshold. For further reading lists, each annotation is interpreted as a text selection and is transformed into a list of word scores.

The scores for each word are then summed across all annotations. If several annotations select the same instance of a word, then the maximum score for that instance is used.

The words along with their scores are used to generate a query. If not many words have been included, then terms that are most characteristic of the document can be added. This padding reduces the chance that a query based on a small number of annotations will return documents that are entirely unrelated.

Ink Annotations as Queries

XLibris recognizes several distinct ink patterns from which queries are computed. These include underlined words, highlighted words, circled words, circled passages, and margin annotations. We emphasize that there is no "vocabulary of marks" that readers must learn; rather, our heuristics are based on general annotation practices. Each type of annotation results in a slightly different query for the search engine. Marks that select specific words translate into queries that retrieve other instances of the same term. Marks that select longer passages generate queries that search for similar passages.

PHYSICAL MOBILITY

The fourth and final document activity supported by digital library information appliances is mobility. Until now we have discussed reading in XLibris; in this section we describe mobile information access in TeleWeb. Desktop access to digital libraries is not adequate for mobile workers.

A doctor making hospital rounds has no desktop with her to access a digital library.

This could have grim repercussions: a recent study concluded that patients for whom prompt MEDLINE searches were conducted have significantly lower costs and shorter hospital stays. Mobile work is not limited to physicians and traveling salespeople; even office workers often work with documents away from their desks. For these people, portable information appliances can provide access to digital libraries anywhere, anytime. Unfortunately, it is not possible to give mobile people the same network access that they would have in their office. Compared to wired desktop networks, wireless networks are slow, expensive (with different billing schemes), and only intermittently available. As workers move from place to place, they are likely to experience three levels of connectivity: high quality connectivity from an office network, lower quality connectivity from a wireless network, and no connectivity at all when disconnected. How can people use digital library appliances to access distributed information sources across this range of operating conditions? Aside from the variable networking conditions, there are two other issues that affect mobile access to digital libraries.

First, downloading a document over a wireless network can be very expensive, and current interfaces for search engines and Web browsers do not help people manage these costs.

Second, user interaction is punctuated by surprises: an information request may return right away (when data is locally stored), take a while (when data is remote), or take forever (when the network is down). The TeleWeb mobile Web browser was designed and built to explore these three issues.

TeleWeb runs on a laptop computer with multiple communication channels: it may be docked to an office Ethernet, used from home over a telephone line, used while traveling over a wireless network such as a cell phone, or operated while not connected to a network. The lessons learned from TeleWeb apply not only to the Web but also to digital libraries. In the design of TeleWeb, we assumed that at least some of the time users would be disconnected but would still want to browse the Web. Some mobile networks are so limited in bandwidth compared to office networks that users may feel like they are disconnected.

How can people browse the Web when disconnected? TeleWeb uses "caching for availability," the standard solution for this problem. This means that the system loads documents into a local cache when fully connected.

Later, if the user needs the document while the network is not available, the locally cached copy is returned. Caching for availability only works if the system knows the user's information needs ahead of time. The system can use past history to predict future needs. In addition, the user can tell the system what documents belong in the cache; unfortunately, in practice people find it difficult to articulate which documents they need.

Furthermore, both techniques share the drawback that information needs often change in unpredictable ways. Overall, caching for availability often works, but is frustrating when it does not.

An alternative solution is to replace synchronous interaction (a user request followed immediately by a response from the network) with asynchronous interaction. For example, when the user requests a document not in the cache, TeleWeb asks the user if the system should download it later.

If so, Tele- Web downloads the information the next time the user connects and adds the document to a "to read" list that the user can browse. This interaction style is analogous to sending a request for a book from an out of state library, and eventually receiving it in the mail.

There are other reasons to postpone downloading a document. For example, if a user is connected over a cellular telephone, downloading a large document is going to be expensive, and can tie up the network connection for hours.

Given the choice, the user might be happy to download this document overnight or upon returning to the office. There is a tradeoff here between how urgently people need information and how much they are willing to pay for it in time and money. With a mobile information appliance, users should be able to decide how much they are willing to pay for each document and how quickly they need that document. With this principle in mind, TeleWeb includes a budget monitor that sits between the user and the network. If a request is made for a document that is not in the cache and downloading the document will break the user's budget, then TeleWeb presents a "conditional download" form instead of the document. Users can override their budget to fetch the document immediately, or they can request that the document be fetched at a later time.

Unpredictable Systems are Frustrating

The third problem of mobile appliances is unpredictable behaviour. Those using computer networks already know this problem: sometimes they hit a key and nothing happens. In wireless computing, this experience is magnified many-fold.

TeleWeb's solution is to show the user what is going on inside the cache and network manager. Specifically, Tele- Web labels links that will be slow to download with a "road work" icon.

If there is no road sign, then either the link destination is cached, or a high-speed connection to the information superhighway is available. This simple change— essentially exposing the state of the system— makes mobile Web browsing much more predictable. This contrasts with the traditional approach of trying to simplify the user's view of the system by concealing the state of the network.

THE FUTURE

The development of tomorrow's digital library information appliances is an iterative process. Our current cycle, however, is not complete until we evaluate the ideas presented in this paper.

Towards this end, we have begun a series of laboratory user interface experiments and are in the planning stage for a real-world deployment. One experiment suggests that free-form ink marks made while reading are better for query formulation than traditional relevance feedback.

People who have tried XLibris agree that our approach of taking a work practice and augmenting it— rather than redefining it— makes the system immediately accessible. Information *appliances* must be accessible. The digital library community must decide whether digital libraries should, as we propose, support users throughout the process of turning information into knowledge.

If so, there are many issues that must be addressed.

One reviewer of this paper asked: "Where is the digital library?" We purposely avoided describing protocols, services, and architectures because we believe infrastructure should *support* the vision of working with a digital library information appliance, not *define* it.

The next step is to understand how users of digital library information appliances should interact with external repositories. For example, should users pay authors to cache documents on their devices, even when they do not read them? How should users search repositories that are not always accessible?

How should searches be distributed between local and remote databases? These and other issues require further investigation. We have shown how information appliances based on the paper document metaphor can support active reading. Because these systems allow people to work on digital documents much as they would on paper, this provides an alternative to the standard "search and print" model of digital libraries.

Furthermore, by integrating a wide variety of document activities, and by allowing fluid movement among them, disruptive transitions between paper and digital media can be eliminated.

The combination of the paper-like and the digital allows us to augment these activities without redefining them. Finally, the mobility of a digital library information appliance supports work away from the desk.

With all these benefits, digital library information appliances can create a rich, universally accessible, digital library experience that improves the way we work. Clearly there is an exciting future for digital library information appliances in the digital library.

3

Library Networks: The Ability to Learn from Successes

Libraries are at the forefront of providing no-fee Internet access to the public. In 1994, just 8.2 percent of public libraries provided this service; as of 2009, 100 percent of libraries do so. While this is a vital role in every community, the library is the only source of no-fee public Internet access in 71 percent of communities.

The core mission of libraries is to connect people with ideas and information. Internet access makes it possible for libraries to fulfill this mission through online resources that can, for example, help people find jobs, improve their skills, access government services, create small businesses, complete school homework, and conduct research.

Libraries have reported high demand for Internet access; indeed, in the majority of libraries, the demand for publicaccess computers far outweighs the supply. As demand for public access to the Internet grows, so, too, does the need for higher bandwidth in the library.

In some communities, libraries play the important role of broadband anchor institution; in other words, by obtaining high-bandwidth connections, they drive the deployment of advanced technologies to communities that might be unable to obtain that level of service through residential demand alone.

In short, libraries that are able to meet the demand for no-fee public Internet access play a vital role in serving both their users and their communities. To help libraries achieve this capability, the Bill and Melinda Gates Foundation initiated the Opportunity Online Broadband Grant Programme. This programme provides funding and support to help State Library agencies in seven states—Massachusetts, New York, Virginia, Arkansas, Kansas, California, and Texas—develop leadership and improve library connectivity to the Internet.

The American Library Association's Office for Information Technology Policy (OITP) is participating in this programme, providing research and consulting services to state libraries, as well as developing publications that address key issues salient to the program's goals. The purpose of this publication is to provide a snapshot of five different library networks that provide users with no-fee Internet access. Strong leadership was an essential element in the development of each of the five networks. At the same time, leadership was distributed among different players at the state, regional, and local levels and was not the exclusive domain of one person or organisation. Moreover, cooperation among these players was a hallmark of the effort. The case studies also illustrate how the various organisations involved often drew on the experiences of other successful cooperative projects to help in the development of their network.

In the formative stage of the Ohio Public Library and Information Network (OPLIN), public libraries that wanted to emulate successful school and academic networks broached the idea of a public library network with the state library association. This association, later called the Ohio Library Council (OLC), assumed a leadership role, and two OLC staff members organised planning and advocacy efforts that led to OPLIN's development.

The West Virginia Network was the first network to centralise the state's computing and data needs. Statewide Library Network (SLN) leadership acknowledged learning from this first statewide network during the project development. Taking a cooperative approach similar to that applied in the development of OPLIN, Wisconsin's local and regional libraries and State Library officials worked together to define the libraries' role in BadgerNet. A past collaborative project to establish a distance learning video network was a key factor in the creation of a 1993 Governor's Blue Ribbon Telecommunications Infrastructure Task Force, which in turn recommended the creation of BadgerNet. The Maine School and Library Network (MSLN) was also the result of cooperation between statewide library associations and the State Library agency. Finally, the member libraries of California's Peninsula Library System (PLS) developed the Peninsula Libraries Automated Network (PLAN) based on their past success with a common circulation and catalog system. Perhaps the most important factor contributing to the success of PLAN is the spirit and habit of cooperation among PLS members. Since, 1982, member libraries have been cooperating to operate a joint circulation system.

Such collaborations require that libraries engage in significant give-and-take to modify longstanding local policies and procedures so as to accommodate a centralised system. This habit of collaboration led to the success of other collective endeavors, including PLAN.

AGGREGATION OF DEMAND AND SERVICES

Aggregation of demand is an acknowledged successful approach to network management. Among its benefits are:

- Improved planning
- Support for a business case for providers to deploy broadband

- More affordable pricing
- Sharing of costs

Aggregation of demand allowed the establishment of each of the five successful networks profiled here, and its benefits have contributed to the networks' continued success. For example, MSLN aggregates library traffic to two nodes, which results in lower recurring expenses for Internet access. Aggregation offers other, less obvious benefits. An example is streamlining and standardisation of members' E-rate participation. All of the statewide networks profiled here regularly file for E-rate discounts on behalf of their members or offer assistance to members in doing so.

A centralised application relieves the burden on individual libraries. MSLN files an aggregated application for federal E-rate discounts and an application for Maine's state universal service fund. Wisconsin files one aggregated E-rate application that includes every K-12 school district and public library on BadgerNet (about 910 sites), and also completes all the required follow-up.

Considering that the most frequently cited reason for libraries' non-participation in the E-rate programme is the complexity of the process, this is a very real benefit with tangible results. Standardisation is a key requirement for aggregation. OPLIN, MSLN, PLS, and BadgerNet require the same router configuration for every library site; SLN requires that all members have the same network equipment; and every school and library on BadgerNet has the same standard Ethernet interface.

Standardisation avoids the logistical challenges associated with customisation. It also allows for aggregation of technical support services. The benefits of aggregating technical support are readily apparent in West Virginia, where these services are typically beyond the means of individual public libraries with limited budgets and staff expertise. MSLN employs a shared project manager to provide planning guidance to individual libraries, a service that would otherwise be too costly for individual libraries.

USE OF DEMONSTRATIONS

OITP's past research suggests that technology demonstrations are necessary to convince a library's community to support a major new effort such as a regional or statewide network. Such demonstrations, while providing essential training to library staff, also serve a critical outreach and public relations function. For example, during the initial phase of network development, OPLIN staff members visited libraries around the state to demonstrate how access to the Internet would help their users. While demonstrations can be very helpful in growing network membership, their usefulness does not end with the network's establishment.

OPLIN and SLN representatives continue to provide information on network services and their use at annual conferences and meetings. Other library systems offer ongoing training on new resources provided via the network and on how library staff can use these resources to improve library services and ultimately benefit the library's patrons. Demonstrations can also help achieve the network's sustainability when used as an advocacy tool for continued funding and support of network projects.

PROVISION OF TECHNICAL SUPPORT AND TRAINING FOR LIBRARY STAFF

Library networks are complex technical entities that support many users and applications; it is unreasonable to expect local library staff, especially those in smaller or rural libraries, to provide comprehensive technical support for the network. All the networks profiled here provide members with some level of technical support and training in how to solve technical problems.

The level of support ranges from handling all network problems to training local librarians in problem solving. Two of the networks—PLAN and Badger Net—continuously monitor network traffic and respond with solutions when they are needed. The case studies demonstrate several innovative approaches to supporting large networks:

- In a centralised model, OPLIN manages a support center that offers members a first line of defence for network troubleshooting.
- MSLN employs one circuit rider whose responsibilities include focusing on resource poor libraries with the most serious problems and developing technical skills among local library staff.
- SLN has network support staff in offices throughout the state and, like MSLN, works to develop the technical skills of library staff.
- In Wisconsin, regional library systems serve as the first point of contact to assist with troubleshooting and the installation of new equipment and software.
- In California, PLS meets the need for network-level support only; its member libraries all have technical support staff on site.

MULTIPLE FUNDING SOURCES

The networks profiled here rely on various revenue streams, such as grant funds, telecommunications settlement funds, universal service funds, state general funds, and local library funding. The five networks were established in economically favorable times, when state and other funds were more readily available for large capital projects than is the case today.

Nevertheless, all the networks face the challenge of securing ongoing funding. Even Maine, which has the most stable source of funding (state and federal universal service funds), struggles with balancing the need for increased network services with limited funding resources. The major sources of funding for the statewide networks have historically been state tax funds and universal service funds (both the federal E-rate programme and state-based programmes).

During the last year, however, tax revenues have decreased sharply in almost every state, and both OPLIN and SLN were in danger of losing significant state funding. California's PLS, funded primarily by member fees derived from local property taxes, has yet to see any significant reductions as assessments of property lag at least one year behind tax collections. Federal universal service funds are relatively stable. However, the total of applications for discounts is approaching fund availability, absent any policy intervention. Additionally, some organisations find the requirements for obtaining such funds to be onerous or contrary to their policies.

ROLE FOR LIBRARY REPRESENTATIVES IN NETWORK GOVERNANCE

The case study networks have widely varying governance and management structures.

For example:

- The Maine Public Utilities Commission (MPUC) governs MSLN.
- Wisconsin's Department of Administration manages BadgerNet.
- The West Virginia Library Commission administers SLN.

All of these networks are dependent on the network's information technology (IT) staff for ensuring the day-to-day management of network operations. But just as there are differences in network management (*e.g.,* some may be outsourced), there are also differences in overall network governance and how much input the library community has to make decisions or to set network policy. For example, the OPLIN governing board in Ohio consists solely of member library representatives. Wisconsin's BadgerNet Advisory Council includes representatives of all network users including libraries, K-12 schools, higher education and state government.

The Advisory Council advises the state Administration Department in areas like member bandwidth needs and planning for the next generation network. California's PLS allows the technical staff of member libraries to be involved with network issues through a committee structure.

INVOLVEMENT OF THE STATE LIBRARY

One common characteristic of the statewide networks is the active involvement of the State Library:

- The State Library of Ohio has strong influence over OPLIN operations and development as a result of its authority to appoint all of the network's board members.
- The State Library in West Virginia operates SLN.
- In Wisconsin, the State Library influences BadgerNet planning and operations through its seat on the BadgerNet Council.

Although MSLN's governing board is the Maine Public Utilities Commission (MPUC), the state librarian is responsible for suggesting policy and for representing the interests of libraries before the MPUC. Furthermore, the Maine State Library has staff members responsible for assessing the needs of MSLN members and for preparing an annual report that outlines the network's needs and presents an annual budget request.

OHIO PUBLIC LIBRARY INFORMATION NETWORK

HISTORY

The Ohio Public Library Information Network (OPLIN) began to take shape in 1994 when a small group of librarians from a suburban library system discussed the need for a statewide public library network similar to the networks used by academic libraries (OhioLink) and K-12 libraries (INFOhio).

This group of librarians reached out to the Ohio Library Council (OLC, then known as the Ohio Library Association), which helped to develop a plan to create the network and lobbied state legislators for the funding to build it. Fran Haley, who had recently joined the OLC, was instrumental in bringing together experienced individuals to develop the network plan and in inviting the entire library community to participate in the process. Greg Byerly, was hired by the OLC to draft the initial plan for OPLIN.

He also worked to allow the state's public libraries to purchase telecommunications services from the statewide SOMACS (State of Ohio Multi-Agency Communications System) contract. The SOMACS contract provides postalised rates for its telecommunications circuits, so that the monthly price remains the same regardless of the length of the circuit or the location of the library.

OPLIN was created by state law in 1995. With the persistence of the OLC and the support of the legislature and then-Governor Voinovich, OPLIN was initially allocated $4.85 million. Before the state budget was passed in 1995, an additional $8 million was added to fund startup costs to network public libraries. The OPLIN board decided to provide funds for the initial installation connecting branch libraries to the network, but not to support recurring costs for these connections.

The board also decided to provide a telecommunications line for one library site (usually the main library) and to support its recurring costs in addition to purchasing computers so that each library would have two public workstations with which to access OPLIN. All but one of the 251 main library systems in Ohio joined OPLIN immediately.

Local boards passed a resolution for each library system to join, and each established its own Internet access policy for the network. The library system pursued funding for the project at the right time, as the state budget was flush, and the overall economic situation in the state was favorable. Funds remained even after OPLIN had been built, allowing the libraries to purchase subscriptions to databases and other electronic materials.

SERVICES

OPLIN provides both broadband Internet connections and information services to Ohio public libraries. Its mission is to ensure that all Ohio residents have fast, free public Internet access through the state's local public library systems, as well as the use of highquality research and reference databases not available free of charge on the World Wide Web.

OPLIN provides these services at no cost to the libraries. Unlike the situation in many other states, OPLIN coordinates the acquisition and installation of the physical telecommunications circuits that connect the main libraries to the network's hub in Columbus. (Most other library networks deliver content and services primarily via a physical network provided by some other organisation.) OPLIN leases circuits for the main libraries under two contracts the state has with telecommunications service providers.

Branch libraries, however, must obtain their own local broadband telecommunications connection to their main library. OPLIN also serves as the Internet service provider (ISP) for all public libraries in Ohio. It manages mail servers and provides the libraries with e-mail services. In addition, OPLIN provides web hosting services for those libraries with their own web site.

User Support and Communications

The OPLIN Support Center serves as the first line of defence for database problems and network troubleshooting. The center received 2,304 library technical service requests in fiscal year 2008, the majority of which related to e-mail issues. The OPLIN Support Center is open only during the workweek; after-hours and weekend calls are directed to the State of Ohio's Network Operations Center. OPLIN communicates with its members in a number of ways. It operates three e-mail lists: one for non-technical topics, one for the OPLIN office to announce new services and important changes to existing services, and one for technical topics. OPLIN also publishes a quarterly newsletter, participates on social networking web sites, publishes three blogs, and has a web site.

Telecommunications and Broadband Services

OPLIN obtains the local telecommunications circuits for all but one of the main libraries in the State of Ohio. These circuits connect the main library to the OPLIN hub in Columbus. As part of a state agency, OPLIN is authorised to lease these circuits under two state contracts: the SOMACS contract, serviced largely by AT&T and used to lease traditional T1 circuits that provide a capacity of 1.5 megabits per second (Mbps), and a separate contract for fibre-based Ethernet services.

OPLIN often transitions main libraries that need upgraded capacity to an Ethernet connection, but these Ethernet services are not available statewide.

OPLIN also provides its members with continuous monitoring of broadband traffic. Every quarter, traffic statistics for each main library are reviewed to see whether traffic patterns warrant an upgrade to a fiberbased Ethernet circuit (or DS1 or DS3 if Ethernet is not available). The additional bandwidth and coordination for implementation are handled by OPLIN at no charge to the main library.

NETWORK STRUCTURE

In addition to the local circuits that connect the main libraries to the OPLIN hub, OPLIN maintains a high-capacity connection from its hub to the Internet over a shared, channelised DS3 connection that is managed by the Ohio Office of Information Technology (OIT). The OIT router manages traffic to OPLIN-provided resources, to the Internet, or back to other OPLIN member libraries.

The bandwidth charge for this connection to the Internet is the fastest-growing expense for OPLIN. As figure indicates, each main library receives a router provided by OPLIN to connect its circuit to the OPLIN hub. Management of this router is carried out collaboratively between OPLIN staff and the engineering group within OIT. The router represents the demarcation point between OPLIN services and the main library's local area network (LAN).

Each main library is responsible for its own LAN management services. OPLIN offers each main library a subnet of 32 publicly routable Internet Protocol (IP) addresses. Each main library administers these addresses following its own policies. As noted, OPLIN does not provide the local broadband connections for branch libraries. The branch libraries associated with each main library system can use a variety of options for connecting to the main library. In many cases, the SOMACS contract allows libraries to pay for a postalised T1, which is available statewide for only $400 per month. Figure shows this option in green.

While the SOMACS contract is available to any branch library, occasionally less expensive options exist. Some branches choose to purchase a digital subscriber line (DSL) circuit to connect virtually to the main library through a virtual private network (VPN). On other occasions, the branch library is located close enough to the main library that a local telephone company can connect both locations with a DS1 for less than the $400 per month under the SOMACS contract.

The line in figure highlights this option. Finally, in some communities, cable TV companies offering telecommunications services can provide a branch library with either a DS1 or an Ethernet connection. Fibre is another option that is gaining popularity among libraries in Ohio. The State of Ohio has signed a separate contract that includes AT&T's Optical Ethernet Metropolitan Area Network (OPT-E-MAN). OPT-E-MAN is typically provisioned via a fibre connection with bandwidth increments as low as 5 Mbps and scalable to 100

Mbps. Libraries that can purchase fibre-based service are ideally positioned to add bandwidth quickly and less expensively than is the case with traditional telephone company services (*e.g.,* T1/DS1, T3/DS3). Pricing for Ethernet services can vary significantly from location to location. The price for a 10 Mbps circuit can range from $600 per month to about $1,000 per month, not including router management fees and Internet access bandwidth.

GOVERNANCE

OPLIN is an independent state agency within the State Library of Ohio. It is governed by a board of eleven members selected by the State Library Board from the staffs of member public libraries and current or past trustees. The OPLIN Executive Director and the State Librarian or his/her designees serve as ex officio board members. Stephen Hedges has served as OPLIN's Executive Director since, 2006 and supervises four staff members.

OPLIN receives fiscal and logistical support services from the State Library of Ohio and contracts with OIT for assistance with network management. OPLIN is now defined in the Ohio Revised Code. Until recently, it was a line item in the State Library budget, meaning that it technically ceased to exist every 2 years. OPLIN is now part of the permanent law, which allows it to take advantage of longer service contracts.

FINANCE

The majority of OPLIN's budget—58 per cent—is spent on purchasing Internet connections to public libraries, which it regards as its most important role. Another 30 percent is spent on databases, which make up about a third of the total cost of the Ohio Web Library database collection. About 2 per cent of OPLIN's budget is allocated by the legislature for grant subsidies to local libraries to help defray the cost of filtering Internet content; another 1 per cent funds conferences and other training for public librarians.

The remaining 9 per cent of the budget is used for all other costs—rent, salaries and benefits (for five staff), supplies, postage, office equipment, etc. Thus more than 90 percent of the OPLIN budget is spent on direct services to public libraries, and less than 10 per cent on administrative costs. From the network's inception in the fiscal year (FY) 1995 budget bill through FY 2007, annual funding for OPLIN varied between $5 million and $8 million each year. Because of the state's recent fiscal problems, OPLIN's budget was reduced in 2008 and 2009, and additional reductions may occur in 2010.

To make up for the loss of state revenue, OPLIN has entered into an agreement with eTech Ohio to manage its E-rate applications this year. OPLIN expects that eTech Ohio's E-rate expertise will lead to more federal E-rate discounts than in the past. Libraries can call on eTech Ohio for E-rate consulting, and eTech Ohio will also be conducting E-rate workshops.

WEST VIRGINIA'S STATEWIDE LIBRARY NETWORK

HISTORY

Many West Virginians depend on their public libraries for Internet access. The West Virginia Library Commission (WVLC) established the centralised Statewide Library Network (SLN) to meet this need. Beginning in the 1990s, the WVLC received a federal grant for a project to connect West Virginia public libraries with 56 kilobits per second (Kbps) frame relay lines leased from Bell Atlantic (now Verizon) and other providers. By 1999, all but 3 of West Virginia's 177 public libraries were connected.

The West Virginia Network (WVNET), the state's Internet service provider, was also instrumental in developing SLN. WVNET was established in 1975 to centralise the state's computing and data needs. It originally connected the colleges and universities in West Virginia to its central hub, and later grew to serve government offices, K-12 schools, and libraries. WVNET established a statewide intranet in 1994 and continues to provide Internet connectivity to libraries today.

WVNET reports to the West Virginia Higher Education Policy Commission and is aided by a Computer Advisory Board, with representatives from higher education and other users of WVNET.

Internet access spurred demand at libraries across the state for such resources as electronic journals, shared library resources, e-mail, and learning programmes. Meeting this demand required more robust connections, so the Library Network 2000 plan was developed to upgrade and standardise the libraries' hardware and software.

Technicians visited every library in the network and installed suitable cabling, reprogrammed equipment, issued new Internet Protocol (IP) addresses, and provided standardised Internet connections. The network staff received a Governor's Award and a National Association of State Information Resource Executives nomination for the planning and implementation of the Network 2000 project. In September 2002, Verizon provided a $1.6 million grant (over 2 years) for the Digital Bridge Project, designed to upgrade the 56 Kbps connections with DS1 (1.5 megabits per second) lines. As of summer 2009, all 177 libraries had been connected with a DS1 line.

Today, the success of this upgraded network is evident in libraries across West Virginia. At a March 2009 WVLC meeting, the Director of Weirton's Mary H. Weir Library, Rik Rekowski, reported that the library's Internet center had 16,000 visitors every year in a town with a population of only 18,748.

Sandy Bumgardner, Director of the Upshur County Library, a service center for several libraries in very rural areas, said that many community residents lack access to highspeed Internet in their homes because dialup access is their only affordable choice. Furthermore, a number of residents who live in areas with affordable Internet access have cancelled their home subscriptions to save money.

These residents use the libraries' public-access computers to search the Internet, write résumés, and complete job applications. Further upgrades are planned for SLN. By 2012, the network will offer Ethernet connections that will operate approximately 10 times faster than T1.

SERVICES

SLN provides all the state's public libraries with Internet access, e-mail communication, data lines, hubs and switches, and technical support. Libraries may also receive funding and support for a shared integrated library system (ILS). In many other states, technical support for network services is the responsibility of the individual library.

West Virginia is different in that the libraries receive, at no charge, the following services:

- Wide area networking, local area networking, and wireless access support
- Help desk services
- Router installation and maintenance
- PC software/hardware replacement and maintenance
- UNIX hardware/software maintenance
- ILS (if shared with other libraries)
- Hubs, switches, and associated cabling (both installation and maintenance)
- Equipment contract support
- Data circuit installation and maintenance
- Network monitoring
- E-rate support

West Virginia made the strategic decision to centralise technology support for its libraries at the state level. As a result, it achieves excellent statewide coverage with just 11 technicians. Each of the technicians directly supports libraries within an assigned region of the state, but he or she also provides support to neighboring regions when the need arises. Most of West Virginia's public libraries had limited access to technical support before the WVLC filled this role.

Libraries now have access to technology assistance for simple problems, such as printer jams, and more complex problems, such as router maintenance. Network technicians also visit libraries to offer library staff members training on various topics, including using the Internet, e-mail, and online databases; establishing remote computer repair options; and completing E-rate applications. Network personnel also provide training sessions during annual library functions and offer classes throughout the year. For example, one SLN technician teaches simple troubleshooting measures to library staff so they can solve technical problems independently instead of calling a technician. SLN's technical support takes a variety of other forms. A series of public service announcements provides basic information about computer viruses, how to perform software updates, and other troubleshooting tips. In addition, SLN maintains four regional desktop computer labs that allow library staff in those regions to access training without driving long distances or staying overnight. Two mobile laptop labs are available for on-site training in more remote libraries. Significant to this centralisation of technical support is the standardisation of the network equipment and configuration and deployment processes.

Any member of the SLN staff, regardless of the region of assignment, can walk into any library and know what equipment and network configuration to expect. In addition, technicians can implement upgrades to the network without having to customise each library's infrastructure. Director of the Wayne County Libraries, "The main benefit of having a statewide network is that it eliminates the need for duplication of service if every county had to run its own network.

The state is able to provide more qualified support than a county could. In the long run, it saves money. If there is a problem, there is one number the local library has to call for assistance. The state office always has somebody on staff qualified to assist with networking issues. Some of the counties may not have access to qualified technicians due to the rural nature of some areas of the state."

NETWORK STRUCTURE

The West Virginia Department of Administration manages a statewide contract for telecommunications services. All public libraries are connected to SLN by purchasing a DS1 from this contract; all of the state's 177 libraries now have a DS1 connection.

Ordering and installation of the circuit are coordinated by the WVLC. Depending on the location of a library, the DS1 connects to either the northern data center in Morgantown or the state capital of Charleston in the south. Traffic destined for the Internet is handed off to WVNET, and the rest remains within SLN. To comply with the Children's Internet Protection Act (CIPA), the WVLC provides Internet filtering using Netsweeper software hosted on the state backbone network.

The WVLC shares this service with other state agencies that must filter Internet traffic, allowing the expense to be spread across a larger pool of members. An advantage of the design of SLN is that only Internet traffic is filtered through Netsweeper. Centralising the filtering tools has eliminated the need for individual libraries or systems to purchase their own filtering software.

This large network requires careful bandwidth monitoring. The WVLC monitors the bandwidth use of individual libraries as well as the statewide network via a monitoring network operations center in Charleston. The monitoring software provides hourly/daily/monthly bandwidth charts for each library, audible/visual outage reports, and battery temperatures.

GOVERNANCE

The WVLC, which established SLN, consists of seven members, all of whom are appointed by the governor and confirmed by the state senate. The WVLC appoints a secretary who serves as State Librarian and manages the WVLC Network Services department, one of the four departments within the commission's office.

As noted earlier, the WVLC centralises support for libraries at the state level and achieves statewide coverage with only 11 staff members. A key to SLN's success is the uniform approach to network design and service, which lends itself to economies of scale. The WVLC has encouraged all libraries to join the network, giving it more power to aggregate demand and further upgrade connections. The WVLC takes a similar approach to technology and E-rate support, centralising these services at the state level to derive benefits from the aggregation of service provision. The WVLC developed and expanded SLN through a combination of advocacy and strong leadership.

It directly recruited public libraries, which were added to the network as funds became available. At its inception, the network also included four academic libraries. As of 2009, there are two. One left the network as a result of a change in administration, and the other joined a private college consortium. The network includes other non-public library participants as well.

The Archives and History Library, a department of the state's Division of Culture and History, shares a catalog server with the WVLC. A few K-12 schools have also been added to SLN. Under state law, the WVLC cannot make direct grants to school libraries, so it pays for the cost of adding them as users of the integrated catalog software.

FINANCE

SLN has enjoyed strong support from the West Virginia legislature and has tapped other funding sources as well. In 1996, the WVLC, WVNET, and the West Virginia Department of Education successfully implemented a $2.5 million grant from the U.S. Department of Education. The first libraries received Internet access under this grant. Additional funding through federal and state grants expanded the number of libraries in SLN. The final public libraries added to the network benefited from federal Library Services and Technology Act (LSTA) funds.

Also in 1996, the legislature provided a onetime allocation of $1 million for upgrades and allocated $1 million for ongoing support. In March 1998, a

$1.9 million grant from the Bill and Melinda Gates Foundation provided computers for the state's public libraries. A July 2002 grant of $991,281 from the State Telecommunications Users' Council allowed SLN to purchase servers. In addition to state and foundation grant funding, the WVLC applies annually for E-rate discounts for SLN. The average E-rate discount rate in 2009 was 76 percent. State legislators cut SLN's fiscal year 2010 budget by 28 percent or $347,000 from its $1.1 million budget in fiscal year 2009. This reduction will most likely slow the upgrading of SLN libraries' local area networks, including evaluating and replacing wiring, switches, and other critical network components. The WVLC also plans to support SLN with some LSTA funds. This funding shift will reduce amounts available for other library programmes typically supported by LSTA funds, including direct grants to local libraries.

WISCONSIN'S BADGERNET NETWORK

HISTORY

Since, as early as the 1970s, Wisconsin has been one of the nation's leaders in creating long-haul video networks to provide distance learning to schools. In 1993, to build on this success, then-Governor Thompson established a Governor's Blue Ribbon Telecommunications Task Force.

The task force was charged to:

- Develop a vision for a statewide telecommunications network for educational institutions and government agencies and
- Recommend changes in state statutes and policy to remove barriers to the realisation of this vision.

In its planning for the statewide infrastructure, the task force also was required to consider and integrate Wisconsin's existing K-12 video network—consisting of more than 8,000 miles of fibre throughout the state at the time—into the network plans.

The Wisconsin Department of Public Instruction (DPI), which houses the State Library Agency, advocated for consideration of library needs in the network's development, and libraries played an active role in the planning effort. The State Library and several members of regional library systems participated in the task force and made their concerns and interests known to the task force participants and to legislators. The task force recommended the creation of BadgerNet in 1993, and the legislature adopted most of the task force's recommendations in 1995. Libraries were specifically included in the statute as eligible to access the BadgerNet network. Shortly thereafter, the legislature created the TEACH (Technology for Educational Achievement) programme to help schools and libraries obtain and sustain their use of technology. BadgerNet was created at a time when the economy was stable and growing. This economic stability allowed the state sufficient time to undertake the 3-year effort and engage many stakeholders in the development of the statewide network.

Additionally, the positive economic climate and the growth of telecommunications services in the late 1990s allowed the legislature to add revenue to the state's universal service fund (which collects funds from in-state telecommunications providers) to fund the TEACH programme.

Following another two-year planning process, in March 2005, the Wisconsin Department of Administration (DOA) entered into a new $116.7 million, 5-year agreement with the consortium of telecommunications providers that deliver BadgerNet services for a new converged, higher-capacity data and video network called the BadgerNet Converged Network (BCN). The transition to the new network was completed on September 1, 2006. The State Library Agency helped coordinate this transition. At that time, BCN was the largest state network of its type that AT&T, the prime vendor, had under contract.

SERVICES

Wisconsin's seventeen regional library systems are required to assist their member libraries in matters related to technology in exchange for state funding. In this regard, they play an important role in addressing local public library broadband and Internet connectivity needs.

Among the services they provide:

- The regional library systems manage wide area networks (WANs) for their member libraries. The WANs are part of the regional network infra-structure that ultimately connects to the BadgerNet backbone at four locations in the state. WANs are used primarily for shared integrated library system traffic and Internet access. Of the services offered through the BCN contract, the libraries most frequently use the WAN service, which links remote libraries to the headquarters of the regional library system in a hub-and-spoke network design.
- All seventeen systems provide consulting for the purchase of computer software and hardware.
- Many systems also offer centralised purchasing for software and hardware, which allows member libraries to obtain a lower price than they could negotiate individually.
- Sixteen of the seventeen regional systems make information technology (IT) staff available as the first point of contact to assist with troubleshooting and the installation of new software and hardware.

BadgerNet also offers high-resolution, real-time interactive video to approximately 350 K-12 schools. Included in these video services are a network scheduling function and specialised equipment that permits three or more locations to be joined together in a videoconference. Classes offered over the network are an integral part of instruction, with as many as thirtytwo separate conferences linking more than a hundred classrooms during a single hour.

Finally, BadgerNet offers network support and help desk service around the clock.

NETWORK STRUCTURE

BadgerNet serves state government, some local governments, universities, technical colleges and tribal nations, and most of the state's K-12 school districts and public libraries. All state agencies are required to use BadgerNet; 900 state agency remote locations use the data network capability of the system to connect to their agency headquarters in Madison.

In total, the network exceeds 2,400 end-points spread across each of the state's 72 counties. Although library participation is voluntary, about 97 per cent of Wisconsin's public libraries have connected to the Internet via BadgerNet since, the mid-1990s. As noted, the libraries generally use a WAN topology such that individual library circuits connect back to the headquarters of the regional library system. The regional system then aggregates the Internet traffic of its member libraries and provides a direct connection to the Internet service provider (ISP). This can be seen in figure.

AT&T serves as BCN's prime contractor, although additional services are provisioned by a consortium of telecommunications providers that includes other local telephone companies. Fortunately for the regional public library systems, the BCN contract allows the local provider to provision service in a variety of ways while ensuring that each library's interface is always the same 10/100 Ethernet port. Routing of traffic through the aggregation and core layers of the network is always the same as well, regardless of the access layer technology. Without exception, Wisconsin's regional library systems have adopted the hub-and-spoke WAN design. Choosing one library, often the headquarters of the regional library system, to act as the hub provides equipment consolidation advantages as well as bandwidth and port access to the Internet.

Two aspects of BCN are somewhat unusual and particularly beneficial to Wisconsin's library connectivity. First, the BCN contract covers all three network layers (a local access connection, an aggregation point, and a core). Most statewide networks provide the backbone, but the library or library system must acquire the local access connection on its own. BCN, through the TEACH programme, subsidises the cost of the local connections in addition to maintaining the backbone.

The network's comprehensive end-to-end service is one reason why almost every public library in the state uses BCN. Second, BCN includes an Ethernet port as the end-user interface. An Ethernet port makes it extremely easy for the library to connect its equipment (such as a firewall, local switch, or router) to the network because the interface will always be an industry standard 10/ 100 Ethernet port. Because BCN uses Ethernet connections, the library can purchase flexible increments of bandwidth. In other words, the library can increase its capacity to 3 megabits per second (Mbps), 5 Mbps, 10 Mbps, 15

Mbps, 20 Mbps, etc. (traditional telephone company offerings are limited to either 1.5 Mbps or 45 Mbps).

Some of the larger telephone companies, such as AT&T and Verizon, and some larger independent phone companies deploy fibre optic cables to libraries requesting highspeed circuits. Typically, fibre is deployed for sites needing 10 Mbps or greater, but some companies deploy fibre to sites with as little as 3 Mbps in anticipation of future growth.

The BCN portfolio of services does not, however, include asymmetrical services, such as digital subscriber line (DSL), microwave, and satellite technology alternatives, because it was too difficult to include every available technology and keep the service consistent. Even though these options are not available through BCN, some library systems purchase DSL services outside of the BCN contract; DSL is often used for patron wireless Internet access.

GOVERNANCE

BadgerNet is the state's telecommunications network; it does not provide Internet service. Most BadgerNet users (*e.g.,* state government, schools, and libraries) receive their Internet access via WiscNet. WiscNet is a not-for-profit association that operates under the auspices of the University of Wisconsin-Madison.

It is governed by a board of directors representing member institutions. A representative from the State Library and a representative from the regional library systems are on the board. WiscNet started providing Internet access in 1991 to 26 colleges and universities in the state. When the first BadgerNet network was built in the mid-1990s, WiscNet expanded its services to include K-12 schools and public libraries. BadgerNet is administered by the network office in the DOA.

The BadgerNet Advisory Council advises the DOA and the service provider on customer issues relating to the network contract, the operation of the network, and the process for developing timely solutions for services provided under the contract; it also provides a forum for planning. The council is made up of representatives from constituent groups, including one representative of a regional public library system and a representative of the State Library.

FINANCE

BadgerNet and its service vendor operate under a 5-year contract, and prices are stable for libraries within this contract period. Under the TEACH programme, schools, libraries, and other eligible institutions pay a reduced rate for their broadband connections; the remainder is paid by the TEACH programme. Schools and libraries pay $100 per month for a broadband connection up to 3 Mbps and $250 per month for a connection between 4 and

100 Mbps. The BCN contract ends in 2011, and the BadgerNet Advisory Council is actively planning for the network's future contract service requirements. The BadgerNet contract charges the same rate to each library regardless of the distance between the library and the aggregation node. These postalised rates ensure that rural libraries pay the same monthly price for access to the BadgerNet network as urban and suburban libraries.

For public libraries in the state, the average membership fee in WiscNet is about $450 per year. More than 90 percent of the libraries have this fee paid by their regional library system.

From its inception, BadgerNet required its vendors to build in rural as well as urban areas and to offer postalised rates.

While this helped reduce the price for rural libraries to connect to the network, it has caused problems in urban areas. Some urban libraries, especially in the Milwaukee area, are finding that they can save money by purchasing service from other providers instead of from BCN.

The TEACH programme uses state universal service funds to subsidise local access connections to BadgerNet for K-12 schools, public libraries, and regional library systems. TEACH pays for equipment, the installation costs for the local data lines and video links to BadgerNet, and a portion of the monthly service costs.

TEACH receives its funding from the state's universal service fund and from the federal E-rate programme. On an annual basis, TEACH spends approximately $13.8 million to subsidise network costs for schools and libraries. The subsidy for public libraries and regional public library systems is approximately $3 million annually.

TEACH received additional spending authority in the fiscal year 2007-2009 budget, which enabled more than 60 percent of the state's public libraries to increase their bandwidth at no direct cost to the library.

Separate from the funding for the TEACH programme, the state's universal service fund also provides an increasing amount of state aid to regional library systems. In prior years, the state universal service fund has generated $5 million for state aid to library systems. The state's fiscal year 2009-2011 budget funds the regional library systems totally out of the state's universal service fund, increasing the contribution by $11 million annually.

THE MAINE SCHOOL AND LIBRARY NETWORK

HISTORY

The Maine School and Library Network (MSLN) was created after a coordinated 2-year planning effort led by Maine's library and education communities. In fall 1994, three organisations in the library community—the Maine Library Association, the Maine Educational Media Association (representing school librarians), and the Maine Library Commission—joined forces to represent the interests of public libraries before the Maine Public Utilities Commission (MPUC). The result of these efforts was the creation of MSLN, one of the earliest and most comprehensive state programmes to improve libraries' Internet connections.

This advocacy effort focused on an investigation by the MPUC into allegations that NYNEX had overcharged its customers. After the libraries formally intervened and participated actively in the case, MPUC Chair Thomas Welch announced on May 1, 1995, that he wanted to permit NYNEX "to use up to $4 million of the rate reduction we require to provide rate reductions or other services to the libraries and schools of Maine."

It was left to NYNEX to work with others, including schools and libraries, to develop a plan for implementing this rate reduction. A group led by librarians and including schools, the MPUC, telecommunications carriers, the cable companies, and the University of Maine negotiated intensely over the summer of 1995. Ultimately, the group settled on a plan to provide 56 kilobits per second (Kbps) frame relay connections for all public schools and libraries in the state, with free Internet access, including equipment and free network support services.

The Internet service provider (ISP) would be the University of Maine System Network (UNET). The MPUC adopted the plan proposed by the librarians and others on January 5, 1996. The initial MSLN plan called for an allocation of $20 million to connect more than a thousand public schools and libraries in Maine for 5 years. Maine's Supreme Court upheld the commission's decision on March 15, 1996, when it issued a decision refusing to consider an appeal of the ratepayer case.

A parallel effort was undertaken in the state legislature to establish the legitimacy of the MPUC action. To guide this effort, the library organisations formed a Joint Legislative Committee to advocate for the expansion of the MPUC's authority to grant discounted rates and services for libraries.

A few weeks after the Supreme Court decision, the Maine Legislature approved a bill that amended the MPUC's authority. In 1999, the Maine Legislature codified the programme and provided funding to continue MSLN beyond its initial 5-year period.

The legislation allowed the MPUC to collect a surcharge on intrastate telephone services and deposit the revenues into the Maine Telecommunications Education Access Fund (MTEAF). Once the legislature had authorised this new source of funding, MSLN became known as MSLN2. Maine is now considering how to upgrade MSLN to accommodate the growth in Internet usage. The bandwidth available through MSLN "is now at its practical limits and is no longer meeting current needs of schools and libraries; in its current structure, it cannot scale to meet future needs." The Department of Education and the Maine State Library are considering how to provide 100 Mbps capacity to all schools and libraries, but acknowledge that doing so will require a new strategy for procuring service and recognition that no single technology will best serve all regions of the state. Schools and libraries are consolidating traffic in central locations to reduce costs, but these central locations require more bandwidth than is currently available. As a result, some schools have opted out of MSLN and negotiated alternative connections from ISPs that can provide them greater bandwidth.

This strategy may meet the individual school's needs, but it does not allow for economies of scale and cost efficiencies that come from a homogeneous network.

The Department of Education believes that it should develop an upgrade strategy based on fibre optic technology. It believes this is a "future-proof" technology that can scale to very high data rates through upgrading of only the end equipment. The department also acknowledges that fibre may be too expensive in some areas.

It notes that wireless service can be a practical solution for service to islands off the coast of Maine, as well as some very rural communities. To move forward on this approach, the department recommends engaging in a collaborative effort with the research and education communities — something several other states, particularly Connecticut, Rhode Island, Missouri, and Iowa, are doing.

SERVICES

MSLN is one of the first statewide networks to provide Internet connections for all schools and libraries. Participation in MSLN is voluntary, and 49 of Maine's 271 public libraries do not receive MSLN Internet services. These 49 libraries have other connections, often through their community's cable company contract; a few have no Internet connection.

MSLN also offers technical support through a circuit rider service that provides advice and assistance by phone, e-mail, and in person to solve MSLN members' technical problems. Currently, MSLN funds a single circuit rider position. The circuit rider visits schools and libraries to assist them, assess their future broadband needs, and hear concerns.

The circuit rider focuses on the sites with the most serious problems and with the fewest local resources to solve those problems. Because the circuit rider cannot address the needs of every library, the programme tries to train local libraries to develop their own sustainable uses of MSLN without ongoing technical dependence on a circuit rider, and to integrate circuit rider efforts with those of other training programmes through the State Library and the Department of Education. Since, 2007, the State Library has been a community partner in WebJunction, the webbased training service for the library community. In addition, Maine's three regional library systems offer workshops and other continuing education activities to member libraries. The State Library also offers limited training through its coordinator of learning and technology, who coordinates training efforts with the regional library systems. In addition, the Maine Association of School Libraries provides some training opportunities for school library media specialists.

NETWORK STRUCTURE

The network supporting Maine's libraries is an interesting case study since, it defies the typical rules for the establishment of a network. Almost invariably, networks emerge from a need to access a resource or application. The need exists before the network is built or significantly modified because few have the vision or the resources to build it otherwise. The State of Maine took the unusual step of creating the network first, when libraries were only beginning to need access to the Internet.

Maine thus developed a very simple design to serve its needs. Two main characteristics of successful library networks are aggregation and centralisation. MSLN achieves both of those key characteristics, but in an unusual way.Rather than three distinct layers that aggregate traffic (a local access connection, an aggregation point, and a core), MSLN allows each school and library to use a local access circuit (56 Kbps or 1.544 megabits per second) to connect directly to UNET (the ISP) and the Internet.

The flat MSLN network structure makes it easier for individual sites to connect directly to each other through the Internet, so that any library can host a resource that any or all MSLN libraries can access.

(A hierarchal design does not necessarily prohibit direct connections between locations, but it often narrows the opportunities.) As noted earlier, the original plan called for each school and library to have a 56 Kbps frame relay circuit connecting the school/library to UNET. In 1998, the MPUC approved upgrading of schools and libraries to a T1 connection if they were exceeding the capacity of their 56 Kbps connection.As shown in figure, the network aggregates library traffic to two UNET nodes within the state (located in Portland and Bangor) rather than a library system's main library.

That design, coupled with standard, ubiquitous transport (T1), allows MSLN to offer consistent service across the state for any library to use. An additional benefit of aggregating all the library traffic is a lower monthly recurring expense for Internet access. The average cost of Internet access measured by the megabit always decreases as more traffic is aggregated.The downside of a flat network structure with only two aggregation points is that traffic destined for a centrally managed library resource (or for another library) must traverse the Internet to reach its destination. This route means that Internet traffic must travel a greater physical distance; the result is added delay, which may cause a potential drop in service. The Internet treats all traffic equally and will not recognise "high-priority" traffic even if marked as such by a library. Therefore, high-priority packets are not delivered over lowerpriority packets. While these can be genuine issues, they have not affected libraries using MSLN.

GOVERNANCE

The MPUC is the governing body of MSLN. The commission decided to retain ultimate responsibility and authority over the network since, ratepayer monies were being used to support it. However, the commission created an advisory board with limited defined functions necessary to administer the fund and the network. In 2007, the legislature disbanded the MSLN advisory board.

The state librarian and the commissioner of the State Department of Education are now responsible for policy and for representing the interests of libraries and schools before the MPUC. Each agency has staff members responsible for assessing the needs of libraries and schools and preparing an annual report to the MPUC that outlines the network's needs and a budget request for the next year.

The project manager provides day-to-day management of MSLN, including oversight of schools and libraries regarding the use of MSLN Internet bandwidth, development of recommendations to the Department of Education and Maine State Library on future bandwidth growth, coordination of circuit moves, and changes of circuits. The project manager also consults with school and library personnel on the impact on bandwidth of their technology initiatives.

FINANCE

Libraries that decide to participate in MSLN have the advantage of requesting service from a contract held jointly between the Maine Department of Education and the State Library. Compared with other library networks, Maine's is unique in many respects but not when it comes to aggregating its purchasing power.

MSLN offers a significantly lower price for T1 service than an individual library could ever hope to obtain for the same service because the MSLN contract offers the telephone company the opportunity to provide the service on a statewide basis. Offering 900 T1s is more economical for a carrier than providing one T1, and the carrier's contract pricing reflects that cost savings. In Maine, T1 services are purchased from FairPoint for any location in the state, even if the provider is an independent telephone company. MSLN can offer a fixed price for T1 service to any library in the state regardless of the local provider.

This aggregation also relieves the individual library of the burden of requesting and evaluating proposals for connectivity to meet the federal E-rate requirements. Certainly one of the factors for success for libraries in Maine is the ability to purchase or upgrade standard service from an existing contract anywhere in the state. MSLN is funded by two surcharges on telecommunications services: the federal E-rate programme surcharge on interstate services and the Maine Telecommunications Education Access Fund (MTEAF) surcharge on intrastate services.

E-rate discounts pay for approximately 60 percent of network costs, and the state programme funds the remaining 40 percent. No later than March 1 of each year, the Department of Education and the State Library file a joint proposal for support for the next fiscal year.

After a prescribed comment period, the MPUC issues an order by May 1 that establishes the amount to be collected from contributing state telecommunications carriers and a level of funding for libraries that do not apply for the federal E-rate programme.

MSLN funding should remain steady for the foreseeable future as the network's revenue is generated through the federal and state universal service funds and not through state appropriations.

The MTEAF collection changes from year to year depending on MSLN needs. MSLN administrators are aware of the need to keep the assessment rate as low as possible, and they lowered the request rate for fiscal year 2008. In fiscal year 2007, the annual cost for MSLN was approximately $4.4 million. Funds from MTEAF pay for telecommunications services, Internet access, internal connections, computers, training, and content.

In addition, MTEAF funds:

- The circuit rider, who helps primarily small schools and libraries
- A consultant to assist with the federal E-rate process
- An administrator to collect the surcharges from telecommunications carriers
- A project manager to work with schools and libraries and track needs
- Free access to a variety of databases

CALIFORNIA'S PENINSULA LIBRARIES AUTOMATED NETWORK

HISTORY

The Peninsula Library System (PLS), located in California's San Mateo County, was established in 1971 to serve the county's eight public library jurisdictions and the San Mateo Community College District. In 1982, PLS decided to automate its circulation system and created the Peninsula Libraries Automated Network (PLAN).

PLAN evolved into a shared integrated library system with a union catalog that allows library users to access materials from all member libraries with one library card number. All branches of the eight public library jurisdictions in PLS have participated in PLAN since, its inception. When the network continued to slow under increased use and bandwidth limitations, PLAN libraries joined with the Community College District library in 1995 to help address the network's broadband issues.

PLAN eventually moved its telecommunications infrastructure to the Community College District. By doing so, PLAN became eligible to connect with the California Internet2 backbone and CalREN. In September 2007, PLS began to evaluate its future network capacity needs.

As part of this evaluation, planners interviewed librarians from each PLS member to assess network strengths and shortfalls. A common challenge identified by many of those interviewed was slow or failing computer applications due to insufficient bandwidth. In December 2007, PLS received two upgrade recommendations from its network consultants:

- Immediately implement hierarchical quality of service (QoS). QoS allows the most important applications to receive preferential treatment while lower-priority traffic utilises the remaining bandwidth.
- Replace the existing frame relay network with a fibre-based network, and upgrade the routers and switches that make up the PLAN infrastructure.

After issuing a request for proposals, PLS awarded a contract to AT&T of California to serve all of the PLS libraries with its fibre-based OPT-E-MAN service. Not only did AT&T offer the lowest monthly recurring service rate, but the company also waived nearly $500,000 in fibre construction fees.

AT&T's initial cost estimate to extend fibre from the curb into each of 33 remote libraries (San Mateo Community College already had an AT&T OPT-E-MAN circuit for its own networking needs at the beginning of the deployment) was $495,000 ($14,500 per library). Fortunately, management within AT&T identified San Francisco Bay Area libraries as strategically important and reduced or eliminated fibre installation costs in order to win or maintain library business.

This ability of the vendor to view libraries as strategic customers was critical to the success of the upgrade project. The only one-time costs incurred by PLS were for the purchase of equipment and professional services (device configuration and project management).

The monthly recurring price offered to PLS for OPT-E-MAN service for a 5 Mbps circuit is $1,025 per month (compared with $1,100/per month for 3 Mbps under the old frame relay service).

The PLS price for a 10 Mbps circuit is $1,225 per month. At the head-end, PLS purchased a 1 gigabit link (1,000 Mbps) for $2,575 per month. By June 2009, PLS had upgraded its network to provide each of its libraries with a fibre connection.

The deployment of fibre to each library and the transition to the new network took approximately 14 months. A number of issues contributed to delays in project completion.

Most of the PLS library buildings are owned by county or municipal governments, so PLS did not have the authority to give AT&T permission to pull innerduct or fibre inside the library. Any work within the building or on the library grounds had to be coordinated among various groups. Site survey meetings included AT&T's conduit subcontractor, its electrical contractor, a PLS representative, an AT&T engineer, a library representative, and the building owner.

Although the need to coordinate among multiple government agencies caused project delays, PLS hired an experienced project manager who relieved the system of coordination responsibilities.

The manager had multiple years of experience with state government and telecommunications companies, and his expertise and presence contributed to PLAN's successful upgrade.

In such large projects, it is essential for library systems to have their own project manager and not rely solely on the telecommunications company to provide coordination and oversight.

Once the fibre had been installed and tested, PLS converted the libraries to the new network within 2 weeks. PLS contracted for implementation services with network consultants to ensure a smooth transition from the legacy network to the fibre network. These consultants were also charged with transitioning knowledge to the local team, allowing them to maintain the network after the conversion.

SERVICES

PLAN is responsible for the day-to-day operation of the network and provides PLS libraries with a variety of teleco-mmunications and broadband services through a centralised information technology (IT) department. In addition to the IT director, PLAN staff members include a database administrator, systems engineer, network administrator, and assistant database administrator/project manager.

These technicians supervise wide area network (WAN) services (network connectivity and network monitoring), local area network (LAN) services (switch and router hardware administration), and enterprise services (integrated library system, patron computer time management, e-mail, web hosting, and 24/7 help desk support).

In addition, PLAN staff members organise training for member library staff and negotiate reduced costs for training and equipment purchases. The community college administers firewall services for the network.

NETWORK STRUCTURE

Until the recent network upgrade to fibre-based services, PLS relied on a traditional huband- spoke frame relay design provisioned by AT&T. San Mateo Community College served as the hub of the network, and the individual libraries (spokes) were served with DS1 connections.

Today, patron and administrative workstations are placed in separate virtual local area networks (VLANs) within each library. In figure, the administrative VLAN is shown in red and the patron VLAN in blue. Creating separate VLANs for patrons and administrators reduces opportunities for security violations. Typically, each library has at least one wireless access point, and some of the larger libraries have as many as five. PLS created a VLAN for wireless users as well, thereby isolating them from administrative traffic.

Each library now has fibre inside the building connecting it to the network. The majority of the libraries connect at 5 Mbps, which is more than triple the 1.5 Mbps (frame relay DS1) they had previously. However, a number of larger libraries implemented 10 Mbps and have already seen usage peak at or near circuit capacity.

The process for increasing bandwidth is simple, requiring only a request that specifies the bandwidth amount desired and the date by which the increase is needed. Each PLS library pays for an increase in bandwidth. In PLAN's current hub-and-spoke design, traffic entering AT&T's fibre-based Ethernet network is routed to the core of the PLAN network at San Mateo Community College.

PLAN centralises services, such as e-mail, the integrated library system (ILS), and firewall services, at the college data center. Any traffic originating at a remote library and terminating at another remote library will travel to the network core and be redirected by the PLAN head-end router. However, most of the traffic originating from remote libraries travels to the Internet.

GOVERNANCE

PLS was one of fifteen statewide library systems authorised under the California Library Services Act. As a result of recent consolidation efforts spearheaded by the California State Library, library systems in California now number eight. In July 2009, PLS combined three library systems to form the Pacific Library Partnership (PLP). This new library system was established through a joint powers agreement; however, the four participating library systems, including PLS, retain a great deal of autonomy and maintain an independent system administrative council and their own joint powers agreement. The PLS Administrative Council, composed of library directors from PLS member libraries, is responsible for overseeing PLAN. PLAN currently serves only PLS, and PLS administrators have no immediate plans to expand it to serve other PLP members.

FINANCE

PLS supports 35 library branches. It is funded primarily by member libraries, which in turn are supported largely through local property tax revenue. PLS also receives support under the California Library Services Act, the federal Library Services and Technology Act (LSTA), and local contracts for special services.

Member libraries share the up-front and ongoing maintenance costs of the central system, the connectivity costs of the transmission system, and the support staff that manage and operate the system. PLS created and maintains the network with funds from its general budget. PLS applies for federal E-rate discounts for eligible costs of operating PLAN, excluding Internet access and internal connection costs. PLS's discount rate is 50 percent.

4

Digital Libraries and Reference Services

INTRODUCTION

Reference services, sometimes referred to as "reference and information services", refer to the personal assistance provided to users in the pursuit of information. Provision of such personalised information services has remained the central theme of the library and information profession. The importance of these services grew over time with the introduction of new technologies and services in libraries.

Researcher categorised reference services into three broad groups:

- Information services that involve either finding the required information on behalf of the users, or assisting users in finding information;
- Instruction in the use of library resources and services; and
- User guidance, in which users are guided in selecting the most appropriate information sources and services.

Reference questions can range from the simple fact-finding type to complex questions requiring consultation, and often analysis, of one or moreinformation sources. An important part of a reference service is the reference interview, which involves a personal discussion between a user and the reference librarian. Through the interview the reference librarian not only tries to understand the specific information need(s), but also collects information about the user, such as the user's subject knowledge, the purpose of finding the specific information, and so on. Based on the reference interview, the reference librarian is often able to filter the retrieved information in order to pick up the most appropriate source(s) for the given user at the given point of time. While reference service is largely a reactive service, *i.e.*, assistance or the service is provided when asked for by the users, libraries have also played a key role in providing information services in anticipation of user needs.

Such services include various forms of current awareness and selective dissemination of information services. These types of service that aim to keep the users abreast of the latest developments in their areas of interest, however, have not been provided only by libraries: online search services like Dialog and institutions like the Institute of Scientific Information (ISI) have provided such services, for example *Dialog Alerts*, *Current Contents* and so on. With the increasing availability of electronic information services, and the emergence of the Web and digital libraries, an obvious question arises: is there a need for such personalised services? To put it in the words of Arms, who is an active researcher and a strong proponent of digital libraries: "could we conceive of an automated digital library that disintermediates all the services that reference librarians now provide?".

This is a very pertinent question for the future of digital libraries as well as the library and information science profession. This is the central theme of this chapter. It is obvious that the current digital libraries, and most of the digital library research projects, have focused on access to, and retrieval of, digital information rather than on the services that have been provided to the users by traditional libraries.

Perhaps the reason for this is the narrower definition of digital libraries formulated by the digital library projects themselves.

This chapter looks at some definitions of digital libraries. However, since, the definitions of digital libraries have been critically analysed by Borgman, the present chapter begins from there. It also looks at some definitions of digital libraries that emphasise services, implicitly or explicitly. The Web has altered the notion of traditional reference services, and a number of Web-based "expert services" are now offered by many non-library organisations. This chapter briefly reviews some currently available Web-based reference services. Although these reference services are not necessarily offered by libraries, and they are termed differently, for example, as "expert services", they are used quite heavily, and they do not require a visit to the library to get answers to the questions.

So, what should be the role of digital libraries? Should they stop providing reference services altogether or should they concentrate only on certain types of reference questions? This chapter looks into these issues. Current digital library research that specifically focuses on providing reference and personalised information services is also discussed. Finally, this chapter points out some research areas that may be looked at for second generation digital libraries in order to change the notion of digital libraries from information access points to information service providers.

DEFINITION OF DIGITAL LIBRARIES AND PERSONALISED SERVICES

While reviewing the definitions of digital libraries, Borgman noted that "in general, researchers (who primarily come from computer science and/or engineering backgrounds) focus on digital libraries as content collected on behalf of user communities, while librarians focus on digital libraries as institutions or services"'. She further stressed that the current state of digital library research and development, especially in the USA, is influenced by the research definition of digital libraries.

The emphasis on the "enabling technologies" for access to digital resources rather than on the services traditionally provided by libraries becomes quite evident when one looks at the two special issues of the *Journal of the American Society for Information Science*, The two issues contain excellent articles reflecting the state of digital library research but none focus on digital library services *per se*. Even the editor of the two special issues did not discuss reference and information services. He mentioned that "digital libraries have the ability to provide a previously unattainable level of service". He emphasised access to information and suggested the various methods, tools and techniques that facilitate improved access to information in digital libraries. However, this is in sharp contrast to the views of the two editors of the special issue of *Information Processing and Management* on digital libraries. Marchionini and Fox in their editorial stated that "digital library work occurs in the context of a complex design space shaped by four dimensions: community, technology, services and content".

The fact that digital libraries should not be regarded only as point of access to digital information was emphasised by a definition of digital libraries given by Borgman as early as in 1992 whereby she contended that a digital library are:

- A service;
- an architecture;
- A set of information resources, databases of text, numbers, graphics, sound, video, etc. and
- A set of tools and capabilities to locate, retrieve and utilise the information resources available.

The definition of a digital library that came up in the March 1994 Digital Library Workshop emphasised that a full service digital library must accomplish all the essential services of traditional libraries and also exploit the well-known advantages of digital storage, searching and communication.

There are many other definitions of digital libraries that mention the services aspect, either explicitly or implicitly. Pointing out the lack of emphasis on reference and information services, Sloan lamented that "human interaction in the digital library is discussed far less frequently. One would almost get the impression that the service tradition of the physical library will be unnecessary and redundant in the digital library environment". He emphasised the point that "technology and information resources, on their own, cannot make up an effective digital library". Emphasising the need for personalised services in digital libraries, Lombardi mentioned that, "helping clients find resources in a digitally chaotic world is the first priority". In a Delphi study of digital libraries it was revealed that "the primary roles librarians play in digital libraries include organisation, selection and acquisition and acting as gateways to the provision of services involving information". This study also revealed that "the best reasons for developing a digital library include: increasing access to information, serving end users' needs and bringing organisation to the unstructured universe of electronically available information".

Thus, this study shows the importance of "serving end users' needs", and the need for the librarians to act as "gateways to the provision of services involving information" in a digital library. Another study conducted by Downs and Friedman indicated that "in the absence of human intermediaries, there is a need for end-user instruction on the use of digital libraries". Covi pointed out that "digital libraries will be used only when workers can readily integrate into social legimitated and legitimatable ways of working". She further suggested that subject specialists, as digital library service providers, help users formulate disciplinary search strategies and provide assistance in developing new resources.

Arms, while trying to answer the question "whether or not we need reference librarians in a digital library", pointed out that automatic tools are steadily reducing the need for reference librarians in fields like medicine that required a significant amount of intermediation in information searching. The essence of Arms' paper is that while computers can do a lot in performing most of the traditional jobs of reference librarians, their skills may be required in case of complex information searches.

Arms, however, believes that there have been significant improvements in the end-user search facilities, provided by electronic database search services and Web search engines, and hence, the need for human intermediaries in information searching has reduced significantly. Perhaps the most comprehensive view of the need for and the nature of personalised services in a digital library has been delineated by researchers.

They maintained that:

- Services reflect the functionality afforded by systems serving the community of users. Access services that facilitate search and browsing have been central to digital library research thus far, but there is great need for attention to reference and question-answering, on-demand help, and fostering of citisenship and literacy and mechanisms to simplify participatory involvement of user communities.

REFERENCE AND INFORMATION SERVICES ON THE WEB

A number of reference and information services are now available on the Web. Interestingly, many of these services are provided by non-library and commercial organisations. While some are free, others need payment.

Detailed discussions on such services are available in a number of publications, McKiernan maintains a site that provides categorised listing of libraries that offer real-time reference services using chat software, live interactive communication tools, call centre management software, bulletin board services and other Internet technologies. Most of these services are designed for registered users of the libraries concerned. Researchers categorised online reference and information services into three broad groups:

- Reference and information services from publishers, database search services, and specialised institutions;
- Reference services provided by libraries and/or experts through the Internet; and
- Reference and information services where users need to conduct a search and find information through theWeb.

Researchers discussed several online information services that belong to the first category.

They have listed various current awareness and SDI services such as: the contents page service from commercial publishers, such as Elsevier's

- Contents Direct Service, IDEAL Alert from Academic Press, and so on;
- Information on new books available free from publishers and vendors, such as the *Wiley Book Notification Service* and Amazon.com;
- SDI services fromonline search service providers, such as Dialog;
- *Current Contents* and *ISI Alerting Services* from ISI, and so on.

Some of these services, particularly the contents page services from publishers of journals, are free, while for others, such as *Dialog Alerts* or *Current Contents* from ISI, users need to register and pay.

Table 5.1 provides a quick overview of some online reference and information services currently available. This is not an exhaustive list, but the table shows the different types of services and some of their characteristics.

It provides the following facts about theWeb-based reference services listed there:

- The listed Web-based reference services are offered by dotcom companies;
- These services use the Web only for communication between the user and the system/answer provider, while the information service is provided by a human expert;
- While most services are free, some charge as high as $250 per question;
- in many cases services are provided by (self-proclaimed?) volunteer experts;
- There are some services offered in specific subject fields.

In addition to those in table, there are also some Web-based reference services where users need to conduct a search for a reference query. Such services provide free access to various online reference sources, and allow users either to select a specific source or conduct a search on a range, or all, of the reference sources.

Examples of such services include the following:

- Internet Public Library.
- Infoplease
- Britannica
- Bartleby Reference.
- Internet Library for Librarians.
- Electric Library.
- Mediaeater Reference Desk.
- ReferenceDesk.
- Xrefer.

While most of these Web-based reference services are available free, some charge a small fee. For example, the Electric Library charges $79.95 for an entire year of unlimited access. Janes *et al.* reported a study of 20 Web-based "expert services".

By asking 240 questions to 20 selected expert services, they noted that the sites gave verifiable answers to 69 per cent of factual questions. An interesting observation of this study was that the kind of reference interview that takes place in traditional reference service environments is non-existent in Web-based reference services.

In fact, the sites did not come back for any discussion or clarification after receiving the initial queries. As a justification, the authors suggested that Web-based information services have been built mainly to answer factual questions, and therefore the experts concerned do not need to go through the reference interview process. Nevertheless, the high rate of success of factual questions shows that more and more end-users will move towards these expert services rather than to libraries for answers to simple types of questions.

SEARCH ENGINE SERVICES

Although Ask Jeeves is basically a search engine, many researchers also see it as aWeb-based information service because of two reasons:

- Unlike in other search and metasearch engines, users can ask a question in Ask Jeeves, and in many cases can get an answer right away; and
- Users can ask a question on a given topic, and Ask Jeeves comes up with a list of questions on the same or similar topics; the user can select any of the those predefined questions, and then Ask Jeeves provides answers to that.

This is an interesting service and may be considered as a useful model for digital library reference and information services.

The Ask Jeeves site maintains that:

- Ask Jeeves is a unique question-answering system that allows users to ask questions in plain English, and then delivers the answer. As one of the most sophisticated navigation systems on the Internet, Ask Jeeves combines a unique natural language engine with a proprietary knowledgebase.Taken together, this mechanism processes the meaning and grammar of real questions in plain English; provides intelligent responses for user confirmation; links directly to relevant, high-quality answers; and, perhaps most exciting of all, becomesmore intelligent as its knowledgebase expands with each question asked and each answer delivered.

The site further says that Ask Jeeves processes each query syntactically and semantically, and then Ask Jeeves' answer-processing engine provides the question template response. When the user clicks on a response, the answer-processing engine retrieves the answer template that contains links to the answer locations. Thus, Ask Jeeves helps users select a query from a pre-defined set of queries on a given topic.

However, there is a debate on whether the kind of service provided by Ask Jeeves matches reference services provided by libraries. Kresh reported an interesting finding: "One consortial system in northern California conducted an informal test of Ask Jeeves by sending it 12 questions its libraries had answered. There were no trick questions, none were arcane, just questions typically received by those libraries. Jeeves was unable to answer any of the questions".

Nevertheless, the techniques and the technology used by Ask Jeeves may be very useful for introducing reference services in digital libraries. Webhelp.com is another service that claims to offer "real-time search assistance with a real live expert I any time, day or night". About.com is a service that shows a number of pre-defined categories related to a search topic given by the user.

For example, a simple search on "e-commerce" not only produces a list of sites, but also provides a set of topics related to "e-commerce", such as e-commerce definition, e-commerce security, advantages of e-commerce, e-commerce disadvantages, e-commerce statistics, etc.

DIGITAL REFERENCE SERVICES AND LIBRARIES

A number of libraries have now begun to offer Web-based reference services and a number of recent studies report the current practice of reference services provided by libraries.

Although this is not an exhaustive review of all the Web-based reference services provided by libraries, the following section provides a quick overview of some that are currently available.

DIGITAL REFERENCE SERVICES FOR THE GENERAL PUBLIC

Ask A Librarian is a Web-based reference service, primarily designed for UK residents, provided by a network of public libraries in the UK. The site says: "Mail us your factual question and we'll send you an answer within two working days, if not before".

A user has to put the query through an enquiry page, which is automatically routed to one of the participating libraries, which receives it as an e-mail message. Within two days the library sends an e-mail message to the user with its response to the enquiry.

The British Library provides special reference services for business, patent, scientific, technical, medical and environmental information. These services range from answering simple questions to finding answers to complex questions involving online database searching, etc. While some of these services are free, for others users need to pay.

For example, users can ask simple business questions using a form, and can expect an answer within ten working days. Similarly, users can send e-mails with simple environmental queries.

A typical answer in such a case may include:

- A list of bibliographies from a British Library catalogue literature search; and/or;
- A list of organisations to contact for more detailed information, and/or
- Information retrieved from Internet sources.

Users are not charged for this kind of service. However, for complex queries users need to pay.

For example, the British Library provides a Science Technology Medicine (STM) search service for which users need to pay at the following rate:

- J 82.00 per hour of staff time divided into 15-minute periods;
- Plus costs of online searching;
- Plus Value Added Tax (VAT).

As stated in the Web site most searches take at least 30 minutes and therefore cost J 41.00 for staff time + costs for online searching + VAT. The site also mentions that the average list of references costs J 80.00 for medical subjects, and between J 100.00 and J 150.00 for other subjects.

Users are also charged a fee if the results are to be faxed. In order to obtain an STM search service, the user has to fill in a form that has three parts. In the first part users need to fill in their personal details, etc., in the second part, users need to enter the query, and in the third part they need to specify the modes of delivery, payment, etc.

In the second part of the form, users can enter the detail specification of the query using Boolean operators and specifying date, language, etc., as limiting factors.

DIGITAL REFERENCE SERVICES FOR USERS OF ACADEMIC LIBRARIES

Academic libraries have also begun to offer Web-based reference services. Wasik and Wasik and Lankes discuss the value of digital reference and AskA services in the K-12 educational environment. They described how AskA services are built and maintained, and also explain how the service works in the classroom.

Archer and Cast emphasised the importance of the personal touch in reference services and discussed how Web technology and the personal element of reference services can be combined to provide Web-based reference services. Tenopir and Tenopir and Ennis reported a survey of the current practices of digital library services in 70 academic libraries in the USA.

These studies noted that the university libraries allow their patrons to pose reference questions in a variety of ways: 99 per cent offer e-mail reference, 96 per cent offer reference services by appointment, and 29 per cent of the libraries offer real-time virtual reference.

Breeding briefly described the various customer relationship management (CRM) software, such as eGain, LivePerson and WebLine, that are used by libraries for providing Web-based reference services. He also suggested that while the CRM software offer a great deal of sophistication to the virtual reference environment, they are more complex and expensive compared to lower-cost chat-based utilities that allow a managed two-way text conversation between the reference provider and the remote library user, thus replacing the need for a face-to-face communication.

Smith discussed the current technologies, such as chat and video conferencing software used by libraries for providing digital reference services. Richardson *et al.* examined the information technology aspects and the key organisational issues involved in establishing an electronic reference desk service in a library. They also reviewed the usefulness of some electronic reference services. Breeding provided an overview of some methodologies and collaborations currently in use to extend assistance to patrons in learning to use virtual resources and in finding the information they need.

DIGITAL LIBRARY SERVICE BY CO-OPERATIVE LIBRARY SYSTEMS

In order to deal with the rising cost of reference sources and staff and also of the huge initial investment required for introducing new services in libraries, many have gone for a co-operative model of digital reference services. Oder and Weissman described the 24/7 Reference Project at Metropolitan Cooperative Library System, a consortia around Los Angeles, and the Bay Area Libraries Project at San Francisco that are co-operative projects for providing Web-based reference services to customers.

One of the advantages of Web-based reference services is that users can ask for such services from a remote location at any time of the day. However, Rogers presented an interesting report of a study analysing Web-based reference services in academic libraries in Illinois.

This study shows a usage pattern that is quite similar to the timing of usage of traditional reference services in libraries, for example, 80 per cent of all usage occurred between 8 a.m. and 10 p.m.; evening use was higher than morning use, and the busiest hour was between 2 p.m. and 3 p.m.

CURRENT DIGITAL LIBRARY RESEARCH ON PERSONALISED SERVICES

Researchers have recently reviewed the status of some digital libraries from around the globe. These reviews reveal that while the digital libraries have very good information access and retrieval mechanisms in place, there is almost no provision for quality reference and information services.

However, these studies show that there is a trend towards the personalisation of digital library service, as in case of HEADLINE and GEMS (presently called iGEMS, a digital library developed at Nanyang Technological University in Singapore). Some recent research efforts have been directed at building personalised digital library environments. These studies can be grouped into three categories: user needs assessment, personalised user interface and personalised digital library, researchers reviewed literature on user interfaces, particularly in a digital library environment, and suggested the need for a task-based digital library.

Researcher discussed the personal digital library (PDL) that acts as a front-end to other electronic library systems and manages the user's information needs. Barry and Barbara discussed the creation of personal digital libraries. The North Carolina University Library developed MyLibrary @NCState as a portal application to the NCSU Library's information resources. This portal allows user profiling to build a dynamic, customised gateway to both general and discipline specific resources.

MyLibrary is a Cornell University Library initiative to provide personalised library services to their students, faculty and staff on the basis of a focus group study to gauge library users.

The MyLibrary project has two components, MyLink and MyUpdate. MyLink allows patrons to save useful information resource links that they found themselves or those suggested by the librarians via a targeted notification in their personal space. Users can access this personal space from any place. MyUpdate periodically queries the online catalogue and notifies users, utilising a pre-defined user profile. Headline is one of the eLib Programme's Phase 3 projects, developing a hybrid library system called the HeadLine Personal Information Environment (PIE), This PIE uses portal-type technology to present an information environment that is personalised to the user's needs and allows user customisation. This project presents users with pages of resources relevant to their courses/department. PIE users are also provided with an "all resources" page that contains all the library resources.

Users can create their own lists of resources on their own pages. Meyyappan reported on ongoing research at Nanyang Technological University in Singapore on the design and development of task-based digital library organisation and a digital work environment (DWE). The major objective of these research projects is to allow users to personalise digital library access so that they can view their preferred resources, and hence, information is automatically filtered. These projects aim to select automatically a subset of the DL collection based on the nature and characteristics of a user.

The user then can add new resources, or delete recommended resources, to his or her page. The DWE project is somewhat different from others in the sense that the main objective of the DWE is to provide filtered access to the local digital library collections, to remote digital libraries, as well as to traditional libraries, and,most importantly, to the vast information resources on the university intranet. The system also allows users to create their own personal workspace to store selected information resources for future use.

CURRENT DIGITAL LIBRARY PROJECTS ON DIGITAL REFERENCE SERVICES

Some research projects aimed at providing reference and information services as part of the digital library services have recently begun. The most prominent is the Collaborative Digital Reference Service (CDRS) project launched by the Library of Congress.

CDRS

Researcher commented that "by applying the best of what libraries and librarians have to offer to the labyrinthine universe of unstructured and unverified information on the Internet, we can begin to bridge the gulf that exists between providers and users of information". With this end in view, the Library of Congress has launched the Collaborative Digital Reference Service, the mission of which is to provide "professional reference service to users, anywhere any time, through an international, digital network of libraries".

The CDRS is a library to library network for asking and answering reference questions. It has three main components:

- *Member profiles*: That contain information on member strengths and features.
- *Request Manager*: A software for entering, routing and answering reference questions.
- *Knowledge base*: A searchable database of question and answer sets.

The system is designed to work in a very simple manner. A participating library sends a question to the system on behalf of a user. The system looks into the knowledgebase for a match. If the answer is found, a response is sent to the querying library by e-mail. If the question is not found in the knowledgebase, then it is passed on to the Request Manager, which forwards the query to an appropriate library selected from the profiles of the participating libraries and their collections, expertise, etc.

This library receives the query, finds an answer and sends it back to the results store, which then sends the response back to the asking library, and stores the query and the answer in the knowledgebase. Hence, the strength of the system lies in the knowledgebase and the Request Manager. Since, June 2000 CDRS has been a "working" pilot with a current total of 220 active members who are routing real questions and answers. The next generation on CDRS is being co-developed by Library of Congress and OCLC. It will integrate local and global e-reference networks, and will be released as a full production service in June of 2002.

AUTOMATIC REFERENCE LIBRARIANS FOR THE WORLD WIDE WEB

The Automatic Reference Librarians for the World Wide Web, a DLI-2 funded project at the University of Washington. The central objective of this project, according to them, "is to create software agents that posses reference intelligence I a limited understanding of complex technical topics, but a very sophisticated understanding of how and where to find high-quality information on theWorld Wide Web". Etioni and Weld reported the basic working principles of the proposed system, which works on a wrapper technology.

The basic steps involved are:

- The user asks a question;
- The Query Router assigns a topic to the query;
- The topic maps to a number of relevant wrappers;
- The parallel Web search module sends requests via wrappers to the sites;
- Responses from the sites are obtained and sent to the fusion engine for collation;
- User gets the response.

SIFTER is an interdisciplinary research collaboration among faculty and students in the Computer and Information Science Department and the School of Library and Information Science at Indiana University. The broad aim of the project is to develop information agents that would perform a number of functions such as culling information from complex resources residing in diverse locations, and conducting analysis, synthesis and customisation according to the requirements of the user.

The specific objectives are:

- Dealing with heterogeneous information sources that may change over time;
- Handling shifting requirements and interest of users with minimal human involvement;
- Creating a robust agent architecture for reactive, proactive and collaborative filtering;
- Supporting agent collaboration based on natural or artificial economic frameworks for multi-agent tasks.

VIRTUAL REFERENCE DESK

The Virtual Reference Desk (VRD) is a project sponsored by the US Department of Education, and its objective is "the advancement of digital reference and the successful creation and operation of human-mediated, Internet-based information services". VRD defines a digital reference service as Internet-based question-and-answer services that connect users with experts. The basic idea of VRD is that when a given user asks a question that cannot be answered by a participating centre, it is forwarded to the VRD network for assistance.

VRD services include the following:

- *Collaborative AskA Service*: A network of AskA services and volunteer information professionals.
- *The Learning Center*: A Web site for the K-12 community with curriculum-related Web sites, frequently asked questions, and other previously asked questions.
- *AskA+ Locator*: A searchable database of high-quality K-12 AskA services.

VRD also supports research on interoperability standards, metadata and other aspects of digital reference services.

LEVERAGING THE DOCUMENT SELECTIONS OF EXPERT PROBLEM SOLVERS

This is a DLI-2 project at the Oregon Health Sciences University and Oregon Graduate Institute. The goals of this project are "to understand how experts select information in a large and complex information space and to develop tools that assist them in this process", The project aims to capture the trace of information used by experts in the health field, for example medical doctors. The basic idea is that as medical experts traverse the large and diverse collection of documents, they make explicit choices about which information resources to examine more carefully and which ones to ignore.

These choices create a subset of documents relevant to a given problem and this subset of documents may be of interest to other users concerned with the same or similar problem. Thus, by capturing this information that is inherent in the selection of appropriate information resources for problem solving, this project aims to come up with models that may be useful for other users.

The project proposed to develop:

- A trace that describes the path taken by an expert in solving his/her problem by using the available information resources;
- A precis of information about each document, its content, and the history of its use by experts; and
- Navigation tools that would assist subsequent problem solvers using the collection by exploiting the knowledge inherent in the existing traces.

Though the project specifically deals with medical experts and looks into their problem-solving processes, the project team expects that the resulting technology will be scalable, because the value of a set of precis and bundles within a collection should increase as the document collection grows and as more experts use the collection.

QUESTION ANSWERING SYSTEMS

A number of question answering systems (QA) are now being developed that aim to provide answers to natural language questions. Research in this area will have tremendous impact on the future of digital reference services. QA systems often use a variety of natural language processing (NLP) tools and techniques to get the correct answer from the source texts. Breck *et al.* reported a QA system that uses techniques from knowledge representation, information retrieval, and NLP. Research reported in the QA track of Text Retrieval Conferences show quite encouraging results. The goal of research in the QA track is to "retrieve small snippets of text that contain the actual answer to a question rather than the document lists traditionally returned by text retrieval systems".

The basic technology involves analysing user queries in several stages. First, cue words/phrases like "who", "when" are identified to guess what is needed; and then a small portion of the document collection is retrieved using standard text retrieval technology. This is followed by a shallow parsing of the returned documents for identifying the entities required for an answer. If no appropriate answer type is found then the best matching passage is retrieved. This approach works well as long as the query types recognised by the system have broad coverage, and the system can classify questions reasonably accurately. In TREC-8, the first QA track of TREC, the most accurate QA systems could answer more than two-thirds of the fact finding type of questions correctly.

In the second QA track, the best performing QA system, the Falcon system from Southern Methodist University, was able to answer 65 per cent of the questions. These results are quite impressive in a domainindependent question-answering environment. However, the questions were still simple in the first two QA tracks. In the future, more complex questions requiring answers from more than one document will be handled by QA track researchers. Such robust QA systems can be used to provide reference services in digital libraries.

EVALUATION OF DIGITAL LIBRARIES AND THEIR SERVICES

Evaluation data of digital libraries and their services are not yet widely available. In fact, very few evaluation studies of digital libraries have taken place so far. The most prominent publications reporting some digital library evaluation experiments appear in *Library Trends.* Saracevic discusses a number of issues related to the methodology and criteria for evaluation of digital libraries. Arguing that digital libraries were still at the stage of research and evolution, he commented that the best practice standards have yet to develop against which the performance levels are to be measured. Carter and Janes reported a study that analysed the log of over 3,000 reference questions asked of the Internet Public Library (IPL), which is one of the most widely used reference services on the Web.

This study has identified different categories of reference questions, such as common questions, quick questions, regular questions and unanswered questions, which were handled by IPL. The study revealed that users seem to have difficulties in assigning subject categories to their questions, and also in determining whether they are factual or require detailed information searching. Since, the greatest part of reference and information services in the past has revolved around assisting users in their information search, and because of the fact that in a digital library environment end users need to search information resources all of which are online, it may be wise to take a quick look at some recent studies involving end-users' search behaviour in the online and Web search environment.

Pending any data from large-scale digital library evaluation experiments involving users, findings of these studies may help us assess the users' online information search behaviour.

Gordon and Pathak compared the retrieval effectiveness of eight search engines: Yahoo!, Excite, Magellan, HotBot, AltaVista, Lycos, Infoseek and Open Text, and noted, among other things, that there were no statistical differences in the retrieval effectiveness among users for recall, though there were for precision.

Although this study talks about the performance of the selected search engines, this observation is very important as far as the need for personalised help in digital library searching is concerned. It shows that the Web search tools differ in terms of search precision, and who can argue that in an online search environment of today, precision is a very important issue since, no one will ever have time to sift through the hundreds of thousands of documents retrieved by an online search tool at any given instant. One million Web queries to discern how the public searches the Web and had some astonishing findings, as follows:

- A great majority of Web queries are short, not much modified, and very simple in structure;
- Very few queries incorporate advanced search features, and when they do so, half of them are mistakes;
- Despite gathering a large number of Web sites as answers to their queries, users do not view beyond the first or the second page of results;
- Web users are notmuch interested in relevance feedback.

Yet another study reveals similar findings. The usage of the MelvylWeb catalogue at the University of California at Berkeley. During the 479-day study period users conducted about 2.5 million search sessions, during which about 7.4 million search statements were executed.

The findings of this study reveal that:

- The length of time research searchers spent at a session grew from six to ten minutes during the 16 month study period;
- During the study period, about 7.4 million database selections were made, out of which the catalogue database accounted for 32 per cent (about 2.4 million uses), Medlars for 22 per cent, magazine database for 10 per cent, periodicals database for 8 per cent, Inspec for 4 per cent and *Current Contents* for 4 per cent;
- The time users spent on each database also varied: about 3 minutes per search in the Medlars database, while 2.2 minutes for the catalogue database;
- Users displayed about four to five citations for each search they performed;
- The length of time users spent displaying results was 30-40 seconds.

The observations of these studies are very useful for designing digital library services. One of the major problems of a digital search environment is the absence of human intermediaries who play a major role in traditional online search services. Appropriate online support for query formulation and modification may improve digital library search results. Again, since, most users do not look at more than a handful of records, appropriate mechanisms have to be developed for filtering retrieved output.

CONCLUSION

The reference librarian in the new millennium will need the ability to read the situation a user is in and find the right information for that situation.

Considering this view and also to keep in pace with the rapid appearances and developments of Web-based reference and information services provided by non-library organisations, many library and information science professionals have now turned their attention to the provision of e-reference services. Oder and Weissman suggested that "the year 2000 brought the advent of live reference.

Several libraries, especially academic ones, have used or adapted chat or commercial call centre software to communicate with surfers in real time and send Web resources to their browser. Indeed, this is a time when digital library researchers should think of the best ways and means to make the optimum use of the technology and experience and expertise of human intermediaries in improving digital libraries from mere access centres to information service providers.

Many recent projects have taken the approach to building software agents to do much of the work of reference librarians. While this is a useful approach, and such programmes will reduce the workload of human experts, it is doubtful whether digital libraries can totally replace human experts and personalised services.

So far as the information filtering aspect of the personalised services is concerned, the personal digital library approach of automatic filtering based on user nature, and the DWE approach of information filtering based on user categories and tasks, seem to be quite promising.

Recent research on online search behaviour of users re-emphasises the need for user training and assistance in online searching. This is in contrast to the views of Arms, who proposed that information retrieval tasks can now be successfully performed by end users without the assistance of reference librarians.

User training, or information literacy programmes, may be conducted regularly and sophisticated online tutorial programmes using digital video technology may be developed to assist users. For assistance in conducting complex subject searches, the current practice of e-mail communications, online chat, videoconferencing, etc., are useful and may be deployed depending on the nature, number, location, available IT resources, etc., of the end users.

The approach taken by Ask Jeeves in the use of templates for storing queries, and the knowledgebase for storing the queries and their answers may be adopted by digital libraries.

The strength of Ask Jeeves is the knowledgebase which, according to the site, "contains links to more than 7 million answers, which contain information about the most frequently asked questions on the Internet". Library and information professionals are trained in organising information and a new research may be conducted for finding the best way to organise reference queries and answers on various topics.

A facet analysis technique may be used in formulating different templates around a given search topic and they may be stored in a knowledge base. A knowledge base, developed on such an approach, will grow fast initially, but after a certain time the growth rate will be minimum. Only when new aspects of a given topic appear in the research and literature will there be a new impetus.

Co-operation in providing ready reference and subject-specific reference services may be a useful cost-cutting measure. Indeed, the high cost of staff in libraries has been a major problem.

However, since, digital libraries can be accessed and queries easily dealt with from remote locations, co-operative mechanisms based on subject specialisation and other criteria may be considered. Specialised search and other forms of assistance need not always be free. In fact, especially where specialised and reliable searches can save end-users' valuable time. Payments for such services may not always necessarily come from the end users. They may be recovered from research projects, business projects and so on. Holmes-Wong suggested that, by combining Internet technology and electronic commerce, libraries may be able to offer customisable electronic reference services to users.

Nevertheless, new research for testing e-commerce models for digital library reference services needs to be undertaken. To sum up, this study re-emphasises the need for, and provision of, personalised information services in the next generation digital libraries.

The current research projects aiming at finding the best means of providing such services through digital libraries are trying a variety of techniques and technologies, including:

- Information filtering mechanisms based on users' personal characteristics and tasks;
- Agent technology for automatic information discovery, organisation, filtering and retrieval based on user nature, need, etc.;
- Co-operative models for sharing the resources and specialisations I both the content and staff;
- Internet technologies such as Internet chat, call centre management software, video conferencing, etc.

These research projects will definitely bring some useful models and approaches that the second generation digital libraries may adopt.

Further research may be carried out in a number of areas, including:

- Building appropriate packages for end-user training involving the best practices for digital library use suitable for specific user needs, characteristics, etc.;
- Testing the query template and knowledge-based approaches in a digital library environment
- Testing e-commerce models for handling the payment and cost

management aspects of sophisticated and resource-intensive personalised services;

- Tracing the techniques of expert information problem-solving processes, and building models for other users in a given domain; and
- Testing traditional library classification tools and facet analysis techniques for creating question templates and knowledge bases for storing answers in specific subject fields.

5

Impact of Digital Library on Higher Education and Research

The library has, since long, been considered to be the source and power of knowledge and also the knowledge base. In higher education ands research, the library has specific functions to facilitate the extensive use of learning resources by students, teachers, and researchers.

With the growth of literature in large numbers even in the same field, these groups of library users have faced problems in identifying the appropriate literature for their use and consultation in a desired timeframe.

Information and communications technology (ICT), particularly during the last two decades, has significantly contributed to open the door of accessing, hidden, knowledge in a highly efficient manner. Initially, the ICT was used in the library environment for developing databases of in-formation resources mainly aiming at storing and retrieving information on various types of publication resources and also to organize various types of information services.

The ICT has put us in the electronic environment to help identify, assess, acquire, record, store, organize, and disseminate information and information resources according to the need of specific requirements and/or of an organization or an individual requirement.

The use of IT in libraries has enhanced efficiency in all aspects of information acquisition, storage, and transfer. Its magical opportunities have dramatically changed the operations of the library and its information services. With the new facilities, the traditional libraries have been modernized to make these as well-equipped and inter-connected electronic resource centres.

In the library and publication fields, computer-based communications have extensively facilitated the transmission of messages, transfer, and exchange of files and text, such as online submission of papers for publication in books and journals, uploading/downloading, access to databases, conduct of interactions, provision of bulletin boards and newsletters, journals, and publications, online orders, inter-library loans, creation of user profiles, consolidation and repackaging of information for specific needs, dissemination of information, and so on.

Uncountable numbers of monographic materials, journals, learning resources, documents, reports, data, databases, and audiovisual materials generated and published by government and non-governmental organizations and commercial agencies/publishers are now available in electronic formats to access even from the remote corner of a country, thereby increasing the use of these materials and enhancing the efficiency of information dissemination.

PURPOSE, SCOPE, AND LIMITATIONS OF THE PAPER

The concept of developing the digital library system is very new in Bangladesh. In Bangladesh, we have 77 (54 private) universities, about 1,800 university colleges, institutes, and colleges, and about 600 organizations and institutions involved in research and related activities.

These organizations and institutions have libraries, but most are run in a traditional way. About 100 libraries have been using IT to carry out various library-related activities, including creation of databases.

Most publications in various fields coming out from Bangladesh are still in printed formats; as a result, the people remain uninformed of these materials.

There have been no formal survey or studies to know the potentials of digital libraries in Bangladesh where the conditions of libraries and information services are rather deplorable in most cases. In Bangladesh, we are moving at database level but not at digital level, except a few cases. The purpose of the present paper is to highlight the potentials and various aspects of digital library and also to highlight its benefits for and impacts in Bangladesh, particularly in higher education and research.

The paper is not based on any research study, rather it is of educative nature. While writing the paper, we had to depend heavily on various publications, particularly the book titled "Introduction to digital libraries" by G.G. Chowdhury and Sudatta Chowdhury published in 2003.

Change in Library-access and use Patterns

Library is used by various categories of people who need to read literature to keep themselves informed, to enhance their knowledge, to meet specific need(s), to educate themselves, to teach and for learning, practical applications, research, and dissemination.

Their major interest is that their desired information/materials are made available at a minimum effort in an appropriate format and when they need these. Library patrons need information, use literature and knowledge, and again apply that knowledge to generate new knowledge and information. Information and knowledge can be obtained from print materials, audiovisual materials, databases, and the Internet.

With the change in the information-provision system over the last few years, libraries are becoming information resource-access centres, while maintaining also the traditional library and modern library services. With the advent and applications of ICT, libraries are now gradually becoming dependent on web-based resources available through the Internet (network of networks), which was first developed and launched in the USA in 1969.

Full-text journals, publications, data, and audiovisuals are available through the Internet, thereby facilitating access to free and priced online information and learning resources.

But monitoring and tracking the availability of, and searching for, needed papers and publications are major problems in the web-based information system because the system is invisible. Library patrons and library professionals can easily register with publishers of journals and other materials through the Internet to be alerted electronically on a regular basis.

These have warranted that both information users and information professionals are well-oriented with the Internet, with web addresses of those organizations/institutions which put materials in their websites, and with searching mechanisms.

Users are now more independent than before, they are self-learners and self-accessors, and they can access web-based information resources even from their home computers and search databases according to their needs.

The technology has been gradually making the traditional libraries to become universal for all those who need, and seek for, information and information resources either from within or out-side the organization or the country where they are located.

Transitions in Library Development

The history of development of libraries started with the preservation of knowledge on bones, wood surfaces, bark, hides, textiles, stones, clay tablets, papyrus, parchment, vellum, etc. and subsequently on paper with the advent of printing machine.

The use of paper in recording knowledge helped spread out the use of knowledge all over the world, even spreading up to rural areas. This also helped preserve knowledge for a longer time.

The mechanism for preservation of knowledge on paper has gradually been transferred to the electronic medium since the advent of the computer system which is used all over the world, including Bangladesh. Now, most publishing houses, national, regional and international organizations are putting their publications and public records in the Internet.

In the early stage of human communication and while transferring knowledge, "man may have even developed an 'oral literature' that was handed down from generation to generation." Initially, library was usually conceived of graphics forms of recorded information, and the library was only one of many means of communication. "The library is a means of communication in the sense that it is a storehouse of recorded information..."

So, the library is the fundamental source of organized recorded or stored information. The process of communication, thus, started first with speech, then writing, then printing, and finally with electronic devices.

Each stage of the development of speech/language, writing, books, earlier libraries, and modern libraries passed though a process of considerable time-span to establish each stage of the conceptualization of each process to development, to organization, to implementation, and to management. "The earliest form of library was what we would consider today an archive, since it was really a collection of government or religious documents."

Based on the growth and change in library systems within the traditional and modern concepts, we have, like computers, several generations in the development of the library system since its inception to up till now.

The generations are:

- *First generation*: Generation of the early archival library system with early writing materials
- *Second generation*: Generation of the traditional library system with collection of printed materials and without the use of modern tools of library organization, such as cataloguing rules and classification schemes
- *Third generation*: Generation of the traditional library system organized with modern tools of library organization
- *Fourth generation*: Generation of the computerized library system with the use of IT/ICT
- *Fifth generation*: Generation of the digital library system without any space, time and language barriers and highly depending on the Internet/web-based resources.

Meaning and Scope of Digital Library

The term 'digital library' has synonymously been used for meaning 'automated library', 'electronic library', 'virtual library', and 'digital library'. The concept of digital library began initially with modernization of libraries with electronic devices.

GG and S Chowdhury reports that "Borgman suggests that the first research-oriented definition of digital libraries appeared in 1992 when the phrase 'electronic libraries' was used for what is now called digital libraries." Another name that we come across is 'hybrid library'.

A hybrid library is a library where both "digital and printed information resources co-exist and are brought together in an integrated information service accessible locally as well as remotely." Whatever may be the name, all mean almost the same, which "support full life cycle of creation, storage, preservation, dissemination, and use of data, information and knowledge." The scope of the functionality of these terminologies is almost same. Unfortunately, as of now, concerned professionals could not conclude an acceptable definition of digital library.

Various researchers and information professionals have proposed various definitions. GG and S Chowdhury say, "Two major categories of definitions are available, one focusing on the access and retrieval of digital content and the other focusing on the collection, organization and service aspects of digital libraries." Borgman presents the scope of a digital library (then defined as electronic library) as a combination of: "

- A service;
- An architecture;
- A set of information resources, databases of text, numbers, graphics, sound, video, etc.
- A set of tools and capabilities to locate, retrieve and utilize the information resources available."

He further says, "Digital libraries encompass two comprehensive ideas, one emphasizing that they extend and enhance existing information storage and retrieval systems, incorporating digital data and metadata in any form; the other emphasizing that the design, policy, and practice should reflect the social context in which they exist."

The 1994 IEEE CAIA Workshop on Intelligent Access to On-line Digital Libraries defined "A digital library is an assemblage of digital computing, storage, and communications machinery together with the content and software needed to reproduce, emulate, and extend the services provided by conventional libraries based on paper and other material means of collecting, cataloging, finding, and disseminating information.

A full service digital library must accomplish all essential services of traditional libraries and also exploit the well-known advantages of digital storage, searching, and communication." The Stanford digital library research team defined a digital library as "coordinated collection of services that are based on collections of materials, some of which may not be directly under the control of the organization providing a service in which they play a role".

Oppenheim and Smithson defined a "digital library as an information service in which all the information resources are available in computer processable form and the functions of acquisition, storage, preservation, retrieval, access and display are carried out through the use of digital technol-ogies."

According to Arms, a digital library is a "managed collection of information, with associated services, where the information is stored in digital formats and accessible over a network."

The Digital Library Federation in the USA defines the digital library as "Digital libraries are organizations that provide the resources, including the specialized staff, to select, structure, offer intellectual access to, interpret, distribute, preserve the integrity of, and ensure the persistence over time of collections of digital works so that they are readily and economically available for use by a defined community or set of communities." Access to the entire collection is globally available directly or indirectly across a network.

Review of the above concepts and definitions suggest that the digital library is "the collection of services and the collection of information objects that support users in dealing with information objects and the organization and presentation of those objects available directly or in-directly via electronic/digital means."

A digital library may contain materials that are already available in digitized format, such as electronic online journals, electronic information resources, or may contain materials that were originally produced in another form, but subsequently digitized.

Need of Digital Library

Many academic and research organizations and libraries in developed countries are building institutional repositories of the institution's books, papers, theses, and other works. Institutional repositories are often referred to as digital libraries.

Cornell University and the Wisconsin State Historical Society are considered leaders in the field of digital archive creation and management. The ICDDR,B in Bangladesh is also in the process of developing an institutional repository of its publications.

With the gradual change in the library-accessing system and with the increased use of IT in libraries, the libraries in Bangladesh will, in the near future, be in a position to put linkages to international online resources and develop their own digital libraries with collection that are relevant to their library patrons.

This is imminent because of the absence of the needed infra-structural facilities in libraries, urgency of the need for information and information resources, information resource-accessing problems in the local environment, e.g. home, shortage of man-power and budget, scarcity of foreign currencies, and pressure from library users and also from the higher authority.

If we consider the advantages and disadvantages of the digital library system, it also guides us to think of developing and establishing the digital library system without wasting any more time.

Benefits and Impact of Digital Library vis-à-vis Traditional Library

A digital library being in the web is not limited by any space/location and time, resulting in an easy and open access to web-based information resources compared to the traditional library system. Any user may access to information resources round the clock, provided he/she has the access facility. The major important benefits are that users from various locations within and outside the country can simultaneously access the required document without any serious hindrances and download the needed documents without loosing the quality. They can also search for documents by word, by subject, by phrase, by author, by title, etc. as the providers of the digital library system facilitate user-friendly search interfaces.

The digital library system takes very little space in storing information resources, allowing unlimited networking benefits, link-age of documents in any site at a lower cost, handling of the system with minimum staff and at a lesser cost, and adoption of new developments compared to the traditional library system where budget, space, and skilled manpower are the important constraints.

The traditional library system is demarked and/or highly constrained by space and print collection and by provision of time-needed traditional library services. In this system, information-seekers and library users are generally required to personally visit libraries to meet their needs of information and literature and to get services.

Unfortunately, the services do not reach them in our country. On the other hand, the open access or digital libraries are demarked by electronic collection, electronic preservation system, and online access facilities. Time and access problems are important factors in the traditional library system, whereas time and access are not barriers in the digital library system.

Digital libraries can serve the user population very fast and with easy access to online resources. The digital library system can cope with the problem of handling information explosion and can manage large amounts of digital contents.

Implementation of the digital library system has treme-ndous benefits and impacts. It brings in-formation and information resources to users, provides a one-stop service, facilitates improved searching, manipulation of information, improved information-sharing, timely access to information, improved use of information, and improved collaboration, and reduces the digital divide.

The digital library system permits offering of digital library services, including personalized information services, reference services, SDI and current awareness services, literature-searching services, bibliographic services, transmission and exchange of literature search results, files, and publications, library-to-library cooperation, removal of barriers of space, time, and language, avoidance of dependence on others, improved communications between receivers and providers, e-alerts of table of contents of journals and publications, and many more.

The digital library helps build own personal collection according to need, lessens the dependence on information professionals or intermediaries, facilitates access to information resources wherever they are located, facilitates the use of same information resources simultaneously by various users, and provides access to information resources not owned by the service-providing organizations.

It brings paradigm shift in the creation, distribution, management, and use of information and facilitates the consumption, creation, and sharing of knowledge. It also facilitates better delivery of information than was possible in the traditional library system.

Limitations, and Constraints in Development, of Digital Library

Digital libraries cannot possibly replace the environment of a physical library as we still like to see and browse reading materials physically and get attracted more to read these. Lack of skills in handling computer viruses and lack of standardization for digitized materials are important limitations. While there are obvious benefits of digitization, the major problem is, however, ensuring the quality of digitized materials.

The other problems are access management, determination of authenticity of materials, and control of unauthorized access and use.

Access being open, through the Internet, many people may be indulged in browsing vulgar resources. Sometimes, it may take a long time to access literature that are immediately needed.

It may happen that computers and other related facilities remain paralyzed in absence of regular maintenance and replacements of necessary equipment.

The development of the digital library system at least involves:

- Digitization (data conversion, data organization, etc.)
- Establishment of linkages to digitized publications. Development of databases only does not mean digital library.

Digitization also involves hardware and software costs, staff cost, outsourcing cost, cost of various related activities before and after digitization, such as movement of physical items, copyright clearance, creation of records, indexes, and so on. The development of a digital library system demands incurring of "large costs for the conversion of print materials into digital format, for the technical skills of staff to maintain them, and for the costs of maintaining online access (i.e. servers, bandwidth costs, etc.)."

Data from the old system to the new system would also need additional costs. The initial cost (cost of hardware, software, groundstations or leasing communication circuit, etc.) is rather high. For fast access and transmit files, the system needs high bandwidth. In the Internet environment, it is difficult to monitor and keep track of information resources used for subsequent use. Users face the problem of 'information overload', receive unwanted information, data, or resources, and provision of services may be disrupted unless access or facilities are ensured.

DIGITAL CURATION AND THE MANAGEMENT OF DIGITAL LIBRARY

This article summarises a presentation given on behalf of LOCSCOT to the 'Google or Bust: Challenging the Profession' CILIPS day event in Dundee on 27 September 2006. The presentation explored certain issues faced by regional and local libraries regarding management, collection and preservation of digital cultural heritage resources i.e. websites and e-journals. The full presentation is available from the DCC and UKOLN websites.

The availability and growing use of digital information and services online has occasioned increasing expectations of digital services from cultural heritage institutions. Many local and national libraries have already embraced the initial challenge of providing basic administrative and collection information online.

Yet the provision of digital library *objects* online takes the digital library challenge to another level: objects and content must not only be collected or created, but also properly managed, stored, and preserved in order to maximise the initial investment and ensure the objects remain available for users for as long as is deemed necessary.

'Digital Curation' is the way to achieve this, with complete life cycle management to tackle these many challenges in a carefully planned, consistent, and ongoing process.

THE UK DIGITAL CURATION CENTRE

In the UK, research and development into digital curation requirements and activities are the core activities of the Digital Curation Centre (DCC). The DCC was founded to support UK institutions which store, manage and preserve digital information, and to help them address the enhancement and continuing availability of digital information for long-term use.

As a centre of expertise in digital curation and associated digital preservation, the DCC provides a national focus for research and development into curation issues and promotes expertise and good practice, both nationally and internationally, for the management of digital outputs.

The DCC is a consortium project with four main partners: the University of Edinburgh; UKOLN at the University of Bath; the Humanities Advanced Technology and Information Institute (HATII) at the University of Glasgow, and; the Council for the Central Laboratory of the Research Councils, the CCLRC in Didcot. The DCC has a strong research and development agenda and maintains numerous services and outreach activities.

These include:

- Organisation of workshops and seminars to explore different aspects of curation such as policies, audit and certification, and legal issues;
- Development of a community-developed digital curation manual to assist data creators, curators and re-users to understand better the

challenges they face and the roles they play in creating, managing and preserving their digital information over time;

- Production of briefing papers, technology watch papers, and standards watch papers on issues relevant to digital curation and preservation, as well as the first journal to focus exclusively on digital curation: the *International Journal of Digital Curation*; Organisation of the annual DCC Digital Curation conference with peer reviewed papers and posters from an international stage;
- Participation in development of an audit and certification framework for trustworthy digital repositories;
- Provision of an associates network, online forum, and helpdesk service offering on-demand support for individuals and UK HE/FE institutions doing preservation planning and solving challenging curation problems. The DCC is funded by the Joint Information Systems Committee (JISC) and the e-Science core programme. More information about the DCC is available from the DCC website.

Digital Curation

As the term 'curation' has only recently begun to be applied to digital materials, we will at this point take a moment to define what we mean when talking about 'digital curation'. Digital curation, broadly interpreted, is about maintaining and adding value to a trusted body of digital information for both current and future use: in other words, it is the active management and appraisal of digital information over its entire life cycle.

The life cycle approach is necessary because:

- Digital materials are fragile and susceptible to change from technological advances throughout their life cycle, i.e. from creation onwards;
- Activities (or lack of) at each stage in the life cycle directly influence our ability to manage and preserve digital materials in subsequent stages;
- Reliable re-use of digital materials is only possible if materials are curated in such a way that their authenticity and integrity are retained.

Approaching digital information management from a life cycle perspective facilitates continuity of service. This in turn supports verification of the provenance of digital resources despite technological and organisational changes in their context, and helps to maximise the initial investment made in creating or gathering them.

Complete life cycle control is an ideal scenario. However, it is not always possible. Many cultural heritage organisations manage and host resources created by external parties; in such instances it is not always possible to exercise influence over creation and external resource management practices. The active area of life cycle management for such heritage organisations is therefore reduced and can begin only at the point of appraisal or transfer.

This scenario exemplifies how responsibility for curation is shared between different stakeholders, particularly when dealing with transfer of ownership. Communication between these stakeholders and documentation of activities is key to achieving life cycle continuity in such a scenario.

Issues in Developing a Digital Library Collection

The types of digital information held by digital libraries can vary considerably. It may include, for example, relatively straightforward images and textual documents, or more complex audio-visual material and websites. Such items may be digitised from an existing original analogue source, or are 'born-digital'. Whatever the nature of the collection item, it should always be accompanied by metadata that describes the resource, helps to manage and preserve it, and facilitates its re-use. Both collection items and metadata need to be properly managed across the entire life cycle.

This is not a simple task; nor merely a technical one. Whilst certain aspects are certainly technical, others are cultural and organisational, whilst others are of a legal or financial nature.

For example:

- Organisational and cultural infrastructure may not be geared towards digital longevity: resources are often created for the here and now, but such practices can be incompatible with the sustainability of authentic resources. Addressing this issue requires not just the proper technical storage infrastructure, but also education, training, managerial support, and dedicated funding;
- Curation and preservation is an ongoing commitment, but what of funding? What are the cost benefits in proper management of digital information? Is there a business model, and what are the options for revenue generation?
- The copying and provision of information online must comply with legal requirements, including Intellectual Property legislation and the Data Protection Act. Which legislation affects the creation of digital surrogates, and how? What solutions would support legal compliance whilst still providing access to the materials in digital form?
- What tools are available to ease the processes of harvesting, acquisition, ingest, indexing, and preservation? Which storage mechanism is most suitable, what metadata are needed, and how can the threat of technological obsolescence be addressed?

The active management and appraisal of digital information over its life cycle – in other words, digital curation – requires that these risks are addressed. Forward planning and an understanding of the life cycle elements is key to achieving this, and a proactive approach is better than a reactive approach although in practice elements of both are usually required. Each stage in the life cycle must be broken down so that the challenges relevant for that stage are identified and tackled.

To complicate matters, challenges cannot necessarily be mapped to a single stage of the life cycle but may persist across different stages: for example, preservation is not simply a storage challenge and may require attention during earlier stages of the life cycle, depending upon time periods and resource availability. Funding and organisational issues such as infrastructure and training can also require attention at several different stages.

Useful Projects and Initiatives

Developing and implementing a curation strategy is not an easy task; yet neither is it one that each organisation must tackle alone. The library, archives, curation and preservation communities have already invested a great deal of time and effort in tacking these solutions. National institutions are a very useful starting point for organisations starting to address curation, and many national libraries have undertaken initiatives for preservation and accessibility upon which local and regional libraries can draw.

A number of further national and international initiatives can also prove useful, including: The Internet Archive, a non-profit organisation based in the US that crawls the Internet to collect websites and make them available to the public through their Internet site. Harvesting takes place at regular intervals and results in a snapshot of site evolution over time.

The International Internet Preservation Consortium (IIPC), building cooperation between the Internet Archive and national and research libraries. The IIPC is developing an open source web archiving toolkit to support acquisition of websites, collection management, storage & maintenance, and access & finding aids.

The UK Web Archiving Consortium (UKWAC), which collects selective web content relevant to the UK. The LOCKSS Project (Lots of Copies Keeps Stuff Safe), an open source solution, harvesting and preserving subscription e-journals through duplication of copies within a prescribed network.

Finally, the Digital Curation Centre is the UK's premiere source of information on curation and preservation. In addition to developing guidance and advice of its own, the DCC resource centre also includes one of the largest virtual collections of international curation and preservation resources.

Addressing the Issues

Recommendations for dealing with some of the challenges introduced above are listed below. This is not an exhaustive list, but is intended to provide a starting point for preservation and curation planning:

- Develop a written policy and strategy to support activities and help secure resources ·Take a life cycle approach to support curation and preservation planning
- If creating resources, provide good practice guidance for sustainability (eg when digitising or accepting digitised resources)
- Assess collection/selection criteria – are they still valid? Do they need expanding? Identify possible resources. (Remember that digital resources can complement and enhance physical ones and do not have to act as replacements.)
- Be aware of externally produced digital resources (eg websites); check other heritage collections before gathering!
- Identify legal restraints in collection/management/access
- Consider whether value can be added to resources during acquisition?
- Store objects in a secure environment
- Plan for preservation activities to maintain access to authentic resources over time and avoid incurring extra costs
- Determine access and user requirements
- Implement an integrated approach to collection accessibility
- Adapt and learn from national and other leading activities

Digital curation is vital if resources created now are to be properly preserved and remain accessible for future generations. This is more than simply a technical challenge and requires commitment at a multitude of levels. This brief article has, I hope, provided some insight into the types of challenges involved and some ways in which they may begin to be addressed. The most useful of these is based on that most fundamental aspects of the human condition: communication.

Digital curation and preservation is an issue for almost any organisation with a responsibility for managing digital information. In the age of the computer, that excludes very few! Whilst these organisations currently have varying degrees of experience, they often have experience in different areas.

Communicating to exchange and share different experiences across a network of curation and preservation organisations can therefore be one of the most fruitful and effective ways to move the practice of digital curation and preservation forwards.

6

E-Books and Library

INTRODUCTION

In the rush to a digital information world we rarely pause to consider the long-term effects on libraries, scholars, and students. Even more rarely considered are the long-term effects that changes in the media of scholarly communication may have on learning and understanding of content. Marshall McLuhan understood the relationship between variations in media and meaning over time and the impacts of these variations on society when he famously declared that the 'medium is the message.' McLuhan was concerned mostly with television, radio, and mass media, rather than with scholarly information sources.

It is difficult to know if such concerns are valid for the materials that academic libraries emphasise—scholarly research reports, journals, and other reference and information resources that are used for finding information rather than for entertainment or news.

If the same scholarly information is available in both printed and digital form, are there differences in how it is used and understood? Or, does the content stand separate from the medium through which it is delivered? How can librarians and other information professionals apply their knowledge about how scholarly materials are organised and used to help people make most of the information available to them?

Many research questions can be posed concerning this general issue, including:

- How does the medium of information affect people's preferences, understanding, and use of the content.
- Do people seek for, understand, and use information delivered in digital form differently from that delivered on paper.
- Does the medium of information resources used make a difference in the new knowledge people create from these information resources.
- How does a library's choice of format for information products affect the library users.

These very broad questions need to be answered in the coming decade as libraries continue to move to digital services, but to answer such general questions, many more specific research questions must be addressed. This article explores three of the specific research questions that are critical to the delivery of effective library service to students and scholars.

- *Medium and Student Work:* How is the change to digital information sources affecting the scholarly work of college and university students.
- *New Models for Scholarly Journals:* When libraries select electronic journals, how do the products offered to them or the models they choose influence scholarship and the way journals are used.
- *Librarians as Intermediaries:* Are librarians—as intermediaries to the search process—still necessary in a digital age? What do human information professionals bring to the online research process that cannot be adequately duplicated online.

MEDIUM AND STUDENT WORK
HOW IS THE CHANGE TO DIGITAL INFORMATION SOURCES AFFECTING THE SCHOLARLY WORK OF COLLEGE AND UNIVERSITY STUDENTS

This Includes Several Subquestions, Including: Are there differences in citing patterns, quality of work, and the research process? When faculty assign papers that require students to use the recorded knowledge, what do they expect and how has this changed? How can educators and librarians influence students' work in a positive way?

WHY THIS QUESTION IS IMPORTANT

It is unclear how the move from paper-based library collections to digital collections is affecting scholarly work. In the past when faculty assigned research papers to their students, the expectations of what types of sources would be used and the role of librarians in providing access to these sources were fairly clear. Today, there is much more variety in media and sources available to students and students often do their research without setting foot in a library. Libraries purchase electronic resources and students access the resources from their dormitories, homes, or offices. Students may not seek help from librarians, either because they have confidence in their online searching skills or because they no longer come to the libraries and librarians are 'out of sight, out of mind.' Librarians have always been concerned that college students demonstrate basic information literacy skills, but in today's virtual library environments teaching these skills may be more important than ever.

In 2000 the Association of College and Research Libraries (ACRL) adopted competency standards for information literacy that recommend: students must be able to articulate information needs, know how to search for and access information resources, and effectively use the information they find. Librarians face new challenges in reaching students who only access library resources online and have grown up with the Web. It is difficult to make sure that such students know how to select appropriate resources, evaluate the quality of what they select, and use these resources well regardless of format or medium.

Academic librarians and faculty members would likely agree that most college students today prefer digital resources to print resources. Even within the realm of digital resources, a majority of undergraduate students seem to choose Web sites or digital resources that include the full text often without regard to how appropriate the source is for their assignment. The impact of this is not yet known, but several aspects of this issue need to be studied. Librarians need to know more about how students make decisions regarding what information sources they use for their class assignments, in order to design better library instruction programmes and so librarians can work more effectively with faculty and with students.

If these decisions are based more on the convenience of electronic full texts or affinity for the Web, we need to understand how the change to digital information sources is affecting the scholarly work of college and university students. The prevalence of electronic resources is likely causing changes in students' citing patterns and may be even changing the quality of work and the research process. Ultimately, understanding these changes in the work habits of undergraduate students may help educators and librarians influence students' work in a positive way.

PREVIOUS WORK

Student Preferences

In the late 1990s, Tenopir and Tenopir and Read recorded academic librarians' observations of online use among students in all types and sizes of colleges and universities. These surveys found that appropriate content, recommendations from trusted people, and ease-of-use are all believed to be important factors that influence which research online resources are selected by students. The one factor, however, that was found to be most important was the availability of the full text.

According to one librarian from a small college: 'Students expect to see the full article pop out. Also, full-text greatly enhances our own, small collection.' Another respondent explained, 'The concept of one-stop information shopping is an important factor in using any electronic information resource". Full text often overrides all other preference factors, in particular for undergraduate students. Librarians who have faith in users to pick the best content sometimes change their opinion when full text is the issue, and, increasingly, not just any full-text will do. One librarian summarised the new expectations: 'End users want full text; preferably with graphics and they want it delivered over a Web interface that provides the flexibility for a variety of output and access options".

When more than one full-text database is available, students may choose the resource that is best suited to their research needs, although convenience and recommendations by peers, instructors, and librarians are influential. Librarians reported in the Tenopir survey that when products are recommended specifically by their instructors or by librarians, students generally use them.

Faculty Concerns

Many university faculties are concerned that students choose the convenience of full-text digital resources without regard to quality or appropriateness for their tasks. One recent study found that although faculty respondents feel positive about the Web, they expressed concerns about their students' ability to evaluate Internet resources and questioned the accuracy and reliability of Web resources. Rothenberg attributed a decline in the quality of student term papers—both in quality of writing and originality of thought—to reliance on the Web for research.

In a recent survey of academic research libraries one respondent commented that 'more and more faculty are unhappy with the Internet resources their students are using and have come to the librarians to help instruct students on reliable resources". Some students may not be aware of the need to carefully evaluate Web and other full text sources. Grimes and Boening found that students are using Web resources in English composition assignments without evaluating the quality and reliability of the sources, contrary to the expectations of their professors.

Preference for resources that are convenient and familiar is natural, of course. Not all faculty, and certainly not all students agree that the Web has had a negative effect on student work. McBride and Dickstein saw no decline in quality of student writing in Women's Studies at the University of Arizona, even though the Web was used more often for research.

A 1998 survey by librarians at Duke University found that 20 per cent of undergraduate students interviewed felt the Web had a positive effect on their work, while another 40 per cent felt the Web made a difference to the quality of their work. Over half identified the Web as a time saver. D'Esposito and Gardner found that undergraduate students are aware that quality is an important factor to consider when selecting Web resources to use for schoolwork. Students in their study reported that government, educational, and reputable business sites are the most reliable. Undergraduate students studied by Wei He and Jacobson felt strongly that the Internet was useful for research and seeking information.

Motivation

Motivations of students who use the Web were studied by Ko from the perspective of media uses and gratification. Ko found that students with higher motivation tended to go more to informational sites, but she did not examine the quality or accuracy of the informational sites they visited. Duggan asked students to self-judge 'valuable educational' Web sites. They found that students who keep track of these sites have a more favourable attitude about using the Web for class assignments.

Many of these studies imply that, contrary to faculty belief as measured in other studies, some students are aware of the need to judge quality of Web sites. The problem may simply be that they do not know how to do so. Instruction by librarians on how to evaluate topical Web sites and integrate them into classes may help solve this problem.

It is not surprising that peoples' motivation levels influence how much effort they put into a task and how long they stick with it. It has been well demonstrated that motivation plays a role in what medium users select. The use of digital research materials is no exception, whether the searchers are students, scholars, or scientists. Research by Nahl and Tenopir and Tenopir, Nahl-Jakobovits, and Howard found that time spent online and search strategies varied if faculty or university students were searching for personal or for work-related purposes.

More highly motivated users spent more time on a search and made more changes to their search strategies. Wildemuth found that the search moves used by medical students varied with motivation. Motivation also plays a factor in what resources are selected. Ko discovered that when users are motivated to use the Web by the need to learn new things or to solve problems they are more likely to visit 'personal identity' and informational Web sites. Users who are online a lot are more likely to visit informational Web sites.

Librarians and Recommendations

Librarians are making adjustments to student preferences for the Web. One librarian responded to the Tenopir and Ennis survey: "we have found in the last couple of years that too many students, because they know how to use the Web are using only the Web itself to find materials for their assignments, rather than trying the periodical indexes that we offer via the Web. We've had to change our instruction efforts to address this problem. We don't discourage them from searching the Web for material on their subject in addition to using the indexes, but we talk a lot about the quality of what they find on the Web—the quality and the provenance". A librarian's recommendation is believed by most academic librarians to be very important, although in most libraries trying to reach a large proportion of students and faculty is a constant effort.

A database demonstrated in instruction classes or English 101 will be selected if students remember it when they need information. For those students who are motivated enough to ask at the reference desk, the recommendation of a specific source is believed to be very influential. Tenopir found that one library saw its usage statistics triple for a particular online system when they introduced a separate instruction class and promoted its use with faculty. Recommendations of relevant sources may be most important the first time a student has to choose a database. After that, familiarity often takes over. If students have had success in a previous use, they are likely to select the same source again, even if 'its use in this instance may or may not be appropriate'. Positive encounters are influential. "If their initial instruction and usage has been successful, I feel they keep returning to what is familiar," says another.

Changes in Citing Patterns

Although there are many opinions among faculty and librarians, only a few researchers have studied what impact these choices have had on scholarship, whether positive or negative. Further research on this topic will help librarians make better collection development choices and will help faculty and librarians design optimal information instruction courses. Philip Davis at Cornell University is one of the few to study changes in the citing behaviour of students over time. Davis and Cohen found a significant decrease in the frequency of citing scholarly resources in microeconomics undergraduate term papers from 1996 to 1999. Scholarly materials are cited less often and non-scholarly materials such as newspaper articles and Web sites are cited more.

The prevalence of newspaper article citations can almost certainly be attributed to the widespread availability of full text newspaper databases such as ProQuest or LexisNexis Academic Universe through university libraries. The Web may be used from home or on campus. Disturbingly, Davis and Cohen found that approximately only one-half of the URLs cited in student papers led to the correct Web site. An update to this research found that the number of citations to Web sites and newspaper articles in undergraduate term papers continued to increase in 2000, but papers submitted electronically had a higher percentage of correct URLs.

RESEARCH METHODS FOR STUDYING THESE QUESTIONS

The importance of changes in what research sources are being used and cited is still difficult to judge. Davis found no significant relationship "between grade and total number of citations, number of Web citations, number of scholarly citations, or number of non-scholarly citations". Further research is needed to examine the intellectual products created by students and their performance in relationship to the resources used. Studying student preferences and faculty concerns answers only a small part of this important question. Librarians and faculty members can guide students to high quality resources in digital formats as well as in print.

More important, but more difficult to understand, is how the inherent properties of a medium influence the learning process. Most of the concerns by faculty and libraries are related to the quality and appropriateness of the content of digital resources used by students. Quality of content is likely independent of the medium, but undergraduate students may be willing to accept online sources without question.

Increased emphasis on teaching evaluation skills, library created portals to authoritative Web sites, and stricter citation guidelines in class assignments are recommended by Davis and Cohen to help solve this problem in the future. If such suggestions are followed, they should be tested to see if the problem truly lies in the quality of student work or in faculty perceptions of what citations are likely to lead to quality information.

Further studies that look at the link between what is cited and the quality of scholarly output will help reveal if a problem truly exists. Academic librarians should work with teaching faculty to conduct such controlled studies. A related research area is to test the effectiveness of user instruction that emphasises Web site evaluation. Other than course requirements, what truly motivates undergraduate researchers? Is instruction in evaluation methods truly effective or is a more prescribed approach to acceptable resources in assignments necessary? Will student achievement increase after such instruction? Finally, the larger issue of medium and understanding needs more research in the scholarly domain, outside of the world of mass media.

The Web combines components of mass media with a wealth of scholarly materials making interdisciplinary research appropriate. The work of communications research and information science research dovetails well in this research area.

NEW MODELS FOR SCHOLARLY JOURNALS

WHEN LIBRARIES SELECT ELECTRONIC JOURNALS, HOW DO THE PRODUCTS OFFERED TO THEM OR THE DELIVERY MODELS THEY CHOOSE INFLUENCE SCHOLARSHIP AND THE WAY JOURNALS ARE USED

WHY THIS QUESTION IS IMPORTANT

Faculty are concerned about what resources students use and cite because there is a long tradition of high quality being associated with peer-reviewed, scholarly journals. Scholarly journals provide scholars with a way to convey their own research findings and to keep up with what others are doing in their disciplines. Peer review provides a quality assurance mechanism. The structure of traditional journals has evolved to provide a forum for research, events, and controversies in each discipline.

Through such devices as topic issues, letters-to-the-editor, book reviews, and editorials, journals have evolved to provide more to a discipline that just a body of individual research articles. It can be argued that a journal with a large following in its field, such as Journal of the American Medical Association (JAMA), Reference and User Services Quarterly (RUSQ), or Tetrahedron Letters builds or reflects the community of physicians, or reference librarians, or organic chemists who read it, subscribe to it, and/or publish in it. Traditional scholarly journals continue to be the single most important information source for scientists and social scientists.

Today, journals may still be delivered on paper but they may also be delivered digitally, either directly from the publisher or through an aggregator such as LexisNexis, ProQuest, or OCLC. Collection development policies for journals now often favour online versions of journals over print. Digital distribution does not necessarily mean the end of the traditional journal, but it does provide many alternatives to journal article delivery.

Publishers may continue to create their journals in issues and merely make each issue accessible on the World Wide Web to subscribers, individual articles can be separated from the journal issue and be made available in large full text databases that combine articles from many different journals, or authors may choose to post their scholarly work directly on e-print servers or their own Web page and forgo publishing in a journal altogether. Electronic publishing clearly has many advantages for libraries, authors, and readers, including a speedier publishing/distribution cycle, desktop delivery, and the possibility of wider distribution.

The move towards electronic journals is well underway and, while it will move more slowly for some journal titles and some disciplines than others, it is a movement that will continue its momentum. There are several aspects to this research question, answers to which will help publishers, librarians, authors, and readers design the best electronic journals for current and future scholars. We need to know if scholarly journals as we know them contribute more to scholarship and the furtherance of science than separate collections of research articles.

If not, databases of separate articles with a good search engine may be the best way for libraries to provide access to the research literature. If so, the scholarly community needs to put pressure on publishers and libraries to continue the journal model. To understand the consequences of such important collection development decisions, librarians and publishers must understand the contributions of a traditional form of a journal. A traditional journal that provides scholars in a discipline with a regularly issued bundled collection of related articles plus substantial non-article materials such as book reviews, letters-to-the-editor, and an editorial voice includes much more material than a database of articles.

We need to understand the extent to which this additional information is valuable to scholarship. Collection development and reference librarians must ask themselves, if we have a good search engine and separate collections of articles is this sufficient for scholarship? Libraries are cancelling subscriptions to print and electronic journals in favour of the collection of articles model, often without asking if it matters to researchers and to research.

Many times the collection of articles model is offered by a third-party aggregator, while the journal model comes directly from the primary publisher. Choosing aggregate models over journal models may, in the long run, cause smaller journal publishers to cease publication altogether. Perhaps the old model of a journal is obsolete and new models of separate articles distributed through e-print servers, author Web sites, or in databases will replace traditional journals.

Librarians now have choices and their choices will help to define the future. These choices should be based on full knowledge of the possible implications of their actions.

PREVIOUS WORK

Models for Access to Electronic Journal Articles

To understand the need for research on these questions, it is necessary to understand the current state of electronic journal publishing. Electronic publishing is still in a state of development and experimentation, with many different variations concurrently available.

Two main models are competing for subscription dollars and readers' attention:

- The journal model; and
- The article model.

The journal model retains the structure and purpose of a print journal, but it is delivered in digital form. It is usually available directly from the publisher as a Web product. The traditional publishing device of issues and volumes may be retained or articles may be put up on the electronic version as soon as they are ready, without regard to issue numbers. Editorials, letters, and short features likely appear with research articles as part of the electronic journal and a table of contents leads readers to the material. Subscription fees may or may not be charged.

All in all, the journal model for electronic publishing retains the sense of community, branding, and editorial voice of the traditional journal, while taking advantage of what electronic distribution and formatting offers. Authors and readers approach an electronic journal much as they do a print journal—by recognition of the journal title as being of interest to them without necessarily knowing what specific information they will find each time they read it. Browsing is the most common method of searching for relevant information and tables of contents with links to the articles are key to browsing. Readers tend to stick to a handful of journals which they consider core to their work.

The 'SuperJournal' research project in the United Kingdom found that scientists tend to favour the journal model more than social scientists. So-called 'journal focussed' users look for specific journals, use them to keep up-to-date in their field, and log on to an online journal system every time new issues of their favoured journals are loaded. The article model is quite different. Aggregators take articles from print or electronic journals and make them available in large multititle full text databases. Readers use a search engine to search for and identify articles of interest to them and they read the specific articles out of the context of a complete journal. Pullinger has called these readers 'topic-focussed' if they search for articles without limiting to specific journal titles or 'article-focussed' if they seek to retrieve known articles from a specific journal title.

Topic-focussed readers likely read articles from a much greater variety of journal titles than do journal-focussed or article-focussed readers, as found by studies conducted by the OhioLink state consortium. A variation on the article model forgoes the first step of publishing in a traditional journal. Authors go directly to an e-print service and post their research papers on this site or post papers on their own or institutional Web site.

As with the more traditional article model, readers may rely on a search engine to locate individual articles of interest to their research and the articles are read out of the context of a bundled collection of material that a journal provides. Adoption of e-print servers varies with workfield, with high-energy physicists notable early adopters. Alternatively, readers may go directly to a known author's Web site to read separate articles by that author or to a university's collection of faculty articles in a standard format such as that promulgated by the Open Archives Initiative.

The Importance of the Journal Model

Research by Amin and Mabe reveals why, in an age that offers both print and electronic publishing, authors choose a particular journal in which to publish. The reputation of a journal within its discipline and its reach to the scientific community are important considerations, in addition to factors such as timeliness and responsiveness to authors. These findings echo earlier studies, in a print-only world, by Kochen and Tagliacozzo and King, McDonald, and Roderer. 'Prestige' of the journal is an important characteristic mentioned in all of these studies. Clearly authors have long considered the journal as a branded bundle, where presence within a high-quality journal title lends cache to a research article. ISI's 'Journal Impact Factors' are another important quality factor for authors, editors, and scholars.

Journal Impact Factors cannot exist without the concept of 'journal title,' as an impact score is calculated for each title in a field based on the number of times articles in that journal are cited, divided by the total number of articles published in the journal each year. Many authors seek to publish in journals with high impact factors and scientists in some countries are given bonuses when they publish in these prestigious journals. Much of the research to date has focussed on the importance of journal articles to researchers' work, rather than the importance of an entire journal.

Exceptions are the periodic studies of the number of personal subscriptions held by scientists. In his 1974 book, Meadows examined the studies through the early 1970s that discussed personal subscriptions of entire journals, concluding that scientists subscribe to major journals they read regularly either in their research field or general periodicals like Nature or Science. More recent studies show a decline in the number of journals that scientists subscribe to on the average, in direct relationship to the increase in journal prices; however, the purchase of full-text separate articles by individuals did not affect their use of print journals.

The number of personal subscriptions has decreased steadily over the last few decades, as the price of scholarly journals has increased. In the past, North American scientists subscribed to an average of six journals each. By the late 1990s this had declined to just over two and the downward trend is continuing. As the number of subscriptions goes down, scientists rely more on library subscriptions and on separates, from electronic full text databases, paper reprints from colleagues or authors, interlibrary loan, or document delivery services. OhioLink, a large library consortium, offers hundreds of scholarly journals to academic libraries across Ohio. They report that many of the journal titles provided electronically as separate articles were never subscribed to by the libraries that now access them. OhioLink research has found that when such journals are available to faculty and students electronically, the number of journal titles from which they read articles goes up.

Beyond those journals considered core to a particular subject, if made readily available, scientists and students read from a variety of sources. Recent data from the NorthEast Research Libraries Consortia, however, suggests that the amount of reading from titles that libraries do not subscribe to in print may be less than that found in the OhioLink libraries, with a majority of electronic readings coming from journals that the libraries already subscribe to.

What Libraries are Doing

Libraries are spending an increasing amount of their overall materials budgets on serials and an increasing amount of their serials budgets on electronic journals. Some of these are journal model products, such as JSTOR, Project Muse, and Springer-Link. Many are article model databases, such as those from ProQuest, LexisNexis, Ovid, and OCLC. Some combine elements of both, such as Science-Direct from Elsevier Science. Since, budget constraints do not allow much duplication, many libraries are replacing print subscriptions with access to electronic journals. Although libraries have always maintained access to both journal and article models in print collections, electronic collections are more heavily weighted towards article models. Some libraries also provide links to e-print servers.

The Pre-Print Network, created by the Department of Energy, Office of Scientific and Technical Information, provides access to many disparate e-print servers. Right now, librarians make the choice whether to purchase a journal model or article model, as both are widely available. If a library changes from a journal model to an article model for electronic journals, will all of the needs of all scholars still be met? Are we, as a recent cover story in Library Journal suggests, in the midst of a revolution in scholarly publishing that means the old models are no longer valid? Many models will be used and tested—only research will tell what the effects will be on authors, readers, libraries, and, ultimately, on scholarship.

RESEARCH METHODS FOR STUDYING THESE QUESTIONS

Studying the potential effects of changes is a challenge and necessarily must include an element of forecasting. Past research into preferences or journal use can provide some insights into possible methodologies for studying this phenomenon.

Two main methodologies have been used to date:

- Surveys to determine preferences of individual scholars; and
- Building prototype electronic journal systems to measure usage and preferences.

Tenopir and King have surveyed nearly 15,000 scientists and social scientists since, the late 1970s to discover a variety of reading variables, including how much they read, characteristics of what they read, what value they get from journal articles, and how much time they spend reading. Questions in the earlier surveys focussed, of course, on reading of print-onpaper articles, those from the mid-1990s to the present also include questions to differentiate print and electronic journals.

Brown and others have surveyed faculty within their respective universities to find out how much they read in electronic journals and their preferences for formats. Surveys can create a statistical picture of current habits and, over time, a picture of how things change, which can provide a basis for forecasting future trends.

They can reveal differences in preferences among work fields and workplaces. They show how things change over time. They can also be used to measure preferences and readers' perceptions of and desires for the future, so both qualitative and quantitative data can be collected. Prototype studies focus specifically on electronic journals and can be used to test preferences for specific search or design features. They borrow methods from both focus group studies and system usability studies. Focus group participants can convey preferences and offer ideas for design features.

When these features are incorporated into the prototype design, use can be observed in a natural or controlled environment. Pullinger's SuperJournal project is the most recent ambitious prototype study; others done in the past include studies by the American Chemical Society and BRS. Several measures can be made in prototype studies, including measures of opinions, preferences as measured by use, and other usage patterns within the prototype system. Both qualitative and quantitative data can be collected as users are studied in an experimental setting. Research methods for studying issues surrounding the impacts of various models for electronic journals include surveys, experiments, and observations.

These methods yield both quantitative and qualitative data. Qualitative data will give a picture of user preferences, opinions, and forecasts of future behaviour. Quantitative data provide information on use, usage patterns, and changes under experimental treatment. Together, qualitative and quantitative studies can provide insights into how journals are now used and will be used in the future. These insights will help us under stand the implications of collection development decisions by librarians and publishing decisions of both publishers and authors on scholarship.

INTERMEDIARIES—ARE LIBRARIANS—AS INTERMEDIARIES TO THE SEARCH PROCESS—STILL NECESSARY IN A DIGITAL AGE

WHY THIS QUESTION IS IMPORTANT

The articles model of electronic journals relies on effective search strategies entered into reliable online systems. Since, the early days of online searching in the 1970s, researchers have studied search strategies, first of expert searchers and later of novices, and observed the interactions of search intermediaries and their clients. These studies have aimed to develop optimal search strategies and procedures that could be incorporated into online systems to make them easier to use and build on the many decades of studying how reference librarians interact with library patrons. It may seem odd to place a phenomenon that has been studied for so long on a list of research topics for the future, but researchers have reached the point with this topic that they are able to build on a firm foundation and compare future research with an accepted body of research from the past.

This is not always the case with library and information science research topics. The ultimate goal of many information retrieval system designers is to create a system that will be so user friendly and 'intelligent' that it can be used independently, so users can answer their information needs with a minimal amount of assistance. The intermediary may not often conduct an entire online search for a user anymore, but even the traditional helping roles of the reference librarian are being questioned in a digital environment.

Many users search online without seeking help from a reference librarian and spend many hours on the Web without ever considering asking for assistance. Even if human assistance is no longer being sought by many users, librarians need to understand what, if anything, a human intermediary or reference librarian contributes to the information search process, which of these contributions can be captured in system design, and which must remain an individualized human process. We need to understand which of these contributions can lead not only to better systems and better library services, but also perhaps to justification for funding librarian services.

PREVIOUS WORK

The literature review here is not comprehensive, due to the vast quantities of articles on this and related topics. Several review chapters in the Annual Review of Information Science and Technology (ARIST) and an early literature review by Fenichel describes in depth related research literature on topics of search strategies, online system evaluation, and expert system design. Lynch studied the reference interview process in public libraries in a mostly preonline era, and Bunge reviewed the traditional reference interview literature in 1984. The current discussion includes only some of the studies that specifically address the contributions of the intermediary in the online searching process.

Seminal Work

Even a limited discussion of this topic must include mention of several seminal studies that form the basis for much of the work that came after them. Most modern studies of the intermediary-client interaction point to Taylor, who, in 1968, differentiated between when users seek information on their own and when they approach a librarian. Asking for assistance usually only occurs late in the search process, and reference librarians are skilled at using questions as filters to elicit the information needed to understand an information need.

Bourne was one of the first to observe strategies of expert online searchers, placing strategies into several broad categories. Citation Pearl Growing, Building Blocks, Successive Fractions, etc., are now recognised general approaches to searching that have been tested and extended by Bates and others. In 1979 Bates developed a set of search tactics that are used to record and measure specific steps used in online searches of standard Booleanlogic based systems. Soon after, Fidel empirically developed a set of operational and conceptual moves used by intermediary online searchers. These specific moves and tactics are still used today to measure search strategies by both novices and information professionals.

Having two accepted measurement scales makes research easier to conduct and to compare, so much of the research on search strategies conducted from the 1980s on uses the work of Bates or Fidel. Borgman examined in depth how individual differences and human characteristics influence choice of search strategies. Borgman found that the time to reach success in computer-related tasks, such as online searching, has a much larger variance than in other types of tasks. Technologically inclined people are able to complete search tasks much more quickly than others and have fewer problems with search techniques such as Boolean logic.

Questioning

The questions asked by both users and intermediaries, and how they are asked, have been shown by many researchers over time to be a crucial factor in the search process and search success. Some early important studies of the human aspects of interaction with information systems show why questions are so important. Belkin observed that users approach a system due to a gap in their knowledge. Belkin expressed this as Anomalous States of Knowledge (ASK) and demonstrated that it is difficult for users to express an information need or ask a question when they have such gaps in their knowledge or understanding. Human intermediaries may, through the reference interview, help users get to the point where the ASK can be resolved, but online systems do not yet do this very well.

Information seeking online involves a range of human capabilities, including the cognitive, affective, and sensori-motor domains. All three domains interact and influence each other. Most systems and documentation confront only the cognitive and sensori-motor domain questions. Human interaction can better address the affective domain than help screens or documentation do. The role of each domain has been identified in studying questions asked during the search process. Nahl and Tenopir and Tenopir, Nahl-Jakobovits, and Howard found that novices ask many questions when they are searching for information online, and, when no intermediary is present, most of these questions are never verbally expressed.

Using the technique of protocol analysis, the researchers tape-recorded novice faculty, undergraduates, and graduate students while they searched for information in a general interest full-text periodicals database. Participants were instructed to 'think aloud' as they proceeded, voicing their internal thoughts. Analysis of the transcribed recordings revealed that, on the average, novices had many questions per search, an average of eleven moves per search. If a reference librarian had been nearby, at least some of these questions would likely have been asked and answered. Questions may get verbalised when a human intermediary is present. Wu recorded the many questions asked of intermediaries by search clients both in the presearch interview and, more frequently, during the search. Although no one session contained all categories of questions, Wu observed nine categories of questions, including questions related to: search terms, search procedures, databases, output, and other information services. Both Wu and Nahl and Tenopir observed a high percentage of reassurance questions—questions that needed no answer but are basically part of the affective side of human interaction. The interaction between an intermediary and a client can take on many dimensions. Spink, Goodrum, and Robins studied interactions both in the presearch interview and during the search session.

They found that intermediaries requested fifteen different types of information from their users, including requests for information about search strategy and terms, output domain knowledge, and database selection. Spink studied interactive feedback between intermediaries and academic clients during presearch interviews and online searching sessions. Data collected and analysed included videotapes, transcripts, online searching logs, and relevance judgements by the users.

This gives a good picture of the various types of interaction that occur between an intermediary and a client during a search and shows how rich that interaction can be. Spink discovered a total of 885 interactive feedback occurrences in 40 mediated online searches, with a mean of 22 per search. She further categorised these occurrences into five types: content relevance feedback, term relevance feedback, magnitude feedback, tactical review feedback, and term review feedback.

White has studied the reference interview over time. In her 1998 study she found that the information specialist dominates the presearch interview, but both clients and intermediaries tend to ask shortanswer questions that are mostly focussed on the subject, search strategy, the service, and the output. The most common types of questions were verification questions. Verification questions are similar to the echoing or rogering questions so commonly held by users, in that the questioner already knows a supposed answer, as opposed to questions that elicit totally new knowledge. Several researchers have studied how different types of questions posed by reference librarians influence the satisfaction and perceptions of users. Findings show that, although both open-ended and closed questions are asked during the interview process, users are more responsive to open-ended questions and questions that probe into why something is needed, rather than close ended or simply factual questions.

Spink observed 'complex interactions' between users and intermediaries throughout a search session. Whether the questions are posed by an intermediary to a user or from a user to the intermediary, the online research process is one in which numerous spoken and unspoken elicitations occur. Robins found that the mediated online search process is highly interactive and that intermediaries and users work together in a non-linear interplay both during the presearch interview and during the search. The search topic even changes focus on the average approximately every seven utterances. Systems today do not yet recognise this important interaction. More research is needed on the effect question asking and question answering have on the success of online research and on the satisfaction levels of users. Most of the studies tape-recorded interactions, with the researchers working from transcripts of these recordings. Transaction log analysis is another method for gaining insights into the searching behaviour of novices. Many researchers in the past decade have analysed the transaction logs from searches of library catalogs, commercial online systems, or Web search engines.

Wallace, for example, examined transaction logs of the online catalog from public access terminals at the University of Colorado libraries. She found variability in the amount of use the search aids available on the system. Quick search and express search features were used rarely; search history and searching other databases were used more extensively. Catalog users prefer to search for natural language keywords and then scan lists of titles.

Information Overload

These studies show that intermediaries help answer factual questions, provide reassurance to affective questions, and help users clarify their information needs. Another role that librarians as intermediaries play is to help users select the best resources and overcome information overload. Information seekers today are much more likely to find too much on their topic rather than too little because most of our online systems are better at locating lots of information than locating only the best information. Extensive studies of Web search behaviour by Spink, Wolfram, and Jansen found that average users of a Web search engine enter only a little over one term per search and review only the first page or two pages of the results.

This either means that the relevance ranking algorithm in the Web search engine works so well that the users find everything they need on the first screen or, more likely, they are overwhelmed by the thought of going beyond twenty or so items and decline to delve more deeply. Many librarians have called for reference librarians to help end users sort through the vast quantities of information to locate the best sources for their needs. Hopkins suggests several possible ways this might be accomplished, including quality filtering by ranking by citation counts or citations in review articles, structured guides to the literature that include quality judgements, and better information literacy instruction.

Teaching Search Strategies

User instruction is another traditional role of reference librarians. Many librarians have commented on the increased need for instruction with the prevalence of independent end user online searching. Mercado surveyed how instruction programmes have changed and recommended that library users need to be taught not only how to search, but critical thinking skills. Beyond the specific techniques of systems, librarians are finding that students need to know overall search approaches and how to choose which databases to search. Developing search strategies is not a natural skill. Taylor and Penhale, for example, found that, even after instruction, students at Earlham College still needed librarians to help them devise and refine complicated searches. Students may have unrealistic expectations of their searching ability and what information they can find on their own. Librarians, through instruction and real-time assistance can help inject some reality as well as skills. Searching is more of an art than a science, however.

Saracevic and Kantor studied search strategies used by experienced searchers on the same topics. They found much variation in the terms selected for searching and the search formulations.

Critical thinking skills, rather than the one best way to search, will help make more independent searchers, but intermediary assistance can help users think about alternatives.

RESEARCH METHODS FOR STUDYING THESE QUESTIONS

Information professionals play many roles in the search process, not only that of an intermediary conducting a search for a client. The roles of question-answerer, affective reassurer, instructor, presenter of alternatives, and quality filter have all been found to be a part of search success. Most of the research into these roles and the effect on search success can fit under the general heading of 'user centered' research.

The methods and methodologies of user-based research are well defined and described by Wang. Observations, protocol analysis, and transaction logs together provide a baseline of mostly qualitative data. In the future, additional observational studies will build on past research, but observations should be combined with experimental techniques. Observational studies generally rely on qualitative data and are often described as 'preliminary' or 'exploratory.'

This is appropriate when a topic is new, but now that specific factors and behaviours have been observed and measures developed, traditional experimental techniques can explicitly test these factors. In the future, we need to discover in more depth how search behaviours vary with different intermediary behaviours and with systematically introduced variations in help screens, real-time online help by librarians, and documentation. Similarly, user satisfaction and the effect on the intellectual output of students and scholars should be measured against the introduction of different treatments in the mediation process. With such a rich baseline of exploratory studies, it is now time to produce more definitive experimental work.

EBOOKS

eBooks are increasingly occupying a large portion of any discussion that involves publishing or publishers. While many of us are told that eBooks are an inevitable part of the future landscape of publishing and, therefore, must receive due attention from publishers that do not wish to be driven to extinction, very little information about it is readily available. Some questions persist: What are eBooks? How are they developed? What are the formatting guidelines, if any? What might be the costs involved? What are the returns on investment? How do they reach customers? These questions have no easy answers. This chapter attempts to answer these questions so that the publisher can make an informed choice when it comes to decisions regarding e-publishing and eBooks.

THE CASE FOR E-PUBLISHING

e-publishing is gaining acceptance among publishers for a variety of reasons and it can be argued that e-publishing, or at least examining its feasibility, is now a necessary step every publisher must take.

Some of the reasons why e-publishing has become so important are:

- *Proliferation of Reading Devices:* If the numbers are anything to go by, it seems like publishers can ill afford to ignore e-publishing. These past few years, e-Readers of all shapes and sizes have introduced into the market, each time at a lower price, and are selling in large numbers. With the proliferation of mobile handsets and the increasingly large screen size available on them, these mobile devices too provide sufficient e-reading capability to its many owners. Thus there is no dearth of e-Readers available to readers. Publishers are therefore scrambling to offer their books as eBooks to these readers. Reading devices, and tablets, have found favour with readers primarily because they are portable devices that allow their owners to work on the move. This means books can be read during a stopover or while waiting to meet someone. Because eBooks can easily be accessed via the Internet, one does not have to be prepared with something to read during an emergency.
- *Availability of Cheap Internet Connectivity:* Internet connectivity, especially broadband connectivity, is becoming increasingly cheaper and, thanks to government and private initiatives, available in many remote locations. eBooks, being electronic files in nature, can be easily distributed over the Internet much like files are sent through e-mail. The easy availability of Internet connectivity thus allows eBooks to be transferred to customers no matter how remotely they might be situated. Thus distribution costs are rendered negligible and the location of the customer does not prove to be a barrier to accessibility of eBooks.

- *Media Assimilation and Content Creation:* eBooks in its most basic form consist of PDF files that the reader can read on a PC or a laptop. However, these eBooks can also be 'enhanced' to make them engaging and entertaining. This is done by incorporating voice and visuals within the context of the eBook. A medical textbook may, thus, explain a disease using a video clip or a children's book may contain a series of animations to depict a situation. eBooks thus become more attractive to the average reader.
- *Access to Distant Markets:* As already explained, eBooks are distributed as files over the Internet. That means that the geographical boundaries that deter sale of physical copies are removed making it possible to sell to readers all over the world. This makes eBooks an attractive proposition especially while addressing small, geographically dispersed markets that cannot be efficiently served with printed books.
- *Always Available:* Given the fact that eBooks do not occupy any shelf-space and can be easily reproduced, publishers need not worry anymore about limited shelf exposure or an out-of-print backlist. eBooks have allowed publishers to have greater visibility for their entire list. From the customer's perspective, readers can access eBooks with great ease and speed so not having a book to read isn't an issue because one can be downloaded and read.

THE CONS

Among the few factors that have discouraged publishers from taking the 'e' route, the primary one is the threat of piracy. eBooks can be easily duplicated and disseminated and can easily lend itself to unauthorised copying and distribution.

The development of eBooks does cost money and publishers must carefully examine the returns they hope to achieve on such an investment. Development of eBooks therefore must be a choice one takes after examining all costs involved and the ability of the market to 'consume' the eBooks. Since, the next eBook costs next to nothing to produce, readers expect eBooks to be priced much lower than their printed counterparts. The jury is still out on this one but discussions on the Internet point towards growing resentment in cases where the paperback and the eBook have been priced equally.

THE NUTS AND BOLTS OF E-PUBLISHING

This section attempts to explain what is involved in e-publishing. Before that, let's understand more about e-Readers and eBooks. eBooks need e-Readers to render them useful. However, e-Readers, or platforms as they may be commonly referred to, are not similar. They are tuned to recognise eBooks that appear only in a certain form, or format. If the eBook is of a format that is different from the one that the e-Reader recognises, the eBook will be rendered incompatible. Think of it as the inability to play vinyl LP records on a CD player. Different e-Readers are tuned to read different eBook formats. The format of an eBook is recognised from the extension of its file name. Prominent eBook formats are.mobi and.azw, which are recognised by the Amazon Kindle, and.epub which is recognised by the Sony e-Reader, the Nook, the Wink and many others.

It is also important to note that some e-Readers do not recognise some eBook formats. Publishers must therefore take care to see that their books are published in more than one format if they wish to reach out to a larger readership.

In most publishing processes, PDF files of the entire content of the book are already produced before the book goes into print. PDF files can themselves be distributed as eBooks or can be converted into.mobi or.epub files for distribution to a larger number of e-Readers.

The costs of producing an eBook will depend on whether or not the process was outsourced and on the quantum of books being converted to the electronic version. Some publishers have chosen to convert their entire list and make them available as eBooks while others have adopted a cautious approach, choosing to produce just a few titles as eBooks and tracking the return on investment before converting the other books. Some publishers choose to convert only their out-of-print back lists into eBooks. Publishers are advised to choose an option that fits their budget and their appetite for risk.

While deciding which books should be converted to eBooks, publishers must also bear in mind the technological constraints imposed on certain types of books. Graphic-intensive books, for instance, are labouriously displayed on e-Readers and need processes that might be expensive to develop. Similarly, books written in other scripts besides the Roman script have encountered problems related to the font that renders them incomprehensible, especially when converted into formats such as.epub and.mobi. Publishers are advised to discuss these issues with their eBook developers before they invest in the process. Since, eBooks are available primarily on the Internet, it is important that they can be searched and located easily.

This is achieved through the use of what is called metadata, data regarding the book such as its title, the names of its authors, its ISBN and other such related data. Publishers should make sure that the appropriate metadata is generated for each book.

NEXT STEPS

The publisher must have an idea of how eBooks will be sold after they are produced. The channels of distribution that will be employed must be determined before the eBooks are produced so that the eBooks can be immediately put up for sale. While the publisher may choose to sell these eBooks on their own web sites, they may choose to do so also on other web sites that aggregate books by many publishers and facilitate their sale.

This is much like having distributors for your book and also choosing to sell your book yourself. They must be extremely cautious about the terms of your agreement, just like they would in the case of printed books. As in all cases, sales must be tracked and returns on investment calculated. If eBooks are indeed the way books will be traded in the future, publishers must be wary of adopting another's way of doing things and devise a method of developing and distributing eBooks that suits it best.

ENVIRONMENTAL IMPACTS OF e-BOOKS

With the growth in the number of e-readers and sales of Ebooks, many have begun to question the environmental impacts of e-readers and e-Books. Currently e-Books make up a relatively small portion of the overall book market and about 9 per cent of the trade book market. However, sales of e-Books are rapidly increasing, as are the number of devices capable or displaying e-Books. With the rapid adoption of e-Books many have questioned what effects e-readers will have on the environmental impacts of the book industry.

At the time of this was written, none of the major manufacturers of dedicated e-readers have published information about the environmental impacts of their devices, however Apple has released an environmental report on its iPad, a tablet computer with a built in e-Book application, and the ability to download applications to read e-Books from other suppliers. Additionally others have estimated the environmental impacts of Amazon's Kindle, and other e-reader devices and attempted to compare them to the environmental impacts of paper books.

This report will summarise some of the information found in these reports and compare the environmental impacts of e-Books to those of paper books. While e-Books can be read on personal computers and smart phones this report will focus primarily on dedicated e-readers and tablet computers.

e-BOOK SALES

Since, Amazon launched its e-reader the Kindle in November of 2007, sales of e-Books have grown rapidly and more companies have released devices capable reading e-Books. The Amazon Kindle still leads the e-reader market, though a recent study indicates that the Kindle is rapidly losing market share to Apple's iPad. Together the Kindle and the iPad make up the vast majority of the e-reader market. A recent survey of e-reader owners showed that 47 per cent owned a Kindle and 32 per cent owned iPads. The Sony Reader and the Barnes and Noble Nook respectively accounted for 5 per cent and 4 per cent of the respondents e-readers. The rate at which e-Book sales have increased in recent years is impressive. In 2009 sales of e-Books totaled over $169.5 million and e-Books accounted for about 9 per cent of all trade book sales from January through August of 2010. It appears that the shift towards e-Books is only picking up steam. In January to August of 2010 e-Book sales were 193 per cent greater than they were for that same period in 2009.

The Book Industry Study Group's 'Survey of Consumer Attitudes Towards e-Book Reading' suggests that we may just be seeing the beginning of the shift in how people choose to read books. According to the study, which was released in January of 2010, 37 per cent of e-Book buyers had purchased their first e-Book in the past 6 months. Furthermore, the data from the BISG survey suggests that consumers of e-Books will purchase fewer printed books. 25 per cent of e-Book owners surveyed said they would buy fewer printed books, 15 per cent said they buy no printed books and 9 per cent said they would not buy a printed book even if the book they wanted was not available as an e-Book.

E-READER LIFECYCLE

Since, the data suggests that sales of e-Books are likely to increase while sales of printed books are likely to decrease, it is logical to question the environmental implications of this transition. In 2008 Green Press Initiative and the Book Industry Study Group commissioned a report on the environmental impacts of the U.S., book industry which included a lifecycle analysis of printed books. That report concluded that in 2006 the U.S., book industry consumed approximately 30 million trees and had a carbon footprint equivalent to 12.4 million metric tons of carbon dioxide, or 8.85 pounds per book sold. Determining the environmental impacts of an e-Book presents a challenge that does not exist in estimating the impacts of a paper book. That challenge is the fact that user behaviour will significantly influence the impact of an e-book. This is due to the fact that the manufacturing of the e-reader device accounts for the vast majority of an e-books environmental impact. Because of this, on a per book basis, a reader who reads 100 books on an e-reader will have almost 1/100th of the impact of someone who reads only one book on the same device.

Additionally, two readers who each read the same number of books per year, can have a very different per-book environmental impact if one buys a new e-reader every year while the other keeps his for four years before replacing it. Because of the impact that user behaviour can have on the environmental impact of e-books, any analysis will either have to make assumptions about the behaviour of a 'typical" reader of e-books, or else identify a break-even point in terms of the number of books that must be read on an e-reader to offset the environmental impacts of a corresponding number of paper books.

However even this can be confused by the fact that it is not clear that reading one e-book offsets one paper book. For example, the ability to instantly download any book at any time may encourage e-reader owners to read more books in which case each e-book read would not necessarily correspond to a printed book that would have been read. Additionally someone who buys a printed book and later lends it to a friend to read would in effect halve the environmental impact of reading that book.

As such any analysis should strive to account for this and determine a break-even point in terms of 'printed books offset' rather than e-books read. Additional complexity is added by the fact that most e-readers can be used for a variety of tasks other than reading books. For example, most can read newspapers and magazines in addition to books and some e-readers can also read blogs and surf the internet. Tablet computers can allow a user to check e-mail, play games, view photos and videos, listen to music and surf the Internet in addition to other things. Thus for the owner of a Tablet computer, who only spends 10 per cent of his time using the tablet to read books, it would seem reasonable to assume that only 10 per cent of the manufacturing impact of the tablet should be counted towards the impact of that users e-books.

APPLE iPAD

Apple is the only manufacturer that has completed an environmental report for its e-reader device. According to Apple's report, over its lifecycle, the iPad will be responsible for 130 kg of carbon equivalent greenhouse gas emissions. 130 kg is equal to about 287 pounds. Using the carbon footprint of the book industry in the Environmental Trends Report, the average printed book is responsible 8.85 pounds of greenhouse gas emissions.

This means an iPad owner would need to offset 32.4 printed books during the iPad's lifetime to break even in terms of the carbon footprint of reading those books. If you are also offsetting printed magazines and printed newspapers with the iPad then the number of books you would need to offset to break even could be much lower.

Daniel Goleman and Gregory Norris conducted their own lifecycle comparison of the iPad with printed books in an article printed in the New York Times titled 'How Green is My iPad' Their analysis concluded that it would be necessary to offset 100 printed books to make up for the carbon footprint of the iPad, however it is not clear if their analysis included the books impacts on forest carbon loss or not. Of course greenhouse gas emissions are not the only environmental impacts of producing e-readers or printed books. Printed books require wood fibre which needs to be harvested from forests while e-readers require plastic metal and glass as well as other mineral resources to make up the various electronic components and battery. Norris and Goleman mention that some materials that are in e-readers, such as columbite and tantalite, are often mined in wartorn regions of Africa and sourcing these minerals can have negative social impacts.

In its environmental report, Apple makes a point of stating that the iPad has a mercury free LED display, that the glass is free of arsenic and that the iPad is free from Brominated Flame Retardants (BFRs) and Polyvinyl chloride (PVC). Norris and Goleman conclude that "With respect to fossil fuels, water use and mineral consumption, the impact of one e-reader payback equals roughly 40 to 50 books".

In terms of health Impacts Norriss and Goleman conclude that in terms of impacts on human health, one e-book has 70 times impact of one printed book, with the primary impact being particulate matter from energy use and production.

AMAZON KINDLE AND OTHER DEDICATED e-READERS

A report by Cleantech estimated that the lifetime carbon footprint of Amazon's kindle is approximately 168 kg of carbon dioxide equivalent emissions. This is equal to 370 lbs. or the emissions of about 42 paper books, which is very much in line with the greenhouse gas estimates for the iPad, however it should be noted that the estimates used in this report have been criticised by some. As with the case of the iPad there are other impacts associated with e-readers besides the carbon emissions.

OTHER FACTORS TO CONSIDER AND ADDITIONAL RESEARCH NEEDS ENERGY CONSUMPTION

Unlike a printed book, an e-reader requires energy consumption during the 'use' stage of its lifecycle. In most of the estimates, this energy consumption used while the reader is reading is baked into the final estimates. Additionally, this number is likely to be relatively small compared to the energy used in manufacturing the device. For the iPad consumer energy use is equivalent to 30 per cent of the tablet's total carbon footprint.

This number is likely to be much lower for dedicated e-readers that use e-ink technology which only requires energy to change the words on the page and does use power while the user is actually reading. Even the iPad uses very little energy when someone is just reading on it. And Norris and Goleman point out that reading at night with a light on can use more electricity than charging an e-reader. What is not clear is the degree to which the studies address the impact of the servers, modems and infrastructure that makes the delivery of e-books possible.

To be certain energy demand for storing and transmitting data over the Internet is increasing rapidly and poses a very serious environmental challenge. However the total portion of data storage that is associated with e-books, while unknown, is at this point assumed to be quite minimal compared to the total content of the internet. Additional research should be conducted to determine the environmental impacts associated with data storage/transmission for e-books.

e-WASTE AND RECYCLING

Paper books can be recycled, though at this point not much data is available regarding the percentage of books that are recycled at the end of their useful life. Electronic equipment can also be recycled, however consumers should make sure they understand exactly what a manufacturer means when they say the will recycle a product. In some cases this simply means the item will be shipped to a developing country where in some cases children will dismantle the product removing only the most valuable components under unsafe working conditions.

The rest of the 'recycled' product is then landfilled or incinerated sometimes exposing workers and the community to toxic materials. It should also be noted that not all e-book manufacturers have recycling programmes.

CALCULATING BOOKS OFFSET

The image to the right is a good way to visualise the environmental impacts of an e-reader. As the number of printed books that the e-reader offsets increases, so do the benefits of that e-reader. At some point these gains offset the impact of manufacturing and using the e-reader. This 'breakeven point' will be different for different metrics of environmental performance but for most it is likely somewhere between 30 and 70 printed books that are offset over the lifetime of the e-reader. For greenhouse gas emissions this number is probably between 20 and 35 books while for measures of human health impacts the number is probably closer to 70 books.

In assessing the impact of an e-reader the idea of printed books offset must be carefully considered. If the owner of an e-reader reads more books because of the ease and convenience of downloading a new title, then every book read on the device does not necessarily correspond to a printed book that is offset. Additionally the numbers in the figure are based on a very simple comparison that is not likely to be replicated in the real world. The assumption is that the reader would either purchase a new printed book once and not share it with anyone else or that the reader would read the books on an e-reader and only use the e-reader for reading books.

If a person would normally share a printed book with others, buy some used printed books, or borrow many of the printed books from the library then the numbers would need to be adjusted to account for that. Additionally, if the e-reader is used for other activities such as watching video, browsing the Internet, checking e-mail, or reading magazines and newspapers, it is unfair to assign the full impacts of producing the e-reader to e-books. More research is needed on typical user behaviour in terms of time spent reading e-books verses other activities on e-readers and Tablet computers in order to make a more accurate comparison.

If the trend of the iPad stealing market share from the Kindle continues, it seems likely that users will spend more time on the other activates that tablets like the iPad are optimised for. Additionally, if someone already owns a tablet computer or an e-reader, the marginal impact of downloading and reading an additional book is quite small. Thus for someone who already owns a device capable of reading e-books, the best choice from an environmental perspective would likely be to read a new book on that device.

e-BOOKS AND e-AUDIO BOOKS

e-BOOKS AND e-AUDIOBOOKS FROM THE LIBRARY

Medicine Hat Public Library pays a company called OverDrive to provide access to copyrightprotected eBooks and eAudiobooks for Library patrons. Anyone with a valid library membership and a PIN number can access these resources from home.

Currently, patrons can have up to 5 electronic titles checked out at once and each title can be kept for a maximum of 3 weeks. At the end of the lending period, each title will automatically expire. There are no late fees! While the file will still be visible on your computer or portable device, you will not be able to open it and it can be deleted. Due to restrictions imposed by book publishers, only one person may have an electronic title checked out at once. So when someone checks out The 9th Confession by James Patterson, that book is unavailable to everyone else until it is returned.

A FEW THINGS TO KNOW ABOUT e-BOOKS

Library eBooks come in two formats: ePub and PDF. The main difference between the two formats is that ePub books have reflowable text: as you increase the text size, the words automatically shuffle to fit your screen. PDF books do not have this feature, so when you increase the text size you may need to scroll from left to right to read everything on the page. Both formats are compatible with PCs, Macs, and most portable eReaders like the Sony Reader, Kobo and Nook.

The iPad, iPhone and iPod Touch are also compatible with ePub files when downloaded directly to the device using the OverDrive Media Console App. In order to read an eBook on your computer or to transfer it to an applicable eReader, you must first install Adobe Digital Editions which is freely available from the Library to Go web site.

A FEW THINGS TO KNOW ABOUT e-AUDIOBOOKS

eAudiobooks from the Library come in two formats: MP3 and WMA. Both formats will work on PCs and most portable audio devices. Unfortunately, WMA files are not compatible with Mac computers. Depending on the type of software your Apple device is running you may be able to transfer a WMA file through a PC. In order to download an eAudiobook and transfer to a portable device, you must first install OverDrive Media Console which is freely available from the Library to Go web site.

LIBRARY TO GO

Library to Go is the library's catalogue for finding and downloading eBooks and eAudiobooks.

BEFORE YOU START BROWSING: DOWNLOAD THE REQUIRED SOFTWARE

In order to read and transfer eBooks you must first download the Adobe Digital Editions software. For eAudiobooks you must first download OverDrive Media Console.

Both are freely available on the Library to Go web site below the green menu on the left-side of the page:

ACTIVATING THE SOFTWARE

After you have installed the software, you need to take steps to activate it before downloading digital materials.

Adobe Digital Editions Requires Activation

You must create an Adobe ID in order to transfer eBooks from a computer to an eReader. When you open Digital Editions for the first time click 'Get an Adobe ID online' and follow the prompts to create your Adobe ID. You can then enter your Adobe ID and password in the relevant boxes in Digital Editions to activate.

OverDrive Media Console Requires a Security Update

The first time you open an eAudiobook with OverDrive Media Console, a message will appear saying that a security upgrade must be performed before the file can be opened. Simply follow the on-screen instructions to perform the quick upgrade.

FINDING TITLES USING LIBRARY TO GO

You can search for a particular title or author using the 'Quick Search' box near the top of the Library to Go page.

The 'Advanced Search' option to the right of the 'Quick Search' box can be used to perform a more specific search. You can also browse for titles using the green menu on the left side of the page or the categories in the centre of the main Library to Go page.

DOWNLOADING AN e-BOOK

When you have found an eBook that interests you, simply click on its title for more information:

If the 'Add to Cart' option is visible in the grey bar under 'Format Information', then the book is available to download and you can click to move to the next step.

If you see 'Place a Hold' instead, then the item is checked out by someone else and you can click to enter your e-mail address and receive notification when the item is available. Once the item is available for download, you will have three days to complete the checkout. After you click 'Add to Cart' you are given the option to 'Continue Browsing' or 'Proceed to Checkout'-if you 'Continue Browsing', your items will stay in your cart for 45 minutes. Clicking 'Proceed to Checkout' brings you to a screen asking for your Library card number and PIN number.

From here you can choose your lending period and see how close you are to your 5 item limit. When you're ready to download, click 'Confirm Checkout' and then the 'Download' button on the next screen that appears.

••If this is the very first time you have downloaded an eBook from the Library, you will need to tell your computer which programme it should use to open the file.

To select the programme to open eBook files, you must click the 'Save' button, choose 'Desktop' as the destination and then click save.

Next, find the file on the Desktop, right-click the icon, go to 'Open With' and click 'Choose Programme'.

Choose Adobe Digital Editions from the list of programmes, click the box next to "Always use the selected programme to open this kind of file' and click 'OK'. If Digital Editions does not appear in the list of programmes, you will need to find it using the 'Browse' button. Usually, it is saved under Programme Files \ Adobe \ Adobe Digital Editions \ digitaleditions.

TRANSFERRING AN e-BOOK TO AN e-READER

To transfer an eBook from Digital Editions to an eReader such as the Kobo Touch, you must first connect your eReader to your computer. If a window opens asking what Windows should do with the connected device choose 'Take No Action'. Then open Digital Editions and follow the steps to authorise your reader if you are using it for the first time. Click on the icon for Library View in the top-left corner of the screen.

Your eReader should appear at the bottom of the Bookshelves area on the left side of the screen. Simply drag and drop the title you wish to transfer onto your eReader. If your eReader does not appear in Digital Editions after you have plugged it in, you may need to download your eReader's software before your computer will recognise it.

DOWNLOADING AN e-BOOK DIRECTLY TO A SONY WIFI e-READER

The Sony WiFi eReader will allow you to borrow eBooks from the library directly on your device without the use of Adobe Digital Editions or any external applications.

To download books onto your device, use the following procedure:

- Turn on your device.
- Go to page 2 and select the 'Public Library' icon.
- If you are asked to set up an account in the Sony eReader store, follow the prompts to do so. This will authorize your eReader to open the library books you borrow.
- In the 'Public Library' section, select the option to 'Discover More' or 'Find a Library'.
- Type in 'Medicine Hat' into the search area and press the small magnifying next to it.
- Select the 'Medicine Hat Public Library System' and then select the 'Library to Go' option—this will take you to the Library to Go homepage where you can login, search for, and download your eBooks.

RETURNING e-BOOKS DIRECTLY ON A SONY WIFI e-READER

To return your eBooks directly from your Sony Wifi eReader use the following procedure:

- Select the 'Books' icon on your eReader screen.
- Press the Menu button.
- Select 'Return Books.'
- Select which books you'd like to return by checking the appropriate boxes.
- Press 'Done'.

Overdrive Media Console Mobile is a free app available for most iPad/iPhone/iPod Touch, Android, Blackberry and Windows Mobile devices. This app allows you to download titles directly to your device over Wi-Fi or 3g. However, not all file formats are currently compatible. Apple devices, for example, only support eBooks in ePub format and eAudiobooks in MP3 format. You can download the app from the app store for your device or the Library to Go web site. You must register your Adobe ID with the Overdrive Media Console Mobile app and you will be prompted for your library card number and PIN before you can download an eBook or eAudiobook.

RETURNING e-BOOKS DIRECTLY FROM YOUR PORTABLE DEVICE

You can also return your eBooks directly from your portable device by using the OverDrive Media Console app. By swiping your finger across the title on the main page you will be shown a button to delete the book. When you click that button, you will then be given the option to delete only, or delete and return the book. Deleting the book only will free up space on your device, while deleting and returning the book will also free up space for another title in your Library to Go account.

Each device is different but most do offer you the option to return items early. To find out if your device has this feature, try to delete the item and see if you are asked whether you want to return the item as well. If you are not given the option, then look in the settings section for each borrowed item.

DOWNLOADING AN e-AUDIOBOOK TO YOUR COMPUTER

The process for finding and checking out titles is the same for eAudiobooks and eBooks. After checking out an eAudiobook click Open in the File Download window. Overdrive Media Console will open automatically. eAudiobooks are divided into parts to facilitate faster download times. You will need to tell Overdrive Media Console which parts to download by checking the boxes beside the parts you want. The default option is to download all parts. Once you have checked the parts you want, you can click the 'OK' button to download.

It could take a while to download depending on the speed of your Internet connection and how many parts you choose to download at once After the eAudiobook has downloaded, it will appear in Overdrive Media Console.

From here, you can click the 'Play' button in the top-left corner to listen to the eAudiobook on your computer. The 'Download' button lets you download any parts of the eAudiobook that you missed.

TRANSFERRING AN e-AUDIOBOOK TO A MOBILE DEVICE

- Connect the device to your PC.
- Open Overdrive Media Console.
- Click the title of the eAudiobook you wish to transfer and click the 'Transfer' button in the topleft corner of the screen.
- Select your player and which parts of the eAudiobook you wish to transfer and click 'Next' to begin the transfer.
- Click 'Finish' and remove your player from the PC.

Special Considerations if Transferring to an iPod

- Some titles are not compatible with Apple devices st have iTunes v9.1 installed on your PC to transfer to an iPod.
- The iTunes setting 'Manually manage music...' must be enabled for Apple devices. Adjust this setting as follows.
  — Connect the device to your computer.
  — Open iTunes.
  — In iTunes, locate the device in the left vertical navigation panel and click the device.

— If it is not already checked, place a checkmark next to the option 'Manually manage music...'and
— Click the 'Apply' button.

Plcasc notc that at this timc transfcrring WMA audiobooks to an Applc device running iOS 5 is not recommended due to compatibility issues between OverDrive Media Console and Apple iTunes. If you do attempt to transfer WMA files to an Apple device then please be sure to back up your files before starting the process. If you are still experiencing difficulty transferring an eAudiobook to your Apple device, please consult the Help section on the Library to Go web site for other possible solutions.

e-READERS

e-BOOK FORMATS

eBooks come in a variety of formats. Some publishers and sellers also place DRM protection on the books so they cannot be copied, viewed on multiple devices, or restricted to specific readers.

There is no consistent licensing as each licence is an agreement between author, publisher and seller:

- ePUB is an open source format and continues to develop. ePUB books can contain video and active links which make the books dynamic. ePUB is the most versatile of all eBook formats. Textbooks developers are looking to this format as it will allow for content and media rich books, moving away from what can be done with traditional text and print media. ePub can be read by most popular devices except Amazon's Kindle. Amazon currently offers an e-mail service that lets you convert ePUB documents and books into the AZW format for a fee, though formaang and interactivity may be lost.
- MOBI also known as MobiPocket is owned by Amazon and is similar to the AZW format for Kindle. The MOBI format can be read by most of the popular readers except the Nook. MOBI was once the most popular format but is losing ground to ePUB.
- PDF is a format that is commonly used to publish documents and images. PDFs are essentially images of pages and therefore do not allow text to flow between pages or to fit the screen size. PDFs are best read on larger computer screens and not mobile devices. PDFs can be viewed in most readers except the first edition Kindle.
- Plain Text formaang allows for a very small file size, allowing large books such as the Bible to be distributed in this format. Plain text is read by major readers except Nook.
- HTML is the markup language for web pages and most eBooks that use HTML can be read in a web browser. Some other eBook formats include HTML in their packaging of books.

- Kindle/ AZW is a version of MOBI and is exclusive to Amazon Kindle. It can be read on a variety of mobile devices with the Kindle App. It cannot be read on other readers such as the Nook or Sony reader.
- eReader was originally developed for Palm. This format supports hyperlinks and images. The Nook can read pdb files while the Kindle cannot.

WHERE TO FIND e-BOOKS

Before you go out and make a purchase for a dedicated reader it might be worth your while to explore what books are available in eBook format. Take some time to read a few books on the devices you already have access to such as your computer or smart phone if you have one. eBooks are not quite the same as print. Some eBooks contain images and some do not. Some free versions were entered by volunteers and may contain a typo or two.

Let's explore a few places to find eBooks:

- Google eBooks puts the power of the Google search engine to work scouring the web for eBooks. Some books are hosted by Google, others from major publishers and distributors. If you are not tied to a particular reader Google books is a good place to start to find the books in a variety of formats. You can find many free books from the public domain, as well as books for purchase.
- Project Gutenberg has a large collection of books in the public domain. Currently there are over 33,000 free eBooks available. The eBooks on Project Gutenberg are found in 3 main formats plain text, ePUB, and MOBI.
- eBooks.com has a wide range of eBooks for purchase including many academic titles for colleges. eBooks.com sells books in PDF, for computer based reading; ePUB, Mobi and MicrosoV reader for mobile devices. eBooks has an eReader app for iPod/iPad/iPhone devices. eBooks from eBooks.com can also be read on a computer
- Amazon Kindle eBooks Books sold at Amazon for the Kindle are primarily in the AZW format, though some may be in MOBI depending on agreements with the publisher. AZW format is proprietary to Amazon and includes DRM protection. Amazon also offers some free ebooks that are in the public domain. Amazon offers the Kindle app for iPod/iPad/iPhone and other mobile devices.
- Barnes and Noble eBook store sells NookBooks formaXed for the Nook. They currently have over 2 million eBooks available. NookBooks are in the ePUB format, eReader and some PDF, though most books have DRM protection on them. Barnes and Noble offers an app called the Barnes and Noble e-Reader for iPod/iPad/iPhone and other mobile devices.

- Borders has adopted the ePUB, PDF and Mobile format for its books; most have DRM protections. Like other book sellers, they also have free books in the public domain. Unlike Amazon and Barnes and Noble, Borders does not sell its own reader but recommends seven different readers on its web site. These are described in the last section on eReaders. Borders also offers a free eReader app for many mobile devices.

The Apple iBookstore currently sells books for reading only on Apple mobile devices, through the iTunes interface. Rumours persist that Apple will release its iBooks app for the Mac and PC in the future but there are always rumours surrounding Apple. Apple prefers the tactile sensation of 'turning pages' with the touch screen on its mobile devices that current desktop and laptops do not have. Apple iBooks are in the ePUB format and allow for interactivity such as viewing embedded video and active web links. Apple also sells fully illustrated books and magazines because of the colour planorm provided by its devices.

e-READERS

Reading eBooks can be done on a variety of devices with a range of apps and programmes. As suggested, begin with a look at reading on computers and multifunctional devices and end with a look at some of the major dedicated readers.

e-READING SOFTWARE FOR COMPUTERS

If you own a computer you can read almost anything though you may need more than one programme to do so. Reading on your computer is not as comfy as reading a book curled up on the couch or siang in your back yard, but you do have access to a vast library of books. Each of the major eBook sellers provides a version of their reader for your computer. If you use a Windows based PC you can choose from Kindle for PC, Adobe Digital Editions, Nook for PC, or Borders eReader for PC. If you are a Mac user you have a similar selection of choices Kindle for Mac, Adobe Digital Editions, Nook for Mac, or Borders eReader for Mac.

EREADING ON MULTIFUNCTIONAL MOBILE DEVICES: iPODS, iPADS, AND MOBILE PHONES

Multifunctional mobile devices are just small computers, some with an added phone. These include iPods, iPads, iPhones, Android Phones, Blackberries and an increasing number of small tablets. Most of these mobile devices have LCD screens which make reading in bright light a bit of a challenge; most are colour and many have touch screens and support the interactivity of the ePUB format. Velocity Micro offers Android based tablets, Borders recommends two, these are described later on.

The device that offers the richest media content support for eBooks is currently the iPad. If you already have a number of gadgets in your bag you may wish for a multifunctional device so you have fewer devices to deal with. Similar to the computer, the devices can have a variety of e-reader apps installed so they can handle a large variety of book formats and work with all the major eBook distributors.

Kindle Reading Apps, Nook Apps and Borders eReader Apps are available for mobile devices including apps for iPods/iPads/iPhone, Android and Blackberry phones. Adobe Digital Editions which reads PDF and ePUB can be used on a variety of mobile devices.

DEDICATED e-READERS

When it comes to dedicated eReaders the ones that get the most coverage are the Amazon Kindle and the Barnes and Noble Nook. These two major book sellers have developed their own eReaders. Borders has taken a more open approach and does not market to a particular eReader allowing the reader greater choice.

As suggested, begin with a brief summary of the Kindle and Nook readers currently available and then look at the 7 that Borders recommends. Amazon currently offers the Kindle 3 and Kindle DX. The two models each come in two flavours—wifi or wifi and 3G. 3G is provided free allowing you to purchase books and download them whereever you are.

The more recent release of the Kindles uses pearl e-ink which allows for crisper images and text, and reading in bright light. The screens are not touch screens, navigation is carried out via a keyboard and side buXons. The kindle 3 has a 6 inch screen and the DX 9.7 inch screen. Kindle supports; AZW, PDF, MOBI, TEXT formats. It does not support ePub, but a programme called Calibre can convert epub to MOBI. Amazon currently offers an e-mail service for a fee to convert files. The Barnes and Noble Nook now comes in two models the original in black and white and the new Nook Colour. Both have two flavour; wifi or wifi and 3G.

As with the Kindle the 3G is free. Both devices use e-ink and can be read in bright light. Nook Colour has a touch screen and designed for those who love reading magazines.

The traditional black and white e-ink did not do justice to the visual images found in many magazines. Nook colour also has extras including some web browsing, e-mail access and games. It is clearly aimed at the iPad, though the Nook colour is not yet a true multifunctional device. The Nooks support the following formats: EPUB, PDB, PDF, MP3, JPG, GIF, PNG, PMB. It does not read Mobi, AMZ, LRX/LEZ, or Text

There are other eReaders on the market that are not tied to a specific vendor. Borders offers a comparison chart for a variety of readers it recommends.

Below is a brief summary of each:

- Aluratek Libre Pro supports books in the ePub, PDF, TXT, RTF, FB2, MOBI, PRC formats. It can play mp3 files and uses an LCD screen that is black and white.
- Kobo Wireless eReader support eReader, ePUB and PDF formats. It uses e-ink and has a 6 inch screen.
- Sony offers 3 models of eReader; the Pocket edition, Touch edition and the Daily Edition. The Sony models all have touch screen navigation and use e-ink. The pocket edition is not wireless and requires a computer to sync books to. They support ePub, PDF, TXT, RTF, and BBeB formats. Sony also has its own eBook store.

Finally rounding out our look at eReaders the Cruz reader and Tablet from Velocity Micro. The Cruz Reader is not a standalone eReader, it more a multifunctional device. It is a colour eReader with 7" screen that also browses the web, plays mp3 files, watch movies, play games and has some productivity apps. The Cruz Tablet is a true multifunctional Android colour tablet. There are two versions of this device—one with Borders eReader and the other with Amazon's Kindle soVware.

There is a great deal of variety in this very fluid technology. It is apparent that eBooks are here and are gaining more and more ground. eBook readers continue to improve as time goes on. Just as with computers, change is inevitable. Reading is a very personal experience therefore each person should make the choice that works for them. It is clearly not a one size fits all experience. Do your research and make the choice that works for you.

7

Online Cataloguing

Online cataloguing, such as Dynix, has greatly enhanced the usability of catalogues, thanks to the rise of *MA*chine *R*eadable *C*ataloguing = MARC standards in the 1960s. Rules governing the creation of catalogue MARC records include not only formal cataloguing rul lges like AACR2 but also special rules specific to MARC, available from the Library of Congress and also OCLC. MARC was originally used to automate the creation of physical catalogue cards; Now the MARC computer files are accessed directly in the search process.

OPACs have enhanced usability over traditional card formats because:

- The online catalogue does not need to be sorted statically; the user can choose author, title, keyword, or systematic order dynamically.
- Most online catalogues offer a search facility for any word of the title; the goal of the grammatic word order (provide an entry on the word that most users would look for) is reached even better.
- Many online catalogues allow links between several variants of an author name. So, authors can be found both under the original and the standardised name (if entered properly by the cataloguer).
- The elimination of paper cards has made the information more accessible to many people with disabilities, such as the visually impaired, wheelchair users, and those who suffer from mold allergies.

TYPES OF CATALOGUING

- *Original Cataloguing:* For MARC records, you input a new master record cataloged according to current cataloguing practices and AACR2. If different rules for descriptive cataloguing are used to create the record (other than rules based on or consistent with AACR2, AACR1, ALA 1949, ALA 1941, or ALA 1908), then code the 040-‡e field with the appropriate MARC coding from the *MARC Code Lists for Relators, Sources, Description Conventions*. If you are using your own descriptive conventions, enter your OCLC symbol in subfield ‡e. Enter subfield ‡e immediately after subfield ‡a. Dublin Core users apply various standards when creating Dublin Core records:

- The Dublin Core Metadata Initiative provides guidance on commonly-adopted best practices in *Using Dublin Core*.
- In the library community, the DCMI-Libraries Working Group publishes the *DC-Library Application Profile* (DC-Lib): library-application-profile/.
- Groups of libraries develop their own specific practices based on more general standards.

- *Copy Cataloguing:* A machine-readable record exists. You modify the record for local use and create a copy of the record with your modifications.
- *Transcribing Cataloguing Copy:* You create a master record using an existing nonmachine-readable catalogue record. Usually, you transcribe pre-AACR2 records, but you may also transcribe AACR2 records. Again, some records are created by other standards.

LEVELS OF CATALOGUING

- *Full-level Cataloguing:* Records that meet the requirements of second-level description (AACR2, rule 1.0D2).
- *Core-level Cataloguing:* Records that meet the requirements of first-level description (AACR2, rule 1.0D1) and some of the requirements of second-level description (AACR2, rule 1.0D2).
- *Minimal-level Cataloguing:* Records that meet the requirements of first-level description (AACR2, rule 1.0D1).
- *Abbreviated-level Cataloguing:* Brief records that do not meet the requirements of Minimal-level cataloguing specifications (*ELvl* code *3*).
- *Dublin Core:* All records created in Dublin Core (*ELvl* code *3*).

ORIGINAL CATALOGUING AND COPY CATALOGUING

Entering ISBD Punctuation

The General International Standard Bibliographic Description (ISBD) prescribes punctuation between elements or areas of bibliographic description for current cataloguing (i.e., AACR2):

- Supply ISBD punctuation that occurs within variable fields. Enter punctuation and spaces between elements within a field as prescribed by AACR2.
- If punctuation separates data that occur in separate subfields, enter the punctuation at the end of the first subfield.
- Do not supply ISBD punctuation (space-dash-space) that occurs between variable fields, *e.g.*, between the 250 and 260 fields.
- Do not supply parentheses around transcribed series statements.

Space-dash-space

The OCLC catalogue card print programme supplies a space-dash-space (-) before the following fields:

- 250 Edition Statement
- 254 Musical Presentation Statement
- 255 Cartographic Mathematical Data
- 256 Computer File Characteristics
- 260 Publication, Distribution, Etc. (Imprint)
- 362 Dates of Publication and/or Volume Designation (First indicator value *0*)
- 4xx Series Statements (First 4xx field)

If the field that precedes one of the listed fields ends with final punctuation (.? !), the print programme supplies a space-dash-space (-). If the preceding field does not end with final punctuation, the print programme supplies period-space-dash-space (-).

Verifying Headings

You must use AACR2 or AACR2-compatible forms for all headings and uniform titles for current original cataloguing. Search the OCLC Authority File to verify forms of entry.

Use current Library of Congress (LC) AACR2 or AACR2-compatible forms. If those forms are not in the OCLC Authority File, construct the heading or uniform title according to AACR2.

INCLUDING NON-ROMAN SCRIPTS

The OCLC provides the capability to include Arabic, Bengali, Chinese, Devanagari, Cyrillic, Greek, Hebrew, Japanese, Korean, Tamil, and Thai scripts in bibliographic records. Include these scripts in your current original cataloguing if you have the knowledge and expertise to do so.

ROMANIZED DATA

If you provide Romanized (Latin-script-equivalent) data, Romanization should follow guidelines in the ALA-LC Romanization Tables on the Library of Congress Web-site.

GENERAL MATERIAL DESIGNATIONS

Use General Material Designations (GMD) for current original cataloguing. GMDs are generic terms describing the medium of the item. OCLC defines subfield ‡h (Medium) in field 245 (Title Statement) for GMD information. Enter GMDs in lowercase letters enclosed in brackets. Example: ‡h [electronic resource].

GMDs and Library of Congress Rule Interpretations

Library of Congress Rule Interpretations (LCRIs), rule 1.1C, lists GMDs and provides standards for use. The LC applies rule 1.1C for only certain types of materials. LCRI 21.29 limits the use of GMDs to the title area only. Follow LC practice except: If one of the following GMDs is applicable, it is mandatory for I-level, Core-level, and K-level records in field 245 subfield ‡h.

Dublin Core users apply different codes:

- ‡h [art original]
- ‡h [microscope slides]
- ‡h [art reproduction]
- ‡h [model]
- ‡h [chart]
- ‡h [motion picture]
- ‡h [diorama]
- ‡h [picture]
- ‡h [electronic resource]
- ‡h [realia]
- ‡h [filmstrip]
- ‡h [slide]
- ‡h [flash card]
- ‡h [sound recording]
- ‡h [game]
- ‡h [technical drawing]
- ‡h [graphic]
- ‡h [toy]
- ‡h [kit]
- ‡h [transparency]
- ‡h [microform]
- ‡h [videorecording]

Notes:

- Use the "graphic" GMD only when applying the "Graphic Materials" descriptive conventions, indicated by the presence of the value *gihc* in subfield ‡e of field 040.

TRANSCRIBING PRE-AACR2 COPY

Master Record

When you create a master record from a non-machine-readable record (often a paper record), you are transcribing cataloguing copy. Usually, the cataloguing copy is pre-AACR2. The National Union Catalogue, for example, has such records. Guidelines in this part apply to all pre-AACR2 cataloguing copy whether part of a retrospective conversion project, reclassifi-cation project or part of normal acquisition and cataloguing workflow.

LATEST ENTRY CATALOGUING

Do not input latest entry cataloguing for serials.

VERIFYING NAME, SUBJECT, UNIFORM TITLE HEADINGS

Use AACR2 (or AACR2-compatible) forms for all name and uniform title headings (including the name and uniform title portions of name and name/ uniform title subject headings) for retrospective cataloguing, even if the transcribed record is pre-AACR2. You must search the OCLC Authority File to verify forms of entry.

If the forms of name and uniform title entries are not in the OCLC Authority File, OCLC encourages you to construct the heading or uniform title according to AACR2, but you are not required to do so. If the subject headings are not in the OCLC Authority File, OCLC encourages you to construct the subject heading according to the *Subject Headings Manual* (formerly called the *Subject Cataloguing Manual*), but you are not required to do so. For entries in other 6xx fields, use the appropriate thesaurus.

If the topical subject heading is not derived from a standard thesaurus but is compatible with the form of headings from that thesaurus and it has value to institutions other than yours, use either field 650 or field 651 with 2nd indicator *4*. Many pre-AACR2 headings for personal names, corporate bodies, etc., are similar to corresponding AACR2 forms.

However, some pre-AACR2 headings will never have corresponding AACR2 forms. Often, these headings include obsolete form subheadings. Their inclusion in WorldCat and in local catalogues usually results in split files of headings for similar materials because of different practices under AACR2 and older rules.

Examples include:

- 100 1 Francesco d'Assisi, ‡c Saint. ‡k Legend ‡p Fioretti. ‡l English. ‡f 1959.
- 110 2 Jews. ‡k Liturgy and ritual. ‡g Tunis.
- 130 0 Arthur, King ‡k (Romances, etc.).

OCLC encourages you to construct the heading or uniform title according to AACR2, but you are not required to do so. Change the heading or delete the heading in favour of an appropriate subject or genre heading. If a heading appearing on retrospective cataloguing copy was incorrectly constructed under pre-AACR2, revise that heading to a valid pre-AACR2 or AACR2 form.

SERIES HEADINGS

- Fields 400, 410 and 411 Series Statement/Added Entry headings are obsolete as described in MARC 21. OCLC has invalidated and removed fields 400, 410 and 411. Enter such series statements as they appear in the retrospective cataloguing copy in field 490, correcting any obvious errors, and supply the series tracing in the appropriate 8xx field.

- OCLC encourages you to construct an AACR2 form for the series but you are not required to do so. The form in the 4xx field should be compatible with the rules used for description. Trace the AACR2 form in an 8xx field.
- If the name portion of a name/title series entry is verifiable online, enter the name portion to match the form in the name authority record.

Using GMDs (Media Qualifiers)

General Material Designators are generic terms describing the medium of the item. Prior to AACR2, GMDs were known as media qualifiers. GMDs have also been called medium designators. Use subfield ‡h (Medium) for GMDs only in field 245 (Title Statement). Use only the current form of the appropriate GMD. Do not capitalize the first letter of the GMD. Enclose the GMD in brackets.

MAIN ENTRY, ADDED ENTRY

If the AACR2 form cannot be verified online and a single surname appears without a forename and is instead followed by a long dash, do not enter the long dash. Enter "Dezauche,- as "Dezauche,". If an asterisk precedes an added entry to indicate that the personal name has been revised, do not enter the asterisk.

TITLE STATEMENT

- If the title portion has underlining, do not enter the underlining.
- Enter the same number of ellipses as appear on the LC copy.
- If ellipses occur within data, enter a space before and after the ellipses.
- If the ellipses are followed by a mark of punctuation (. , : ; ! ?), do not enter a space following ellipses.
- If two vertical parallel lines (| |) appear on the copy, enter space-slash-space (/) instead of these vertical lines. Such lines show that the title of a work is printed in verse or distinguish two editions or versions of a rare book.
- If the title has superscript and subscript alphabetic characters, enter the characters as regular lowercase characters, except in formulas.

Printed on LC Copy	Enter
A-BA (n^{-1})	A-BA ([superscript] n^{-1})

- If the record (usually a non-English language record) has place and/or date of birth and death identified with an asterisk (•) for birth data and a single dagger (†) for death data, do not enter the symbol or the birth or death data.

Printed on LC Copy	Enter
El caballero del romanticismo; primer centenario de su natalicio. †Usiacuri 7 de	El caballero del romanticismo; primer centenario de su natalicio. Chiquinquira, 21 de mayo de 1867. febrero 1923.

IMPRINT STATEMENT

- If the reprint statement has the appearance of a double imprint (*e.g.*, "Bonnae, Apud Henry and Cohen, 1856; Frankfurt/Main, Minerva, 1967"), separate the reprint statement from the imprint by a period. Enter the first (original) imprint as part of the preceding field (title or edition). Enter the reprint data in field 260 (Publication, Distribution, Etc.).
- In the following imprint, the place of publication appears to have a street address: "72-Souligne-sous-Ballon, l'auteur, 1968." But "72" is a postal code and "Souligne-sous-Ballon" is the name of the town. Enter both (as they appear on the card) as the place of publication.
- If a place name (*e.g.*, "Rio") is incomplete, enter the complete name with brackets around the data not appearing on LC copy (*e.g.*, "Rio [de Janeiro]").
- If two places of publication are separated by a conjunction (*and*, *und*, *u.*) or by a hyphen, enter a comma instead of the conjunction or hyphen and treat the two places as two separate places of publication.

GERMAN IMPRINT STATEMENTS

Separation of two place names by a hyphen usually (although not always) indicates that one place is located near a larger, better known place (*e.g.*, "Hamburg-Altona"). Treat such entries as a single place of publication. Two place names separated by "bei" or "b." (*e.g.*, "Ratingen b. Dusseldorf") constitute a single place. Treat two place names separated by *und* or *u.* as two separate places of publication.

COLLATION

Do not enter the statement *Cover title* in the collation. Enter *Cover title* in the first note field. When illustration information is given in the title paragraph or in a general note, but not in the collation, enter the collation as is. Do not add the illustration information to the collation. Do not enter illustration codes in the fixed field. If a statement of reprint is included, do not enter *reprint* in the 300 field. Use a 5xx note field for reprint information.

SERIES STATEMENTS

Omit information not used under AACR2.

Printed on LC Copy	Enter
Half-title: Library of philosophy Ed. by J.H.Muirhead	Library of philosophy

Some records have a "bound with" note in the series statement position and a series statement in the note position. Use the 4xx and/or 8xx fields for series statements and the 5xx fields for notes. Disregard the position on the card. Tag each field according to what it is rather than where it is.

LOCAL NOTES

Do not include copy-specific or institution-specific details (such as binding, imperfections, incompleteness or copy number) in the master record. If you want such notes to appear on cards or in OCLC-MARC records, include the notes in field 590 (Local Note).

- 590 L.C. copy imperfect: bibliography wanting.
- 590 L.C. has v.1, 3-5 only

Optionally, if the copy-specific or institution-specific details are of interest beyond the inputting library, enter them in a 500 field (General note) with subfield $5, Institution to which field applies.

TITLE TRACINGS

Follow local practice when entering the title added entry indicator. Some title tracings are inverted (*e.g.*, "Title: Retail Terms, A Manual of."). Use field 246 (Varying Form of Title) for such titles. LC copy for a work published in English but translated from a non-Roman language may have a phrase in the form "Russian title: [title in Cyrillic alphabet] (transliterated: [title in Roman alphabet])" following the tracings. Do not enter these phrases and titles. They are not part of the tracings because they are not preceded by a Roman numeral. Limited cataloguing records (identified by a double dagger after the card number) do not have series tracings. If you add series tracings, treat the resulting record as having been upgraded by your library. Enter your library's symbol in field 040 (Cataloguing Source) subfield ‡d (Modifying agency).

SUBJECT HEADINGS

- Enter only these subject headings: LC (including Library of Congress subject headings for children's literature), National Library of Medicine (NLM) and National Agricultural Library (NAL).
- Spell out in full, according to current LC practice, abbreviations that appear in older LC subject headings (*e.g.*, spell out "Bibl." as "Bibliography").

- Do not enter non-LC, non-NLM or non-NAL subject headings enclosed in brackets.
- Do not enter portions of subject headings enclosed in brackets.

If a portion of a subject heading is enclosed in sub-script parentheses, enter the data, but do not enter the parentheses.

Printed on LC Copy	**Enter**
[Labour supply–Stat.–Russian]	(Do not enter)
Fruit [–Hardiness]	Fruit.
Wages–(Furniture Workers)–United States	Wages ‡x Furniture workers ‡z United States.
Spraying and dusting residues (in agriculture) [–Testing]	Spraying and dusting residues in agriculture.

FULL NAME NOTES (SECULAR NAME, NAME ORIGINALLY, ETC.)

Do not enter full name notes that appear in brackets between the tracings and the card number.

COPYRIGHT NUMBER

Do not enter copyright numbers that appear in the lower left corner below the LC legend.

CONTENT DESIGNATION

Use the following guidelines (New and Old) for tagging and entering data in subfields used for pre-AACR2 bibliographic data.

GUIDELINE 1–NEW CONTENT DESIGNATION

Use the new content designation when an old, corresponding content designation has been replaced. Use the following guidelines:

- Enter an alternative title in subfield ‡a (Title) of field 245 (Title Statement).
- Enter adjacent publisher statements (different publishers or agencies) in separate subfield ‡b's (Name of publisher, distributor, etc.) of field 260 (Publication, Distribution, Etc. [Imprint]). Use punctuation as a guide. If in doubt, use separate subfields.
  - 260 Washington, ‡b Published for the Library of Congress by the Gertrude Clark Whittal Poetry and Literature Fund; ‡b [for sale by the Superintendent of Documents, U.S. Govt. Print. Off.] ‡c 1964.
- Enter printing dates in field 260 subfield ‡c (Date of publication, distribution, etc.) in pre-AACR2 records, regardless of whether the printing dates are enclosed in parentheses on the copy. Do not enter the parentheses.

  - *260 London:* ‡b J. Lane, ‡c 1902 (1907 printing)
  - *260 London*: ‡b J. Lane, ‡c 1902, 1907 printing.
- Enter accompanying material data in subfield ‡e (Accompanying material) of field 300 (Physical Description).
  - *300 6 v.*: ‡b ill., maps; ‡c 22 cm. ‡e and atlases (3 v.: ill.; 30 cm.)
  - 300 3 l., 100 p. ‡b illus. ‡c 25 cm. ‡e and portfolio (24 plates) 30 cm.
- Use subfield ‡v (Volume number/sequential designation) in field 490 (Series Statement).
  - 490 1 ACRL monographs, ‡v no.8
- Repeat subfields ‡a (Series statement) and ‡v for a subseries that follows the main series number (first subfield ‡v) in field 490.
  - 490 1 Biblioteca de arte hispanico; ‡v 8: ‡a Artes aplicades; ‡v 1

GUIDELINE 2–OLD CONTENT DESIGNATION

Use the old content designation when no new designation has been defined. For pre-AACR2 conference names entered under place (AACR2 form not verifiable online), use subfield ‡q (Name of meeting following jurisdiction name entry element) in x11 fields.

- 711 Hague. ‡q International Peace Conference, ‡n 2d, ‡d 1907.

Use the following guidelines to delimit short titles (field 245 subfield ‡a) in pre-ISBD records:

- If a title has a date or a range of dates, terminate the short title after the date.
  - 245 10 Disarmament and Soviet policy 1964-1968 ‡c by Thomas B.Larson.
- If a title has a colon as the first mark of punctuation, terminate the short title at the next logical break following the colon.
  - *245 10 Canada 2067:* Canada in the next century ‡c by John Smith.
- If a title has brackets, terminate the short title at the next logical break.
  - 245 10 Catalogue of musical instruments [in the] Victoria and Albert Museum ‡c [by] Raymond Russell.

SCORES

Use subfield ‡d (Plate or publisher number) for a plate or publisher number that is part of the imprint (field 260). In addition, enter the plate or publisher's number in a nonprinting field 028 (Publisher Number).

- 028 20 18315 ‡b Breitkopf and Härtel
- 260 Leipzig, ‡b Breitkopf and Härtel ‡c [1888 or 9] ‡d Pl. no.18315.

SOUND RECORDINGS

Use field 262 (Imprint Statement for Sound Recordings [Pre-AACR2]) for a pre-AACR2 imprint. Enter the publisher number in a nonprinting field 028.

- 028 00 SLT 43091 ‡b Telefunken
- 262 ‡b Telefunken ‡c SLT 43091. ‡d [1966]

If the retrospective copy consists of separate bibliographic records for each separately titled work, you are encouraged but not required to recatalog the item (AACR2, rule 6.1G) to describe the sound recording as a unit. (A record for a sound recording described as a unit may coexist with the records describing its separately titled works.)

Treat the new record as original cataloguing and use the following guidelines:

Element	Guideline
Srce	Use code *d* (other).
Desc	Use code *a* (record is in AACR2 form).
010	If the retrospective copy is LC copy, include the LC card numbers for each separate description in subfield ‡z (Canceled/invalid LC control numbers).
050	If present on LC retrospective copy, include the LC call number.

AUDIOVISUAL MATERIALS

Use field 261 (Imprint Statement for Films [Pre-AACR2 Revised]) for pre-ISBD production and release information.

- 261 Archers Film Production, ‡f London, ‡d 1947. ‡b Released in the U.S. by Universal International Films, ‡d 1948.

MAPS

Use field 507 (Scale Note for Graphic Material) for a scale note:

- 507 Scale 1:500,000; ‡b 1 in. equals approx. 8 miles.

RECATALOGING

If you have retrospective copy and the item in hand, you may recatalog the item according to AACR2.

Use the following guidelines:

- The record must meet at least the K-level input standard.
- Use the OCLC Authority File to verify each heading. If an AACR2 or AACR2-compatible form is present, use that form. If no AACR2 or AACR2-compatible form is present, you must create an AACR2 form.
- If you are entering Library of Congress subject headings (6xx with second indicator value *0*), you must follow current LC cataloguing policy.

RECATALOGING NON-LC COPY

If the retrospective copy is non-LC copy, treat the record as original cataloguing and recatalog to AACR2:

Element	Guideline
Srce	Use code *d* (Other).
Desc	Use code *a* (record is in AACR2 form).

RECATALOGING LC COPY

If the retrospective copy is LC copy, use the following guidelines:

Element	Guideline
Srce	Code for the source of the cataloguing copy: • National bibliographic agency • Cooperative cataloguing programme
Desc	Use code *a* (record is in AACR2 form).
010 ‡a	Enter the LC control number from LC copy.
040 ‡d	Enter your OCLC symbol.
050, 082	Enter the LC call number and the Dewey classification number if present on the LC copy. You may change field 050 (Library of Congress Call Number) to field 090 (Locally Assigned LC-type Call Number) if the author number or the classification has been changed.

TRANSCRIBING AACR2 COPY

Because OCLC loads current LC and National Library of Medicine (NLM) cataloguing, you seldom transcribe printed AACR2 cataloguing. This part provides guidelines for such transcription in these rare cases.

LC OR NLM COPY

The legend *AACR2* in the lower right corner identifies current LC printed cataloguing. Transcribe the data exactly as shown on LC or NLM copy.

LC cataloguing

Enter *DLC* in field 040 subfield ‡a (Original cataloguing agency) and assign the code *b*/(National bibliographic agency) in *Srce*.

- ELvl: I
- Srce: b/
- 040 DLC ‡c XXX

NLM Cataloguing

Enter *NLM* in field 040 subfield ‡a and assign code *b*/(National bibliographic agency) in Srce.

- ELvl: I
- Srce: b/
- 040 NLM ‡c XXX

Supply other fixed-field elements and variable fields, indicators and subfield codes. Include the LC call number (field 050), the NLM call number (field 060) and the Dewey Decimal call number (field 082) if they appear on the LC or NLM copy. If you cannot transcribe the record exactly because of the limitations of the machine-readable record, modify the appropriate data. If you modify LC or NLM data, supply the appropriate MRec code.

MODIFICATIONS TO LC AND NLM COPY

The following table identifies the modifications permitted for pre-AACR2 and AACR2 coding of MRec.

Characteristic	Modification	MRec
Incidental non-Roman characters not in character set	Romanize the incidental characters and enclose within brackets.	ϕ
Incidental mathematical symbols or other special characters not in	Add a descriptive word or phrase in brackets. character set	ϕ
Two or more fields (245–260, 4xx) require romanization	Romanize. With the OCLC Connexion Client, users may enter non-Latin script only records.	r (or) o
Obsolete subject entries or forms of name	Replace with current form of entry. If the change affects author-number portion of call number, change the author-number portion and tag the call number as local (fields 090 or 096–Locally Assigned Call Numbers).	ϕ
Lacks certain volumes in contents note	Add volumes to contents note.	ϕ
Lacks final volume number and date for completed set or serial	Add final volume number and date.	ϕ
Lacks a useful access point (*e.g.*, ISBN, subject added entry or other added entry)	Add access points, including subject added entries (6xx fields) and other added entries (7xx fields).	ϕ

If more than one MRec code applies, assign a code in the following order of preference: *s* (Shortened record), *r* (Record is completely romanized; corresponding LC manual record is in the original script), *o* (Record is completely romanized; corresponding LC manual record is also romanized). Enter your OCLC symbol in field 040 subfield ‡d to indicate that you have modified LC or NLM cataloguing:

- 040 DLC ‡c XXX ‡d XXX
- 040 NLM ‡c XXX ‡d XXX

Data Elements Defined in the MARC Formats but Not in AACR2

Some important data elements (*e.g.*, fixed-field *Lang* and field 041 [Language Code]) do not appear on printed LC or NLM cataloguing, but must be included in the record. Follow the I-level input standard for such data. Do not use a MRec code.

LC CATALOGUING IN PUBLICATION

You seldom transcribe AACR2 printed LC Cataloguing-in-Publication (CIP) because OCLC receives most CIP directly from LC. Contact OCLC if you have printed LC CIP which is not represented in WorldCat. Verify that LC has not used the LCCN appearing in CIP for cataloguing an earlier edition or different title. Do not add such records as LC cataloguing copy.

REPRODUCTIONS FROM LC COPY

You may use LC cataloguing for the original item to create a new record for a microform or photocopy reproduction. Treat the new record as your institution's original cataloguing. Use Srce code *d* and enter your OCLC symbol in field 040 subfield ‡a:

- Srce: d
- 040 XXX ‡c XXX

LIBRARY AND ARCHIVES CANADA COPY

To transcribe cataloguing (including Canadian CIP) from the Library and Archives Canada (NLC), treat the new record as your institution's original cataloguing. Use Srce code *d* and enter your OCLC symbol in field 040 subfield ‡a:

- Srce: d
- 040 XXX ‡c XXX

GUIDELINES

Use the following guidelines for selected variable fields:

Element	Guideline
015	The Canadian national bibliography number is structured like an LC card number but is derived from a Canadian source. Enter an uppercase C before the number.
055	Enter the LC-type call number assigned by the NLC. Field 055 prints as a call number for those libraries profiled for Canadian call numbers.

082	Enter an uppercase *C* before the Dewey DecimalClassification number assigned by the NLC.	
092	Since field 082 does not print as a call number, use field 092 for a local call number for card production.	
6xx	Use *Library of Congress Subject Headings* (LCSH) and the subject authority file to verify topical subject headings.	online

Table Contd...

Element	Guideline

If a heading corresponds to LCSH, code it as LCSH (field 650 [Subject Added Entry–Topical Term], second indicator value *0*). If a heading does not appear in LCSH or differs from the LCSH form, treat it as an NLC subject heading (*i.e.*, field 650, second indicator values *5* or *6*), or treat it as a local subject heading.

OTHER NATIONAL LIBRARIES

Treat current cataloguing records (including CIP) from other national libraries, such as the British Library and the National Library of Australia, as original cataloguing.

FULL, CORE, MINIMAL AND ABBREVIATED-LEVEL CATALOGUING

Historically, in cooperation with OCLC advisory groups, OCLC established input standards for entering bibliographic data into WorldCat. Unless noted otherwise, these standards conform to national standards. In addition, OCLC adopted the core-level standard that was defined in 1994 by the Cooperative Cataloguing Council (now known as the Programme for Cooperative Cataloguing (PCC)).

FULL-LEVEL CATALOGUING

Records that meet the requirements of second-level description (AACR2, rule 1.0D2). Correspondence between data in Full-level records and data required for second-level description is not exact. Input full records when possible.

CORE-LEVEL CATALOGUING

Records that meet at least the requirements of first-level description (AACR2, rule 1.0D1) and meet some requirements of second-level description (AACR2, rule 1.0D2).

The core standard is a less-than-full standard, but is more inclusive than Minimal-level. The standard is optional. Use it as appropriate.

MINIMAL-LEVEL CATALOGUING

Records that meet the requirements of first-level description (AACR2, rule 1.0D1). Correspondence between data in Minimal-level records and data required for firstlevel description is not exact. Data required for online cataloguing may not be required by cataloguing rules. Input Minimal-level records as appropriate. Users may upgrade Minimal-level records.

ABBREVIATED-LEVEL CATALOGUING

Brief records that do not meet the requirements of Minimal-level cataloguing specifications. Because Abbreviated-level records may not meet Minimal-level standards, users with Full-level cataloguing authorization or higher can upgrade these records. Depending on the authorization level, users may upgrade to *K*, *I*, *4* or *b/*.

ENCODING LEVEL

The code in ELvl identifies the standard to which a record conforms. In ELvl, use code *I* for Full-level, code *4* for Core-level, code *K* for Minimal-level, and code *3* for Abbreviated-level.

GUIDELINES FOR CORE LEVEL

When entering data in Core-level records, use the following guidelines:

Topic	Guideline
Notes identification	Include only those notes that support the of an item. Criteria for inclusion vary by form of material. In some cases, you may provide alternative justification of added entries through other data, for example, the tagging or the use of relators.
Assigned subject or MARC 21	If appropriate, assign from an established thesaurus headings subject heading system recognized by at least one or two headings at the appropriate level of specificity.One heading is not the absolute upper limit. You need not decide between two equally appropriate headings, nor must you stop with two headings if the item calls for more.

Topic	Guideline
Added entries	Use a complement of added entries that cover at least the primary relationships associated with a work (*e.g.*, corporate bodies, joint authors).
Determining primary relationships	Determination of primary relationships and relative importance of title access information reflect either cataloger's judgment or institutional policy.
Series practice	• Authenticated Core-Level Records (042 ‡a contains pcc). If a national authority record for a series already exists, follow the tracing practice recorded in that record. If one does not exist and you want to trace the series, you must create (or request creation of) an authority record. • Non-Authenticated Core-Level Records (no 042 ‡a

	pcc). If a national authority record for a series already exists, follow the tracing practice recorded in that record. If an authority record does not exist and you want to trace the series, follow AACR2. In either case, untraced series need not be supported by an authority record.
Choice of main entry and	Practice is identical to Full-level for main entry choice and form, title page and series transcription and bibliographic physical description of the item. description
Form of heading	• Core-Level Records (042 ‡a contains pcc). All headings in Core-level records must be verified in the appropriate Authority File (Name, Series or Subject). If an authority record does not exist, you must create one in order to authenticate the Core- level record. If a heading is unverified, you cannot enter the record as an authenticated Core-level record.
	• Non-Authenticated Core-Level Records (no 042 ‡a pcc). All headings in Core-level records must be verified in the appropriate Authority File (Name, Series or Subject). If a heading is unverified, you may still enter a Core-level record and the heading must be established according to AACR2.

PROGRAMME FOR COOPERATIVE CATALOGUING

Various programmes (CONSER, BIBCO) support input of Core-level records. Cooperative programme participants create Core-level records under the auspices of the Programme for Cooperative Cataloguing (PCC). Programme participants identify "Programme-created Core-level records" by entering *pcc* in field 042 (Authentication Code) and code *4* in ELvl. They may also create Fulllevel records (ELvl: blank) under the auspices of the Programme. They enter *pcc* in field 042.

Example of a Programme-created Core-level record:

- ELvl: 4
- Srce: c
- 040 System-supplied OCLC symbol.
- 042 pcc

Example of a Programme-created Full-level record:

- ELvl: b/
- Srce: c
- 040 System-supplied OCLC symbol.
- 042 pcc

Example of a Non-Programme created Core-level record:

- ELvl: 4
- Srce: d
- 040 System-supplied OCLC symbol.
- *[Omit field 042.]*

Programme participants must supply the applicable elements of the Core-level standard. They may supply additional elements, up to Full-level.

NATURE AND FUNCTIONS OF ONLINE CATALOGUING

During the past decade, the widespread adoption of the online catalogue has launched the library visibly into the computer age and has made the library a center stage for information access in academic institutions and in the communities served by the public library.

A whole generation of library users has traveled the path to computer and library literacy through the use of the online catalogue. Implementation of online library catalogues has given new impetus to programmes for user education, formal bibliographic instruction, and information desks, building, in the process, an infrastructure for electronic access to the resources of the library and the community.

Within the profession, the online catalogue has led to a host of conference programmes, workshops, and professional discussion groups. Not the least of these changes is the gradual redefinition of the 'catalogue.' Ten years ago, most librarians and library users would agree to a definition of the catalogue as displaying the bibliographic information for monographs and serial titles physically held in a specific library. Today, it would be harder to get agreement on the definition of a catalogue. Present day online catalogues are beginning to provide access to abstracting and indexing databases, full text, and 'pass through' access to catalogues of material housed in physically diverse locations in different institutions.

In addition to the simple find and display functions, online catalogues are providing printing, downloading, electronic mailing of results, requests for document delivery, and access to electronic full-text. Notwithstanding the lack of clear definition of the online catalogue, large libraries now typically have online catalogues or are actively planning to install them. The effort and resources required for adoption are very substantial: choosing between numerous different systems; finding funding; installing and connecting terminals; connecting to local area networks and the Internet; training staff and users; harmonizing the online catalogue with other computerized systems; and so on.

Recent catalogue records were generally already in machine-readable form but the conversion or upgrading of older records has involved and continues to require a major effort. The widespread adoption of online catalogues is clearly a major advance in library service and yet, in another sense, there has been relatively little progress in the basic functionality of the online catalogue. The searching functions of the best online catalogues of 1992 were not much better than the best online catalogues of ten years earlier.

Online catalogues have evolved through 'generations,' a categorization proposed by Hildreth, to differentiate catalogues in terms of the sophistication of their search functions and user interface. A 'first generation' online catalogue allows searching in the same manner as a card catalogue, typically has one mode of interaction, limited help, and simple displays. A 'second generation' catalogue supports, in addition, the searching of individual terms within the main entry, title, and subject headings, Boolean searches, two modes of interaction multiple display options, and help and error recovery facilities.

The phrases 'third generation' and 'next generation' are used to describe the catalogues that do, or will in the future, include advanced functionality and broader access. Over the last ten years, there has been a gradual development from first to second generation catalogues facilitated by the increasing awareness of the librarians and users of the potential of online access as well as by the rapid drop in costs of computing. Almost everything else around the online catalogue has changed more substantially: extensive installation of infrastructure; massive conversion of existing catalogue records to machine-readable form; the mounting of additional bibliographic databases in conjunction with catalogues or on CD-ROMS; and the mounting of full-text documents online.

During the past ten years there has been a limited relationship between the users and the designers of online catalogues. The origin of both the first and second generation online catalogues are deeply rooted in the card catalogue. We have often been constrained and our purposes determined, to an extent we often discount, by the types of technological advances currently available that happen to be more or less useful in the context of an online catalogue. With the card catalogue as their frame of reference, most of us were not in any better position to provide meaningful input to the design process than the trailblazers who took the first steps.

It turned out that online catalogues were easier and more rewarding to use than the card catalogue and users responded by expressing high levels of satisfaction with the online catalogue and using them more. The online catalogue has brought with it relatively sophisticated tools for automatically gathering data on catalogue use.

For example, transaction logs, combined with various other kinds of studies, provide a continuous flow of information on the strengths and weaknesses of online catalogues on the basis of patron usage.

The information gleaned from these studies has been used to improve the catalogue and the library environment of the catalogue. Though most of these improvements, such as better help messages, new indexes for special functions, orientation programmes, glare-free locations for terminals, etc., have been small, the cumulative effect has been a gradual improvement of the catalogue and a rapidly broadening perception of its potential.

Although the state-of-the-art in functionality of online catalogues has evolved little, numerous constructive proposals have been made, increasingly by researchers interested in, but not responsible for, operational online catalogues. It is clear, however, from the research reviewed that users are experien-cing significant problems in making effective use of online catalogues in spite of expectations.

When the users don't go away empty-handed, they may feel satisfied even though in reality they have received incomplete search results. Because users may be unaware of what information they are missing, they have been slow to articulate these types of problems.

This review examines problems with online catalogues, examines some actual and proposed solutions, and seeks to understand the changing position of the online catalogue. Although some of the solutions draw on other kinds of online bibliographic retrieval systems, our focus is on online catalogues, concentrating on recent literature, and is deliberately selective. From this analysis it is hoped to provide not only a convenient summary of recent developments, but also to contribute to the agenda for research, development, and design of future online catalogues.

The review is in five parts:

- The introduction defines the scope of the review and summarizes briefly the present situation;
- Difficulties encountered by users are then examined;
- Opinions and evidence concerning users are noted;
- Solutions for identified difficulties are examined; and, finally,
- Conclusions are drawn.

PROBLEMS

In this part identified problems of online catalogues are noted.

FORMULATING A SEARCH

Researchers have been observing users, conducting user surveys, and examining online catalogue trans-action logs to develop a picture of what is happening when users interact with the system. The results of these studies have been used to improve levels of search effectiveness. However, recent studies suggest that users continue to experience discoura-gingly low levels of search effectiveness using online catalogues. Larson conducted a transaction log study of the University of California's MELVYL online catalogue and concluded that subject searching had declined 2.15% per year over a 6-year period, while title keyword searching increased by a comparable amount. He attributed the likely causes to the high incidence of search failure for subject searches and the problem of 'information overload' in successful subject searches as the size of database grows.

In 1986, Shaw reported that novice searchers choose the wrong database, search several concepts in a single statement, and use unlimited truncation. It has been widely observed that users do not base subject searches on known documents.

Hildreth reports survey results indicating that 75% of users would be more likely to look up "any publication that may have information on a specific topic or subject area" rather than look up specific books they know about on the topic. People inevitably make mechanical errors using computers.

Seaman found that 40% of user errors were due to incorrect author or title and 9% due to unsupported abbre-viations. They also make spelling errors and have trouble with conjunctions, ellipsis, and missing or incorrect punctuation. A small, but significant, portion of search failures have been attributed to typographical and spelling errors (9.9%-15%) and system failure (9.7-18%), but an even larger proportion (29%) arise from the failure to match user terms with controlled vocabularies. Studies are showing that library users still do not find the use of Boolean operators intuitively obvious.

Bellardo observed that searchers misuse logical operators. Peters found that 73.5% of Boolean AND searches fail while 84.8% of Boolean AND searches between two subject headings also fail. In her recent study of online catalogue use, Ensor shows that there is still widespread lack of familiarity with Boolean operators. Ensor also found that computer 'literacy' affects the degree of facility with which users are using online catalogues. Peters found that remote users of online catalogues are more sophisticated in terms of search patterns than in-library users. For example, he found that 38% of remote users used right truncation while user-initiated truncation was almost non-existent among in-library users. Users still make errors of basic strategy.

Very early on, researchers noticed that catalogue users were failing to develop successful search strategies. A decade ago, searching on broad single terms that trigger large, unmanageable retrievals and missing obvious synonyms that could increase results of small retrievals were common user errors. In fact, most subject queries used "whatever popped into the searcher's mind". The situation has not improved much a decade later. In a transaction log study of academic library use, Hunter found that subject searching was used most frequently, but least successfully.

In addition to typographical errors and using uncontrolled vocabulary, she attributed this failure to a misunderstanding of how to use the system. Bates made the important observation that searchers fail to consider the inverse relationship between recall and precision in searching, *i.e.*, that expanding a search to find additional relevant records will also increase the number of non-relevant records and refining a search to exclude non-relevant records will also exclude some relevant ones. The other side of the coin is search failure. Searches, even in large databases, frequently retrieve sets that are either null (*i.e.*, empty or 'zero-hit') or perceived by the user as too small.

Ten years ago, between 23% to 45% of searches were reported as resulting in null sets. This problem has not changed significantly. Markey found that 34% of subject keyword searches retrieve no records and 53% of subject keyword searches retrieve only one relevant citation. Peters reported a 40% zero-hit rate for searches of an online university catalogue. Hunter came to the daunting conclusion that 58% of searches fail. Of course, not all zero-hit searches are search failures. It is possible that in fact no relevant record in the database matches the search query.

Perhaps the user was seeking to confirm the absence of a citation. However, researchers examining zero-hit searches are demonstrating how minor changes in search statements succeed in retrieving the type and quantity of records desired (Berger, personal communication). For example, if a searcher queries a database indexed with Library of Congress Subject Headings (LCSH), a subject word search on 'Vietnam War' will fail where a subject word search on 'Vietnamese Conflict' will succeed. An experienced searcher might find this by searching submitting a title word search on 'Vietnam War', look at the subject headings and discover that the material on this topic is in fact entered under 'Vietnamese Conflict'.

This example reveals the effect of not implementing LCSH cross-references in MELVYL, but it is also characteristic of how LCSH terminology can differ from natural language that people really use. Another example of this type of failure is the perfectly reasonable subject search on 'Bayesian statistics' which retrieves no records, because LCSH uses 'Bayesian statistical decision theory' for this subject category and provides no cross-reference. If these variant phrases were linked, the user would retrieve records on these topics. As these examples clearly demonstrate, zero-hit search results do not necessarily reflect a lack of records in the database. Several researchers have reported that users have difficulty using subject headings.

MODIFYING SEARCHES

Not only do library users have difficulty formulating searches, they also fail to modify them effectively. System features currently available on most online catalogue systems for dealing with problematic search results include truncation, Boolean operators, and date, language, and location limits. But users rarely use advanced features even when they are available. Harter reported that only half of searchers use these system features, usually the 'limit' command or a change of output format. Shenouda found that most changes are related to the deletion and addition of terms and facets.

Even many experienced users do not use all system capabilities. Are users unaware of the existence of advanced features? Are the advanced features too difficult, too complicated, or too much trouble to use? That library users rarely base subsequent searches on previous results seems to be a characteristic pattern. Tolle and Hah found that 15% of users quit immediately after receiving an error message. Both problems are perhaps due to incomplete understanding of how the database is structured.

No satisfactory solution has yet been developed to cope effectively with null and 'too small' sets. Novices generally accept null sets unquestioningly.

Not only do searchers accept defeat rather quickly when confronted with a zero-hit result, they also flounder when rewarded with a few worthwhile records and want more like them. Ercegovac reported 46% of users having difficulty increasing results when too little is retrieved. More records on the search topic may very well exist in the database, but the necessary link that would lead to their successful retrieval has not been made, either on the part of the searcher or the system. To compound the problem, indexing techniques and retrieval methods that work well with small and medium-sized catalogues tend to fall short and fail when catalogues become large.

An increasing problem is the retrieval of excessively large numbers of records. Factors related to large retrievals include size of the database, keyword indexing, and use of the Boolean OR. Physical limitations of the display screen and inadequate search assistance compound the large retrieval problem, especially for untrained users.

When the retrieved set is large, users must decide whether to continue displaying more records, whether to reformulate the search query, and at what point to discontinue the search. Early studies showed users retrieving large sets 22%-53% of the time and 26% of users experiencing problems reducing the result when too much was retrieved.

Repeated negative experiences with large retrieved sets without adequate online tools to cope with them continue to discourage users from using online catalogues. Kantor found that the number of positive and negative reinforcements affects when users stop. As the size of the database increases, legitimate types of searches tend increasingly to retrieve large, unwieldy sets. Even though Bates observed in 1984 that a 30-hit response is considered an optimal search by many searchers, the reality is more often than not 'information overload'. The average subject search by a skilled user in MELVYL in 1987 was yielding over 181 records.

A decade ago, Bates observed that users typically responded to searches that retrieved one hundred or more citations by either walking away from the terminal or displaying all of the citations. Larson found that the average number of records retrieved by searchers in a large online catalogue was 77.5, but users only displayed 9.1 records.

In 1992 MELVYL users were still finding many more records than they were willing to display, retrieving an average of 100 records, but only displaying about 15 records per search.

With a large system like MELVYL, with 7 million records in its catalogue database, it has also been necessary during times of peak usage to implement a policy of blocking resource-intensive searches that typically return very large sets. Such searches would normally be considered reasonable in smaller databases. How can methods for modifying a search query be conveyed to users when search results are too large? As of 1992, online search aids provide little strategic help for higher-level problem-solving tasks involved in selecting, evaluating and modifying queries.

HANDLING RETRIEVED SETS

Having retrieved a set of records, what next? A search on a large database that presents the user with an unmanageably large retrieved set is only accomplishing part of the task. What assistance is available to help the user cope with a large set of records and make decisions about it? How can the user satisfactorily determine if any records in the set are likely to be relevant and where they are within the large set? How can a view of the set be presented so that the user can make reasonably informed decisions about how to proceed?

How can the user quickly obtain a summary of features that characterize the set and identify subsets likely to be of interest? Are there functions that can be applied that will sort and display views of the entire set from various perspectives, *e.g.*, language, publication date, location, subject headings, title words? Does the average user have, and know about, the tools to reduce the set size in an appropriate, helpful way? Short of moving on to a new or modified search, the user ordinarily has only one option: to display screen after screen of records that have been sorted into alphabetical order of main entry, a tradition carried over from the card catalogue.

There may be alternative forms of display for individual records, but, as of 1992, responses to a query on PACS-L indicated that few options were available and that it was still rare for an online catalogue to allow the user to choose any other ordering or to provide any tools for understanding anything about the retrieved records other than how many there are. It is, therefore, not surprising that users look at a limited number of items and select a few.

SYSTEM DEFICIENCIES

In spite of the afore-mentioned problems, online catalogues are still proving to be remarkably useful and popular. It is, therefore, fortunate that libraries can benefit from the continuing, dramatic improvements in the power and cost-effectiveness of computing, networks, and data storage. Un-fortunately, increased speed, memory, and disk space are not enough to cope adequately with the problem of providing effective access to large numbers of records. Searching is computationally intensive. Second generation online catalogues consume substantially greater computing resources than those of the first generation because of the need to support keyword indexes, keyword truncation, and Boolean combinations. This results in system slowdowns.

In 1989, Farley reported that about 10% of searches on the University of California MELVYL system were resulting in large retrievals that took 60 or more seconds to report back findings. There is also an emerging need to provide high speed downloading of records. This requirement was not expected a decade ago when the need was to support terminals at relatively low speed, but is now implicit in the expectation that high speed networks will be used to search and download results from remote catalogues.

DATA DEFICIENCIES

Data deficiencies affect the quality of search results. Close examination of any large bibliographic database reveals errors in the data. When searching is extended to non-indexed fields, the error rate will probably rise. This will present significant problems when more fields become searchable. Ballard and Lifshin have commented on the need to eliminate spelling errors in bibliographic databases. Large database size is an inhibiting factor in tracking down duplicate records. Software designed to analyse retrieved sets will also prove useful in identifying deficient data. The recent achievement of OCLC in correcting up to 30,000 records a day should be an inspiration to all.

TOPICAL ACCESS AND SYSTEM VOCABULARIES

The present review makes no attempt to duplicate Larson's review of subject searching in online catalogues in volume 15 of Advances in Librarianship to which reference should be made. In general, users have trouble expressing questions in subject terms and matching terms to information systems. Bates found that there is only a 10% to 20% likelihood that two people will use the same term for a concept. Peters and Kurth found that 58% of search sessions begin with terms not used in the system's controlled vocabulary. Several researchers have reported that users have difficulty using LCSH for subject searching.

In 1983, Markey found subject searchers did not consult LCSH even when it was easily available. Bellardo noted the failure to use controlled vocabulary. Even when users do attempt to base searches on LCSH, they are confronted with a formidably complicated maze of relationships. Although modifications have been made, the loose structure of LCSH does not fit well into the typical thesaurus organization with highly structured broad, narrow, and related terms. Not only does this present problems in searching, but it also interferes with the presentation of retrieved sets to the user in a coherent fashion.

LCSH phrase headings and inverted syntax disrupt the logical sequencing of subject heading subdivisions. Not surprisingly, Butkovich concluded that users do not understand the organization and structure of LCSH. Hancock-Beaulieu argues that online catalogue systems at present do not offer any opportunity for a contextual approach to searching. There are no tools for negotiation or experimentation that the user can call upon to further define queries. She also believes that browsing system indexes is of limited value and that alphabetical listings of LCSH do not offer an overview of related subjects.

In addition, there is the problem that browsing records ordered by class number fails to convey the structure of the classification scheme to the user. She points out that combining pre-coordinate subject headings (LCSH) with post-coordinate keyword indexing can cause confusion. Larson reported that title word searches are being increasingly favoured over subject searches and Frost found that, as in a card catalogue, faculty do mostly known-item searches. One explanation for this is that faculty do not search for books in their own field by subject because they are already familiar with the books and authors they are investigating. However, this suggests that users are not basing their searches on the indexing system offered by the system.

USERS

WHAT DO LIBRARY USERS WANT

Unquestionably, online catalogues are enjoying high use, and perceived success in service leads to demands for more services. Librarians are becoming familiar with requests that the online catalogue be extended to provide access to records for articles held in the library as well as records for books and, indeed, to the texts themselves.

Gradually, many of these additional functions are being put in place. Meanwhile, several comments have been made about the features users want in an online catalogue. Bates found that searchers want a sense of control over the search, to know what is going on during the search, and what information is being included and rejected and why. Crawford thinks that it is important to users to feel in control, but understanding all the mechanics involved is not critical. Ensor has found that about two-thirds of library catalogue users tend to look at a long list of results rather than take some action to narrow it.

She attributes this to two reasons:

- Users have difficulty learning and remembering appropriate actions to take to narrow a search; and
- Users want to maintain control over the whole process.

In her study of keyword and Boolean use in a university online catalogue, Ensor found that users do use Boolean operators when a search retrieves too much or too little, but faculty and graduate students find Boolean operators easier to learn than undergraduates. Interestingly, she also found that undergraduates use keyword searching more than either graduate students or faculty. Sixty per-cent of all users felt that keyword searching is easy to learn, but this was affected by possession or lack of computer experience. Recent literature includes several comments concerning users' preferences. Ercegovac states that 45% of users want to see related terms. But online catalogues do very little to support this. Forty-two per cent want to search tables of contents or back-of-book indexes and 24% want to search title words. Fox and Harman say searchers prefer document-ranked retrieval, *i.e.*, with documents individually ranked according to an estimate of the probability of being relevant, to other methods. Saracevic and others found that precision was associated with high satisfaction. This points to a need on the part of the users for additional points of access and more options to organize result sets that will allow them to judge relevance. As for how many records are wanted, a 30-record response is widely considered a typical optimal result, and professional searchers view 50 to 70 references as optimal. Kinnucan found satisfaction relatively unaffected by retrieval set size but sensitive to precision, though less so as retrieved set size increased.

WHAT DO EXPERIENCED SEARCHERS DO

There is good reason to examine what experienced searchers do. What works for experienced searchers could form the basis for redesign of the system to make the strategies adopted by experts more accessible to novice searchers. Experienced searchers tend to adopt stereotyped sequences of tactics which could be embedded, more or less, in the interface.

Providing for 'strategic commands' that would trigger such a pattern of tactics might empower the novice as well as provide an appreciated labour-saving amenity for the expert. Fidel has studied that informal, highly intuitive methods used by experienced searchers to select 'search keys' and how they can be formalized in a decision tree and incorporated into knowledge base of an expert system.

Harris observed that experienced searchers view large sets as intermediary sets, *i.e.*, as a basis for a more refined, secondary search. Successful searchers tend to view large sets as being presented with a wider range of choices rather than feeling overwhelmed by information overload. Hancock noted that searchers who consciously adopt a broad search formulation strategy are more successful than those who take an exact matching approach.

Starting with more general terms to gain an overview of the domains they cover can often give a searcher a better idea of how to phrase a narrower search. If novices and successful searchers start their searches in much the same way, does the difference lie more in how they view and continue the search process? If so, how is that 'broad view' conveyed? Katzer sees user interaction with the system as a process of enhancing and refining the original query. In all cases, support for providing tools for analysing retrieved sets is indicated.

MODELS

Inevitably any but the most sophisticated design will be based on a set of assumptions concerning the expected users. Similarly, any but the most trivial usage depends on a set of expectations by the user concerning system behaviour. Ordinarily, 'cognitive model' is used to denote the system's assumptions concerning the user and 'conceptual model' to denote the user's assumptions concerning the system. People do not operate like machines, and some researchers have pointed out that people do not approach problems in a linear, logical fashion. They have memory limitations and tend to organize information idiosyncratically.

Several authors have urged that the development of cognitive models of how users process information ought to lead to the design of better systems. We still need to look at how people process information when solving problems. Belkin has urged the importance of discovering users' goals, tasks and behaviours. This has led to attempts to base system design on a conceptual organization of knowledge and human information processing limits. One approach has been to study information-seeking activity at the catalogue and at the shelves as an interrelated process. An-other problem with developing concise models of users is that data from user studies is more often qualitative or impressionistic than quantitative.

Although Bellardo did not find searching performance to be related to cognitive or personality traits, there have been several studies that found observable differences among groups. Horne found that solvers and non-solvers use different self-questioning strategies. Harter reports that re-searchers in the 'hard' scientific and technological disciplines tend to share a common paradigm and agree more on terms than researchers in 'soft' literary and sociological disciplines. This makes agreement on terminology outside of narrowly specified domains much more difficult. For more on user models, see Ellis who analysed the search behaviour of academic social scientists in terms of six types of procedure: starting, chaining, browsing, differentiating, monitoring and extracting.

Dickson concluded that gaps in users' conceptual models were a significant source of errors and several writers have urged the use of metaphor, maps, or models to orient users by providing a conceptual map of the system. Mental models are effective for complex tasks according to Borgman, who has argued that conceptual training is superior to procedural training, at least for complex tasks. Brown suggested helping the user develop a search strategy using an outline metaphor. Using a flowchart to create a conceptual map of the search is one way to convey mental models of systems and teach users conceptual models.

A flowchart model would include six basic steps: initiation, selection, exploration, formulation, collection, and presentation. Researchers are more successful when they think in categorical terms and concluded that users who have difficulty lack a model of information flow, knowledge of the bibliographic chain, knowledge of relationships between subjects, and an under-standing of knowledge creation. Borgman observed that front ends tend more to ease mechanical rather than conceptual problems of use.

Library activists made the interesting observation that people who learn to use a complex device without instruction modify their theories with experience, but these changes may be based on limited evidence and can instead reinforce incorrect understanding.

Reviewing the literature on what users want, how experts search, and, especially, cognitive and conceptual models, suggests that it makes little sense to study online catalogues in isolation from other retrieval systems. In the next part, we take a look at some solutions that have implemented or proposed.

SOLUTIONS

FORMULATING A SEARCH

Retrieval Techniques

The current state-of-the art of operational online catalogues is solidly based on the retrieval of sets of records and basic Boolean operations. This is in marked contrast to a quite separate thirty-year tradition in information retrieval experimentation which is almost as solidly based on probabilistic retrieval models and that rank each document by an estimated probability of relevance to each query. Predictably, the dominance of Boolean techniques in online catalogues has been challenged.

Exact-match Boolean retrieval systems show major performance and user deficiencies and partial match techniques and ranking of retrieval output to be more useful than Boolean logic. Prabha has observed that the limitations of keyword indexing and Boolean logic become more pronounced as databases get larger. Boolean techniques are widely used but are generally unsatisfactory, that all retrieval techniques perform better for some queries than for others, and that experimental techniques perform better than Boolean techniques, but these have not been implemented on any large scale.

Fortunately, experimental prototypes, such as Larson's Cheshire are becoming available. At the same time, standard Boolean systems are based on unweighted binary values: to retrieve, every record must have the specified attributes and all other, unspecified attributes are deemed irrelevant. Standard Boolean systems can be considered relatively undeveloped given the possibilities for weighted search terms and for supporting conditional search modifiers that can be invoked heuristically.

As Buchanan noted, Boolean systems can be used for creating and ranking small subsets. For example, sorting by date in reverse chronological order can provide a very useful ranking. There has been little systematic comparison done and since probabilistic systems and existing Boolean systems both have the potential to be refined considerably, there is much work to be done in this area.

Search Aids and Interfaces

The use of search profiles and searcher profiles has been examined by several writers. Interfaces can be designed to support searching in order of defined priorities. The OASIS front end to MELVYL supports a repeating FEWER command for progressive retrieved set reduction that invokes stored statements of users preferences. Researchers have examined different information retrieval models that integrate user profiles into the system.

SAFIR is an expert system that offers information on search strategies based on information already known about the user and the domain. One challenging area for research and development is the design of systems that can help searchers formulate a search strategy.

Slack points out that most failed searches could be turned into successful ones with minimal guidance by such techniques as limiting searches by date or identifying several relevant records to find subject headings used by the system. It has been suggested that users be offered a variety of tools that they can adapt, mix, and match.

Library activists suggest that systems automatically determine the best search approach based on characteristics of search queries. Such an approach would take into account the number of words in the query and extent to which queries match the controlled vocabulary. Belkin suggest providing online maps, tables of contents, and the capability to browse by genre. Navigation has been suggested as a key concept crucial to building successful systems that empower the user.

Among other recommendations, that menus and help screens should provide enough information to teach a person to navigate through the system. A prototype intermediary system called Knowledge-based Intermediary System for Information Retrieval (KISIR) has been under development in Finland since 1986. In the KISIR system, users can request information about the search at any point in the session.

The type of information KISIR provides includes:

- Current context;
- Status of the search; and
- Instructions on how to do the next step.

Current context is indicated by displaying defaults and other parameters in effect. Search status tells the user the stage they have reached in the process and suggest possible next steps. It also offers an option of saving displayed records in either a separate file or marked inside a general session history file. There seems to be general agreement that simple functions like automatic spelling and search statement format correction should be implemented.

At first glance, spell-checkers seem simple to implement but the existence of multiple languages poses problems immediately. Although the CITE system was using error-correction techniques and expert system spelling correction systems could identify phonological and sequential errors in the early 1980s, these features have not yet to be widely implemented in online catalogues and researchers are still reporting the need for automatic spelling and search statement format correction.

Although interface design is out of the scope of this review, work relevant to this review includes looking at functional components of browsing, offering novel graphical interfaces that offer with direct manipulation approaches to query formulation, using forms-type interfaces and weighing the completeness of information against number of screens needed for display. Berger has discussed the need to allow the user to configure a number of elements in the interface, such as modifying the interface appearance, location of windows icons, and buttons.

Researchers argues against low-density displays: "The more relevant information within the eye span the better". For a recent review of interface research see Shaw. Online catalogues are generally hierarchically structured. Searches can be prog-ressively narrowed, but branching is generally unsupported. This means that one typically backs out of one search before entering a new search.

Moving sideways or using one feature of a record to browse other records sharing the same feature is not usually an option. Hickey and Prabha have suggested browsing records and access to more fields, and Larson recommended the browsing functionality associated with hypertext. Dynix offers a 'related works' option and BLCMP offers 'titles on this subject' option.

Improved Use of Data

Because of the complexity involved in dealing with subject access, the use of non-topical attributes for searching and, especially, for search modification, may be an effective and easier first step. Searchers typically have basic preferences concerning such non-topical attributes such as date, language, and location. Furthermore, the values of such attributes are relatively easy to manipulate in Boolean systems. Harter discussed the use of identifying such non-subject search parameters as document type, date of publication, language, author, and corporate source.

Databases are often organized by document type, making database selection crucial to search success. But this is not always clear to the user. Rubens has proposed actively soliciting the user for information on format, date, intellectual level, and subject. Researchers found that although personal name-matching techniques have been developed, they are being applied to databases where no significant name authority work has been done. There is also considerable scope for improved use of topical data.

Most systems offer a very limited subject searching approach. This is usually offered in the form of exact LCSH with implicit right truncation and, in second generation catalogues, keyword searching of terms derived from LCSH, but more should be offered. One option is to use more of the existing data. For example the classification numbers present in catalogue records could be used to extend or modify the subject headings to help the searcher make relevance judgments. The keyword matching in the personal name and subject heading fields would increase both precision and recall.

A second option is to make more sophisticated use of existing data, using, for example, probabilistic ranking techniques. Cheshire, an experimental online catalogue developed by Larson at the University of California, Berkeley, uses a classification clustering approach. For each *Library of Congress Classification* (LCC) number, the title and subject keywords of all documents assigned to it are used to increase the number of terms associated with each individual bibliographic record.

Micco proposes a term weighting scheme in which weights are based on the MARC tags the term is drawn from: the first 6xx field gets highest weight because it represents aboutness. The lowest ranking goes to natural language keywords from titles, notes, tables of contents. She also suggests extracting and displaying in scrolling windows the x, y, and z subfields containing modifiers of the LCSH. Connell also recommends searching the subdivisions of LCSH. The use of surface matching of stems and syntactic phrase types to generate a hierarchical display of phrases showing equivalence, hierarchical, and associative relation-ships. This category could include almost any non-standard matching algorithm, such as, for example, *Latent Semantic Indexing* (LSI) which accepts keywords in any order and returns hits with an index of relevance. One development of great promise is 'entry vocabulary' capability whereby whatever words the searcher uses are converted automatically to the system vocabulary terms with a high probability of corresponding to what the searcher wants. A simple approach is to use the existing indexes or cross-references of the system vocabulary, possibly enriched with additional cross-references to anticipate use of non-standard terms.

A more advanced approach is to use statistical relation-ships between, say, title words and assigned LCSH. The inferred system vocabulary terms can be presented to the searcher for adoption or rejection. The Cheshire online catalogue provides a working example, deriving, from whatever combination of terms the searcher may enter, a ranked listing of the LC classification numbers most likely to denote what the searcher is seeking. Buckland nominated the development of entry vocabularies as the most promising single innovation for online catalogues. A third promising line of development is to use additional resources beyond the standard catalogue record to improve or modify searches.

Bibliographies are an obvious source. Providing access, online, to dictionaries or thesauri could be helpful to the searcher in modifying or extending topical queries. As networked information resources grow, there is also a need for directories of online library catalogues, file archives, online journals, and information servers.

Another suggestion is to give the user more help in finding the most significant literature, the 'classics' in a field. 'Classics' could be based on citedness, identification by subject experts, or other indicators. A fourth option is to use the 'nearest neighbour' technique: Never mind what the specific heading is, what other record resemble this one most closely when all features are compared? Blair noted that one of the simplest, but infrequently used, approaches is to begin with a highly useful document. Using a closest match search strategy along with a dynamic feedback to the user for search refinement.

Modifying a Search

Mechanisms for Modifying Searches

Successful modification of a search depends heavily on the user's assessment of what has happened in response to a query and ideas about what the best next steps would be. How can the system assist with these two tasks? There is no reason why the system's response should not be automatic. Functionality that would provide the prompt analysis of retrieved sets, although generally a precondition for search modification, has received little attention until recently. There has been more attention to built-in support for automatic search modifications by the system.

Researchers reviewed user studies and reported that systems should provide such recovery mechanisms as:

- Searching first word of author name followed by the first letter of the second word (ie., truncated);
- Searching unmatched terms in the appropriate index;
- Displaying alphabetically adjacent terms;
- Passing unmatched terms (other than author names) against a spell checker; and
- Forcing users into a help routine after one or more identifiable errors.

Bates suggests monitoring searches at the tactics and strategy levels rather than at the moves level. When there seems to be a need for other terms or the wrong terms seem to have been used, particular tactics should be available to the user as options. When there is a need to revise terms, a different set of tactics could be applied.

Search Expansion

Two fundamental strategies for dealing with zero or too few hits are to widen the scope of the search and process the search against all reasonable information sources. Standard practices are to relax Boolean ANDs and to use the Boolean OR to add broader, narrower, and related terms, including synonyms and variant spellings.

Other techniques include using LCSH to enhance access, using LCC for subject retrieval, using both DDC and LCSH, adopting strategies to use LCC, and using LCC for term clustering and ranking has identified a number of tactical responses for query expansion: neighbour, trace, parallel, fix, super, relate, and vary. Connell suggests manipulating the grammar of LCSH and providing access to fields not usually searched.

Search Reduction

Approaches to dealing with excessive retrieval center around Boolean operations that limit both topical and non-topical parameters. When applicable, Henry recommended reducing ORed terms. Markey thought the user should be prompted to limit his or her search when retrieved sets exceeded 20 records. Bates has distinguished a variety of descriptively-named search tactics. Harter proposed moving truncation characters to the right and limiting the search to a specific subject area by a classification code as effective methods of reducing large retrieved set sizes.

Fidel suggested restricting fields, tightening proximity, limiting by language, or limiting by type of literature to deal with large sets. Morris recommended intersecting with another concept; adding narrower terms; applying more stringent proximity; limiting to one or fewer fields; using NOT and AND NOT; and limiting by language, document type, year, and first few items.

Prabha also supports the traditional approach of managing large retrievals by extending the use of restrictors such as language, format, and date of publication, but she has also suggested using library classification schemes as a limiting feature.

Lesk pointed out the benefits of exploring uses of *Library of Congress Classification* (LCC) to deal with 'too many hits'. As Prabha has pointed out, there is much to be learned about the incidence of large retrievals, measures for evaluating retrieval performance, evaluating existing search features for increasing retrieval precision, and using additional data for managing large retrievals.

The problem of excessively large retrieved sets does not arise with systems that rank documents, one simply accepts as many as one wishes. Similarly the problem could be reduced in Boolean systems if they included built-in mechanisms for creating subsets and ranking them.

HANDLING RETRIEVED SETS

The analysis of retrieved sets to examine the characteristics of what has been retrieved can provide an important basis for search modification decisions.

Retrieved set analysis can also be used for database analysis, identifying erroneous data, and collection analysis.

Hickey and Prabha suggest making tools available online that summarize large retrieved sets. These summaries could be presented in the form of tables, pie charts, and bar charts. Several writers have suggested trying new, more compact, approaches to managing browse displays. The size of LCSH displays could be reduced by suppressing the display of geographic and chronological subfield headings.

An important new function is now being added to online catalogues for retrieved set analysis. The European Space Agency's Information Retrieval Service (ESA-IRS) offers a command called 'zoom'. For any retrieved set, zoom provides a frequency analysis of the values for a number of attributes that can be specified by the user. Among the options ESA-IRS provides are arrangements by dates, authors, corporate sources, words, classification codes, molecular formulae, and titles.

One good use of a 'zoom' command is to identify the most frequent subject headings in a set, perhaps a set initially defined by use of title keywords. Similar capabilities have been included in CITE, RUBIKON at Roskilde University Library in Denmark, and OASIS at Berkeley. In OASIS the 'summarize' command summarizes subject headings or holding libraries. Norway's national online catalogue, BIBSYS, offers sorting on the author, title, author and title, publication and issue fields. The publication and issue fields can be sorted in either ascending or descending order.

SYSTEM IMPROVEMENTS

Fortunately, recent advances in computer technology have made accelerated speeds, massive disk storage capabilities, and expanded memory capacity available at rapidly dropping costs. How-ever, the improvements in hardware are so substantial that new designs are indicated, such as, for example, a shift from traditional line-by-line displays to bit-mapped images and graphical user interfaces.

The increasing affordability of more powerful personal computers and workstations facilitates moving some of the processing to the user's desk top both for the experimental prototyping of enhanced systems and also for routine use.

There is a growing recognition that the 'intelligence' necessary for aiding the searcher could and, perhaps, should reside in a front-end system. Post-processing tools can help users refine searches and browse records more easily. Other specific recommendations include adopting a multi-tasking interface that allows users to download bibliographies while carrying out other searches and providing online catalogues with more user-friendly and adaptive X-Windows graphical interfaces.

DATA IMPROVEMENT

Enhanced hardware, software, and searching techniques are still liable to be hampered by deficiencies in the data. Errors and variant forms create the additional problem of duplicate records, often separating records for different copies of the same title. These records need to be consolidated. The OCLC Duplicate Detection Project uses matching algorithms that look for duplicates resulting from typographical errors and cataloguing differences.

Hickey initiated several techniques for comparing records, of which the 'matching trigrams' technique proved to be the most effective. Another form of improvement is to make records more complete, adding optional fields and/or additional fields. This could include enriched subject voca-bulary, standard non-roman scripts, more cross-reference structure for variant forms of names and subject headings and enhanced use of the LCSH Subject Authority File. Cataloguing rules, subject headings, classifications, and data format rules change over time.

Card catalogues tended to receive rather minimal retros-pective modification to bring older records into line with newer practices. With databases both the need and the means for maintaining standards change over time. The rapid trend towards mounting multiple databases implies the need for support for searching across databases. Since databases overlap in coverage, problems arise in identifying which records are variant representations of the same work and, more generally, linking works of similar nature across databases.

TOPICAL ACCESS AND SYSTEM VOCABULARIES

There are problems and opportunities that arise in the process of moving from the searcher's terms to the catalog's terms. Micco suggests guiding the user to select the best search strategy by mapping user's terms to the controlled vocabularies in the database. Bates recommends the provision of a super thesaurus with a large entry vocabulary that includes colloquial terms and spelling variants. Warner advocates showing the user how language is mapped in the system by organizing both natural language and controlled vocabulary into a single display.

The online catalogues that force users through a thesaurus lead to more satisfaction with search results than catalogues that do not. Gomez report that user success is improved when the number of terms indexed is increased. However, larger retrieved sets are also a likely consequence. Many suggestions have been made to wrestle with the deeply-entrenched LCSH. Lester recommends modifying user input to match LCSH. Markey-Drabenstott and Vizine-Goetz report that exact matches with LCSH are usually queries for topical subjects, but queries with combinations of topical subjects and names rarely match LCSH.

The incorporating subject terms from the *Dewey Decimal Classification* (DDC) and other library classifications into online catalogues would enhance subject access and provide additional subject searching strategies. Possible solutions to the semantic problem include a semantic network approach for generating synonyms and related terms and a classification knowledge-base that could store the semantic components for each LC class or subject heading with which the user would form a query by selecting relevant facets.

Additional problems arise when the catalogue provides access through multiple vocabularies or several foreign languages, as is often the case in European systems. Mandel describes several strategies online catalogues are now using to provide access to multiple vocabularies: segregated files, mixed vocabularies, integrated vocabularies, and front-end navigation.

EXPERIMENTAL SYSTEMS

A development that deserves special note is the increasing viability of experimental prototypes. It used to be that only those responsible for operational catalogues were in a position to develop them, but now the prevalence of powerful, yet relatively inexpensive, workstations, reduced data storage costs, and increasingly available datasets enable anyone with sufficient expertise to experiment and develop a functioning experimental online catalogue. Further, remote access to a wide variety of databases over the Internet offers the opportunity for widespread testing.

In this way new techniques can be tried, tested, evaluated, and, perhaps, adopted and developed by others. Experimental systems are beginning to use natural language techniques developed by artificial intelligence researchers. A good example of a promising experimental system is the Cheshire system developed by Larson. For nearly thirty years the advantages of probabilistic retrieval techniques have been advocated.

Yet it was not until the Cheshire system was developed on a unix workstation at Berkeley with very little funding, using the MARC records of a nearby library, that one could actually use a probabilistic online catalogue with probabilistic document ranking. Another good example is the Okapi system, developed initially at the Polytechnic of Central London and later at the City University, London. Okapi has been used for numerous interesting studies over the years. Okapi currently develops a query by selecting the best terms from a list of the original query terms as well as terms from records judged relevant by the user.

The OASIS system, also developed at Berkeley, takes low-cost prototyping one stage further. OASIS, running on a unix workstation acts as a front-end to the massive MELVYL online catalogue of the University of California. Ordinarily operating as a terminal connected to MELVYL, additional functionality can be supported through the pre-processing of new commands and new retrieval results can be achieved through the post-processing of records downloaded from MELVYL.

The result is, in effect, a prototyping of enhanced MELVYL functionality using the MELVYL database and achieved without any interference with MELVYL software or service. Although there are limits to what can be done this way, the OASIS system has been successful in developing strategic searches and performing useful retrieved set analysis. As search and retrieve protocols are adopted, any workstation could, in principle, develop and demonstrate enhancements to any online catalogue supporting a standard protocol. In Norway, BIBSYS provides access to a 5 million-record database with searching on 33 different fields. BIBSYS also handles e-mail search requests and offers a choice of eight output formats.

Records can also be downloaded with FTP or Kermit. Users have a choice of either a simple menu-driven or a command-driven search. In Finland, KISIR provides several browsers, including thesaurus-dictionary browsers, retrieval system description browsers, and database description browsers. As the online catalogue becomes less and less isolated from other retrieval activities, so less catalogue-like systems become of potential interest. Also, as the role of libraries expands to include many of the resources provided by the online environment, many new forms of information are falling within the domain of the online catalogue.

Full-text resources, for example, commonly have little or no human indexing and bring with them a whole new set of problems for both users and the catalogues. Second generation online catalogue techniques, particularly Boolean keyword searching, perform poorly, for many reasons, when applied to full-text documents. Indexing and retrieval techniques new to the catalogue world will be needed. Fortunately there is much interesting research and experimentation going on outside of libraries. The Information Visualizer is a project at the Xerox *Palo Alto Research Center* (PARC) where researchers are experimenting with visualizing large amounts of data.

The Information Visualizer uses colour and interactive real-time three-dimensional animation to depict complex aspects of in-formation. Information is represented as 3D objects. The user is given the sense of moving around the objects to view them from different perspectives. Thinking Machines Inc. has designed a group of applications that work together to locate and retrieve documents. Known as the *Wide Area Information Server* (WAIS), WAIS accepts queries in natural language and translates them into key words that are used for a search.

A query is entered in the user's own words which can then be sent out across the Internet, accessing the wide variety of servers and databases now available. Thinking Machines Corporation is collaborating with Apple, Dow Jones and KPMG Peat Marwick to simplify information retrieval from personal files, corporate records and remote databases. The aim of the project is to develop approaches to the problems presented by the overwhelming surplus of electronic data now confronting large organizations.

The long-range goal is to develop technology for a scalable system that will allow users to access a variety of data sources, including large commercial databases, through a common interface.

The WAIS system is based on the client server model consists of server software distributed by Thinking Machines and an open protocol for transmitting queries and responses. Thinking Machines has also undertaken a project with Columbia University's Law School.

Project Janus is implementing a full-text retrieval system that deals with both text and graphics. This means including full-text documents such as the United Nations library human rights collection. Online versions of the legal texts like the Maastricht Treaty and the Rio Conference on the Environment are receiving high usage, with the North American Free Trade Agreement getting 200-250 hits per day.

The project is aimed at alleviating storage problems in libraries, making fragile items accessible, and providing access to information increasingly only available in electronic form.

The system will include user-friendly interfaces, better search methods, and the ability to make scattered databases appear to be a single one database. Keyword searches will be replaced by natural language queries, allowing users to search an unknown domain in their own words.

The search strategy uses weighting and focuses on uncommon words to direct the search. Portions of full-text documents can be used to form new queries and find more documents on the topic selected. The library is also planning to work with publishers to load copyrighted text onto their system.

Apple's Advanced Technology Group has used WAIS to create Rosebud, a personally customizable electronic newspaper based on the metaphor of reporters and news-papers. Basically an Internet search and text-filtering programme, Rosebud enables users to create a personal news-paper daily from wire-service reports, arrange documents by priority for action or reading, or locate specific items of correspondence.

Rosebud finds information with user-defined keyword lists and provides a statistical content analysis. Aimed at non-expert information users, Rose-bud searches numerous remote databases and presents its findings in a newspaper-like format, prioritizing documents according to user preferences.

A commercially-available object-oriented information system called Topic uses a knowledge-based approach based on the idea of concept retrieval which uses hierarchically arranged 'topics' to search for entire concepts instead of words or phrases.

Topic uses typical Boolean retrieval techniques, but allows the user to create topics with rules about relationships to more specific topics. Topic handles data from databases as diverse as news wires, intelligence reporting services and electronic mail. AT&T Bell Laboratories is prototyping.

The RightPages electronic library, the first phase of a plan to create an electronic analog of the traditional library environment. The RightPages library alerts users to incoming scientific and technical journal articles that correspond to their interest profiles.

It also allows them to view pages of the articles, browse other articles in the database and order printed copies. The United States *Defence Advanced Research Projects Agency* (DARPA) has specified research on three methods of intelligent document-retrieval for investigation under its Tipster intelligent document-retrieval project. Keyword searching limitations and inaccurate queries present serious problems for searching documents.

DARPA has is focusing on context vectors, conceptual graphs and inference networks as 'the most promising technologies' for detecting and retrieving desired documents. Context vectors automatically summarize and compare the meaning of portions of text.

Conceptual graphs perform pattern-matching to detect the relationships between concepts in multiple bodies of text. Inference networks are used to detect larger patterns in texts using statistical information retrieval and natural language processing techniques. The Sloan School of Management at MIT is engaged in a research project called Information Lens, which focuses on ways to handle large quantities of on-line messages.

Information Lens is based on the concept of 'intelligent assistants' used in artificial intelligence applications and graphical user interface design. The intelligent assistant in Information Lens can sort, prioritize, and seek out incoming messages. General Electric Research and Development Center is working on a system called Scisor that can handle large input and output of information. Scisor uses artificial intelligence, natural language, and database management to collect relevant financial data from the Dow Jones wire services. To do this, Scisor locates key words and 'reads' them before deciding to keep or discard them.

Scisor is able to process news items at the rate of about six stories per minute. The system has also been used to obtain information from other subject areas. Scisor uses information retrieval techniques such as word-based text search and lexical analysis. In addition, special mention should be made of several other experimental 'environments' or test beds being developed for experimental techniques such as:

- I3R,
- CODER, and
- FERRET.

MULTIMEDIA RESOURCES AND ONLINE CATALOGUING

DEFINITION

AACR defines an electronic resource as material encoded for manipulation by a computerized device. This material may require the use of a peripheral directly connected to a computerized device or a connection to a computer network. Electronic resources that do not require the use of a computer, are not included in this definition.

For cataloguing purposes, electronic resources may be treated in one of two ways depending on whether access is direct (local) or remote (networked):

- Direct–a physical carrier can be described. This carrier, (*e.g.* disc/ disk, cassette, cartridge) must be inserted into a computerized device.
- Remote–no physical carrier can be handled. Remote access can only be provided by use of an input-output device.

CONTENT VERSUS CARRIER

Until 1997 electronic resources were coded for carrier and not content. In June 1997 MARBI (the committee that governs MARC changes) revised the definition of code "m" in the fixed field Type. Electronic resources are now cataloged and coded according to their content and not the carrier.

Type code "m" is now used only for the following general classes of electronic resources:

Computer software (including programmes, games, fonts):

- Numeric data
- Computer-oriented multimedia
- Online systems or services

Examples:

- Census data on CD-ROM or the Internet – Type "a" (book)
- Online maps – Type "e" (cartographic materials)
- Maps on floppy disks – Type "e" (cartographic materials)
- Most web pages – Type "a" (book)
- Multimedia encyclopedia on CD-ROM or online –Type "m" (electronic resource)
- Computer games online or on CD-ROM – Type "m" (electronic resource)

GUIDELINES FOR CODING ELECTRONIC RESOURCES IN LEADER/06

DOCUMENTATION

- *MARC 21 Concise Format for Bibliographic Data* defines the codes and conventions that identify data elements in MARC bibliographic records. It is updated on an annual basis.

- OCLC's *Cataloguing Electronic Resources: OCLC-MARC Coding Guidelines* assists catalogers creating biblio-graphic records for electronic resources and includes information on the proper coding of fixed fields, including Leader/06 (Type of record).
- *Guidelines for Distinguishing Cartographic Materials on Computer File Carriers from other Materials on Computer File Carriers* helps catalogers working with carto-graphic electronic resources to distinguish them from other types of electronic resources and to select the correct Leader/06 (Type of record) based on that distinction.
- *Relationship of Fields 006, 007, and 008* explains the general model adopted to indicate how repeti-tions of field 006 (Fixed-length data elements-Additional material characteristics) and a single field 008 (Fixed-length data elements-General information) coexist in bibliographic records, especially in relation to the values in Leader character positions 06 (Type of record) and 07 (Bibliographic level), and clarifies the relationship of field 007 (Physical description fixed field) to fields 006 and 008.
- *Use of fixed fields 006/007/008 and Leader codes in CONSER records* presents guidelines for coding in CONSER records.

PRINCIPLES AND GUIDELINES FOR CODING LEADER/06

An electronic resource is a manifestation of a work that requires the use of a computer for access. Peripheral devices attached to the computer (such as a CD-ROM drive) may also be required.

The manifestation's carrier is accessed either directly (*e.g.*, via CD-ROM, etc.) or remotely (*e.g.*, via the Internet). Items that do not require the use of a computer, such as audio CDs or movies on DVD-videodiscs, are excluded from this definition.

The Leader/06 (Type of record) character position in the *MARC 21 Format for Bibliographic Data* contains a one-character alphabetic code that differentiates MARC records created for various types of content and materials. The definition of code "m" (computer file) in Leader/06 was revised in June 1997 as a result of *Proposal No. 97-3R*.

The new definition narrowed the choice of code "m" to the following types of electronic resources:

- Computer software (including programmes, games, fonts)
- Numeric data
- Computer-oriented multimedia
- Online systems or services

Code "m" is defined as follows in the MARC 21 Format for Bibliographic Data:

- *m-ComputerFile:* Code m indicates that the content of the record is for the following classes of electronic resources: computer software (including programmes, games, fonts), numeric data, computer-oriented multi-media, online systems or services.
- For these classes of materials, if there is a significant aspect that causes it to fall into another Leader/06 category, code for that significant aspect (*e.g.*, vector data that is cartographic is not coded as numeric but as cartographic). Other classes of electronic resources are coded for their most significant aspect (*e.g.* language material, graphic, cartographic material, sound, music, moving image). In case of doubt or if the most significant aspect cannot be determined, consider the item a computer file.

This revised definition stipulates that catalogers code electronic resources for the significant aspects of their content, as opposed to their carrier. The Leader/06 determines which 008 code (Fixed-length data elements-General information) is used and the appropriateness and validity of other fixed data elements in a record.

PRINCIPLES AND GUIDELINES FOR CODING FIELDS 006, 007 AND 008

The 008 field contains character positions that provide coded information about the record as a whole and about special bibliographic aspects of the item cataloged. This field is not repeatable.

Field 006 (Fixed-length data elements-Additional material characteristics) permits coding for additional aspects of an electronic resource (including any computer file aspects) if the 007 and 008 fields do not adequately describe it. Some cataloguing utilities and groups (such as CONSER) require the use f 006 fields under certain conditions. Sample records in this document include 006 fields for those who may wish to use this field. Coding all of these positions involves making a series of decisions.

Consider the following when deciding what code values to select:

- What are the primary characteristics of the content of the resource (as opposed to the physical format or carrier)? Look at the definitions of the various Leader/06 codes. Is the content primarily language material, notated music, cartographic material, a computer file, a musical sound recording, etc.?
- Does the resource match the Leader/06 definition of a computer file? If so, "m" (for computer file) goes in Leader/06, and the 008 field is coded for computer files. Position 008/26 contains the code for the type of computer file described in the record.
- If Leader/06 is coded "a" (language material), is the resource a monograph or a continuing resource? This determines the code in Leader/07 (Bibliographic level), which in turn influences 008 field

coding (Books or Continuing resources). For other material types, the Leader/06 code determines 008 coding.

- Does the cataloger wish to add a 006 field to record characteristics that cannot be coded in the 008 field? Some electronic resources might need more than one 006 field. For others, a 006 field may not really add any additional information and could be left out.
- Note that *Proposal No. 97-3R* specifies that a 007 field (Physical description fixed field) for electronic resources is mandatory regardless of the Leader/06 code value when the physical form of the resource is an electronic format in order to provide an explicit indication that the item is in an electronic format.
- Some combinations of 006, 007, and 008 fields may result in a certain amount of redundancy, in the sense that the same information about an electronic resource might appear in more than one of these fields. Catalogers must decide whether the infor-mation added as a result of recording additional characteristics of an item justifies the redundancy.

In case of doubt, or if the most significant characteristic cannot be determined, code the resource "m" in the Leader/06 position.

Coding for Different types of Electronic Resources

- Bibliographic database on the Internet
- Collection of databases on the Internet
- Textual continuing resource
- Textual continuing resource with search software
- Textual continuing resource received via e-mail
- Textual document
- Cartographic material
- Still images
- Notated music
- Census in textual form
- Database containing manipulable numeric data
- Computer operating system
- Computer software
- Computer game
- Internet search engine
- Web portal
- System or service on the Internet, such as an E-commerce site
- Web site with significant audio and video content
- Streaming video
- Streaming audio

Notes:

- The sample records are partial records.
- Some of the records have a Leader/07 with a value of "i" (for integrating resource). Bibliographic Level "i" for integrating resources was fully implemented in June 2006.
- Some of the 006 fields in the sample records do not necessarily provide much additional information but were added for illustrative purposes.

GUIDELINES FOR THE USE OF FIELD 856

Field 856 in the MARC 21 bibliographic, holdings, authority, classification, and community information formats is used for electronic location and access information to an electronic resource.The field may be used in a bibliographic or holdings record for a resource when it or a subset of it is available electronically. In addition, it may be used to locate and access an electronic version of a non-electronic resource described in either the bibliographic record, a portion of the resource described, or a related electronic resource.

Field 856 contains the following elements:

FIELD 856-ELECTRONIC LOCATION AND ACCESS (R)

Indicators:

First Indicator	Access method
#	No information provided
0	E-mail
1	FTP
2	Remote login (Telnet)
3	Dial-up
4	HTTP
7	Method specified in subfield $2
Second Indicator	**Relationship**
#	No information provided
0	Resource
1	Version of resource
2	Related resource
8	No display constant generated

Subfield Codes:

- *$a:* Host name (R)
- *$b:* Access number (R)
- *$c:* Compression information (R)
- *$d:* Path (R)
- *$f:* Electronic name (R)
- *$h:* Processor of request (NR)
- *$i:* Instruction (R)
- *$j:* Bits per second (NR)
- *$k:* Password (NR)

- *$l:* Logon (NR)
- *$m:* Contact for access assistance (R)
- *$n:* Name of location of host (NR)
- *$o:* Operating system (NR)
- *$p:* Port (NR)
- *$q:* Electronic format type (NR)
- *$r:* Settings (NR)
- *$s:* File size (R)
- *$t:* Terminal emulation (R)
- *$u:* Uniform Resource Identifier (R)
- *$v:* Hours access method available (R)
- *$w:* Record control number (R)
- *$x:* Nonpublic note (R)
- *$y:* Link text (R)
- *$z:* Public note (R)
- *$2:* Access method (NR)
- *$3:* Materials specified (NR)
- *$6:* Linkage (NR)
- *$8:* Field link and sequence number (R)

GENERAL INFORMATION

The data in field 856 may be a Uniform Resource Identifier (URI), which is recorded in subfield $u. The necessary locator information may also be parsed into separate defined subfields. Note that separate subfields for locator data was provided when this field was first established in 1993, but generally, these are seldom used. An access method, or protocol used, is given as a value in the first indicator position (if the access method is e-mail, FTP, remote login (telnet), dial-up, or HTTP) or in subfield $2 (if the access method is anything else). The access method is the first element of a URL. The field may also include a Uniform Resource Name or URN [(*e.g.*, a DOI (Digital Object Identifier) or handle)].

Uniform Resource Identifier

For any access method, a Uniform Resource Identifier (URI) is generally recorded in subfield $u. Separate subfields may be used if it is desirable to display data in a particular way.

The most commonly used data elements in field 856 are as follows:

- 1st indicator = 4 for HTTP (earlier records may use blank)
- Subfield $u = [HTTP URL]
- Subfield $3: data specifying to what the URI refers, if applicable
- Subfield $z (Public note): data relating to the electronic location of the source that is adequate for public display

Required Subfields

A URI in subfield $u is required unless electronic location and access information is parsed into separate subfields, in which case no single subfield is required. When using this technique, the subfields used largely depends on the access method indicated in the first indicator or in subfield $2 (if first indicator = 7).

Encoding Non-MARC Characters

In February 1994, Proposal 93-10 defined additional characters in the MARC character set to both accommodate existing bibliographic needs and to align it with the ASCII and ANSEL character sets. Both the spacing underscore and the spacing tilde were added at the time because of the need in directory and file names for electronic resources. Many systems have implemented these characters.

For systems that have not implemented the spacing underscore and tilde, the following alternative characters may be used:

- Spacing underscore%5F
- Spacing tilde%7E

Since these characters are valid ASCII strings, the method allows for the functionality supported by Z39.50 clients and Web browsers which permit users to click on links to access resources represented by URLs.

When the additions to the MARC 21 character set are implemented to support the encoding of the spacing characters, it will be possible to replace all instances of the%xx strings.

Multiple 856 Fields

There are many reasons to include multiple 856 fields in records.

The following are the most common:

- Location data elements vary (the URI in subfield $u or subfields $a, $b, $d, when used)
- Different access methods (*e.g.*, a document available through HTTP and from an FTP server)
- Different parts of the item are electronic, using subfield $3 to indicate the part (*e.g.*, table of contents accessible in one file and an abstract in another)
- Mirror sites (the same resource is made available at two different locations, often to facilitate access, perhaps internationally)
- Different formats/resolutions (*e.g.*, the ASCII version of an electronic journal vs. the Web home page for that journal; a thumbnail vs. archival copy of a digitized photograph)
- Related items, using subfield $3 and second indicator value to specify

Field 856 in Bibliographic or Holdings Records

Since field 856 is valid in both bibliographic and holdings records, institutions may favour recording it in the holdings record. It is intended to be an electronic equivalent to field 852 (Location), which contains information used to identify the holding organization and other detailed information required to locate a physical item in a collection. In early 1999, the Network Development and MARC Standards Office elicited opinions on whether it is desirable to use the field in bibliographic or holdings records. Responses received generally favoured recording the field in the holdings record where practical. However, for a variety of reasons, such as the wider exchange of bibliographic records, many institutions use the bibliographic record despite the benefits of using holdings records.

The following advantages of using holdings records have been expressed:

- Ownership to an electronic resource may vary by institution. Such access information belongs in local holdings.
- The holdings record is a means to bring together various versions.
- Use of a single record approach for the bibliographic item has been implemented widely. This practice makes it clearer to use holdings for the specific versions.
- Having a hot-linked 856 field in holdings forces users to think of it as holdings information, and to separate information about the universal bibliographic item.
- The "universal URL" that is for general access and any general information on access in note fields should be in the bibliographic record. Specific local access URLs should be in holdings (although this may result in unpredictability).
- Bibliographic field 856 might usefully be limited to links that do not apply to the entire bibliographic item (*e.g.*, finding aid, table of content, abstract).

In order to move towards this approach in the future, it will be necessary to persuade vendors to make the following changes to their ILS systems:

- Allow for hot links from holdings records
- Allow for the ability to do link checking from holdings records
- Provide indexing of holdings records
- Allow for the ability to export the fields from holdings, to be exchanged either as separate holdings records or embedded in an exported bibliographic record
- Provide for more logical displays of bibliographic/holdings information where necessary
- Allow for sequencing multiple holdings records

At this point, it is a local decision whether to use the field in bibliographic or holdings records.

SPECIFIC DATA ELEMENTS

First Indicator (Access Method)

The first indicator contains information about the access method to the resource and has values defined for E-mail, FTP, Remote login (Telnet), Dial-up, and HTTP. Access methods without defined values may contain a first indicator value 7 with the method indicated in subfield $2. Older records may contain value 7 and subfield $2 (with content http) if created before value 4 (HTTP) was defined.

The list of indicator values and the values used in subfield $2 is specified in the URL standard (RFC1738) and maintained by the Internet Assigned Numbers Authority (IANA).

For those access methods that have an indicator value defined (ftp, telnet, electronic mail), the URI is included in subfield $u with the appropriate indicator value recorded, even though it is redundant with the first element of the URI. Value # (blank) (No information provided) may be used if only a URN is recorded in subfield $u.

If using a URI in subfield $u with one of the access methods that has a value defined in the first indicator, the access method may be repeated in subfield $2. Value 7 and subfield $2 is used for electronic access to host-specific file names (*i.e.*, files stored locally) with the access method, "file." This designation is also a defined URL scheme.

Second Indicator (Relationship)

A second indicator is provided to show the relationship between the information in field 856 and the resource described in the record. This may be used for the generation of a display constant or for ordering multiple 856 fields.

Suggested display constants for the indicator values are:

- # (blank): Electronic resource:
- *0:* Electronic resource:
- *1:* Electronic version:
- *2:* Related electronic resource:
- *8:* [no display constant generated]

Subfield $3 (Materials Specified)

Subfield $3 is used to specify to what portion or aspect of the resource the electronic location and access information applies.

Specific situations may be:

- A portion or subset of the item is electronic
  - *Example:* $3table of contents; $3v. 2-5; $3abstract; $3b&w copy negative
- A related electronic resource is being linked to the record
  - *Example:* $3author's self-portrait

Subfield $q (Electronic Format Type)

Subfield $q was originally defined as File transfer mode to include "binary" or "ascii". It was redefined in June 1997 as Electronic format type to accommodate an Internet Media Type (MIME type), such as text/html. Alternatively, textual information about the electronic format type may also be recorded.

Subfield $u (URI) Repeatability

Subfield $u may be repeated only if both a URN and a URL or more than one URN are recorded. Field 856 is repeated if more than one URL needs to be recorded. Some institutions may wish to record a persistent name (URN) as well as a resolvable HTTP URL in field 856.

Persistent Uniform Resource Locators (PURLs) at OCLC are intended to deal with the problem of changeable URLs. Functionally, a PURL is a URL, but it is intended to point to an intermediate resolution service. Its persistence depends upon the updating of a PURL database when the location of the resource changes. When recorded in field 856, it is intended to allow for persistence so that each record containing the URL need not be updated when the location changes.

Since the PURL is supposed to provide persistent access to the resource, it can be argued that there is no reason to retain a URL that might become invalid. However, this is an internal decision, and institutions that use PURLs should use subfield $x (Nonpublic note) for the original URL if they wish to retain it. This is an appropriate subfield, since it may not be desirable to display the URL to the public because it could cause confusion. The CONSER programme has, however, repeated subfield $u to include both the PURL and cooresponding URL in the past.

Subfield $y (Link Text)

Subfield $y contains link text which is used for display in place of the URL in subfield $u. Often URLs are difficult to read and most systems do not display them to the user. Since subfield $y was not approved until June 2000, there have been various practices in terms of systems using data in the field as link text. Some systems have used subfields $3 or $z in the past for this purpose. It is not clear how widespread the use of subfield $y is since its approval.

Subfield $z (Public Note)

Subfield $z may be used for any additional notes about the electronic resource at the specified location. Examples include subscription information or access restrictions. Institutions have used subfield $z in various ways. Some have created a note for display repeating the URL in subfield $u. It would be preferable for systems to display subfield $u rather than have those preparing records to include information redundantly.

URIS IN OTHER FIELDS AND FORMATS

URLs in Fields other than Field 856

Several proposals resulted in the definition of a subfield $u (URI) in other fields.

These fields include:

- 505 (Formatted Contents Note)
- 508 (Creation/Production Credits Note)
- 511 (Participant or Performer Note)
- 514 (Data Quality Note)
- 520 (Summary, Etc.)
- 530 (Additional Physical Form Available Note)
- 538 (System Details Note)
- 555 (Cumulative Index/Finding Aids Note)
- 583 (Action Note)
- 670 (Source Data Found) *in the MARC 21 Format for Authority Data*
- 678 (Biographical or historical data) *in the MARC 21 Format for Authority Data*

As with field 856, subfield $u should be repeated only when both a URL and URN is recorded.

Field 856 in Other Formats

Field 856 is also defined in the authority, classification, and community information formats.

It may be used as follows:

- *Authority Format:* Field 856 was defined in June 1998. Guidelines will be needed from policy making bodies to further describe its use, especially in cooperative projects. The intent of Proposal No. 98-13 (Define Field 856 in the MARC 21 Authorities Format) was to provide electronic access to Web sites for organizations and other supplementary information within an authority record.
- *Classification Format:* Field 856 provides a link from a MARC classification record to a related electro-nic resource. This allows for accessing visual aids from an online database of MARC classification records.
- *Community Information Format:* Field 856 provides a link from a MARC community information record to community information available on the Web, *e.g.*, Web pages for organizations, events, services, etc.

LC USAGE

Field 856 has been used at the Library of Congress as follows. Records for resources that have been digitized (or otherwise made available electronically) as part of the National Digital Library Programme (American Memory) may contain field 856. Generally, the field is added to the record for the original item, rather than a new record created (unless it consists of components that have been gathered together and only exist as an entity in electronic form). In some cases, LC has also recorded a handle, which is a URN. Older records may contain a URN in subfield $g (which is now obsolete).

LC uses local codes in subfield $q to indicate the different categories of a complex object. This is because digital reproductions created by the Library of Congress are not single files and thus, Internet media types recorded in subfield $q are not applicable. For example, the reproduction of a book usually combines page images and text marked up in SGML.

MAJOR CHANGES INCLUDED

The following are major changes made to the August 1999 revision to create these (March 2003 revision) guidelines:

- Added a table of contents, along with making other struc-tural changes to enhance the document's readability.
- Updated the element list to include the changes made to the repeatability of subfield $u. Subfield $g was also deleted because it was made obsolete in 2000.
- Added and revised the repeatability guidelines for field 856 and subfield $u.
- Updated the "Encoding non-MARC characters" section to include implementation information for the spacing underscore and the spacing tilde.
- Added descriptions of subfields $q and $y to the "Specific Data Elements" section.
- Expanded the "URLs in fields other than field 856" section to include a complete list of bibliographic and authority fields that include subfield $u.
- Expanded and added examples to the "Field 856 in other formats" section.
- Expanded the "LC Usage" section to include updated information about how the Library of Congress uses field 856 in various projects.
- Deleted the "Attachment B: Subfield Use When Not Using $u (URL)" section.
- Updated the examples in the "Examples" section to match current usage of field 856.

CATALOGUING ELECTRONIC RESOURCES: OCLC-MARC CODING GUIDELINES

This document originally combined and superseded two older sets of OCLC guidelines for dealing with electronic resources: "Cataloguing Electronic

Resources: OCLC-MARC Coding Guidelines," by Rich Greene, first published in February 1998; and "OCLC Guidelines on the Choice of Type and BLvl for Electronic Resources," by Jay Weitz, first published in March 1998. This consolidated document was originally prompted by the issuance in June 1999 of "Guidelines for Coding Electronic Resources in Leader/06" by the Library of Congress Network Development and MARC Standards Office.

Like the two superseded OCLC documents, this revised set of guidelines is intended to assist catalogers in creating records for electronic resources in WorldCat, the OCLC Online Union Catalogue. These guidelines pertain to OCLC-MARC tagging (that is, content designation). Cataloguing rules and manuals (such as AACR2) govern the content of records. You should implement these guidelines immediately.

In addition to LC's valuable June 1999 "Guidelines for Coding Electronic Resources in Leader/06", which should be consulted for helpful details, sources for further information include the following documents:

- *CONSER Cataloguing Manual*: Module 31—Remote ccess Electronic Serials (Online Serials)/CONSER.
- *Integrating Resources:* A Cataloguing Manual/Programme for Cooperative Cataloguing.
- Draft Interim Guidelines for Cataloguing Electronic Resources/Library of Congress.
- Guidelines for Distinguishing Cartographic Materials on Computer File Carriers from Other Materials on Computer File Carriers/Library of Congress.
- Guidelines for the Use of Field 856/Prepared by the Library of Congress, Network Development and MARC Standards Office.
- *ISBD(ER):* International Standard Bibliographic Description for Electronic Resources/recommended by the ISBD(CF) Review Group. (Munchen: K.G. Saur, 1997).
- Use of fixed fields 006/007/008 and Leader codes in CONSER records/ Library of Congress.

All of these documents remain primary sources for guidance in the cataloguing of electronic resources. The recommendations made here are meant to be extensions of these documents, not replacements for them. Note that Nancy Olson's "Cataloguing Internet Resources: A Manual and Practical Guide, 2nd edition," formerly listed here, has been withdrawn because it is out of date.

Remember that these guidelines affect mainly (although not exclusively) the choice of certain fixed field elements, particularly the Type of Record, Bibliographic Level, and Type of File codes. The descriptive rules in AACR2 for cataloguing electronic resources continue to apply, as do most other MARC coding decisions.

DEFINITION OF ELECTRONIC RESOURCE

According to AACR2, 2005 Update, an electronic resource is: "Material (data and/or programme(s)) encoded for manipulation by a computerized device. This material may require the use of a peripheral directly connected to a computerized device (*e.g.*, CD-ROM drive) or a connection to a computer network (*e.g.*, the Internet)." This definition does not include electronic resources that do not require the use of a computer, for example, music compact discs and videodiscs.

"TYPE OF RECORD" CODING (FIXED FIELD "TYPE")

The definition of Leader/06 ("Type of Record") code "m" (Computer file) was revised and greatly narrowed in June 1997 (LC Update No. 3 to *USMARC Format for Bibliographic Data*) to allow for the coding of electronic resources for the significant aspect of the content, rather than their physical form. Code "m" is now used only for the following general classes of electronic resources:

- Computer software (including programmes, games, fonts)
- Numeric data
- Computer-oriented multimedia
- Online systems or services

For these classes of materials, if there is a significant aspect that causes it to fall into another Leader/06 ("Type of Record") category, code for that significant aspect (for instance, vector data that is cartographic is not coded as numeric but as cartographic). Other classes of electronic resources are coded for their most significant aspect (for instance, language material, graphic, cartographic material, sound, music, moving image). In case of doubt or if the most significant aspect cannot be determined, consider the item a computer file. If the resource is essentially the equivalent of a print item but in electronic form, use the same Type code you would use for the print version.

FIELD 006

In records for electronic resources where the Type Code is not "m," OCLC mandates including the field 006 for the electronic aspects so that the "COM" search qualifier will continue to retrieve these materials. Remember to code the "File" value correctly, usually "d" for textual materials.

"TYPE" AND "FILE" CODING

In keeping with the current definition of Type code "m," OCLC is recommending the following choices of "Type" code and CF 006/09 and CF 008/26 "File" ("Type of Computer File") values for the following categories of electronic resources. Included below are resources accessible directly, such as on CD-ROMs or computer disks, and remotely, such as from Web sites and online files.

In its definitions of certain values for the Computer File 008/26 ("File"), *MARC 21 Format for Bibliographic Data* clarifies coding for electronic resources that include search software. The presence of search software does not alter the basic intent of the resource and does not mean that the resource should be coded as software. If its primary purpose is, for instance, textual or bibliographic, it remains textual or bibliographic and is coded as such.

In the area of online systems and services, consider whether the system itself (for example, a library system providing an interface to several databases), or the content of the several constituent databases, is being cataloged. When cataloguing the system itself, use "Type" code "m" and "File" code "j".

"FORM OF ITEM" CODING

As part of the MARC 21 format changes implemented by OCLC in April 2000, a new code "s" was validated for the "Form of Item" fixed field, 008/23 and 006/06 in the Books, Serials, Mixed Materials, and Scores formats, and 008/29 and 006/12 in the Maps and Visual Materials formats. On 2002 December 1, the code "s" was also implemented in the "Form of Item" fixed field, 008/23 and 006/06 for the Sound Recordings format. When cataloguing an electronic resource that includes a significant aspect in any of these bibliographic formats according to current definitions, use "Form of Item" code "s" in the fixed field "Form" and/or in the "Form element of any 006 fields for that aspect, as appropriate.

FIELD 007

According to LC's Draft Interim Guidelines for Cataloguing Electronic Resources, the computer file 007 is mandatory in any record representing an item whose carrier is a computer file. OCLC endorses this recommendation.

FIELD 856

Please be careful about the correct coding of the field 856 second indicator:

- "Blank" is used when no information is provided about the relationship of the electronic resource to the bibliographic item described in the record (for instance, use "blank" when the subfield $u contains a URI that is no longer accessible but there is another 856 with a currently accessible URI). Display constant: None.
- "0" is used when the electronic location in the field is for the same electronic resource described by the record as a whole. Display constant "Electronic resource:" may be generated.
- "1" is used when the electronic location in the field is for an electronic version of the resource described by the record (for instance, an electronic version when the record is for a nonelectronic version). Note that the Library of Congress uses code "1" in

conjunction with subfield $3 to indicate the electronic location of tables of contents. Display constant "Electronic version:" may be generated.

- "2" is used when the electronic location in the field is for an electronic resource that is related to the bibliographic item described by the record. In this case, the item represented by the bibliographic record is not the electronic resource itself. Use subfield $3 to further characterize the relationship between the electronic item identified in field 856 and the item represented by the bibliographic record as a whole.
- The display constant *Related electronic resource*: may be provided. Limit this use to electronic resources that have a specific bibliographic relationship to the resource described in the body of the record. This would include links to such resources as a finding aid for an archival collection or the Web site of a musical group on a bibliographic record for a sound recording. This would not, however, include Web sites that have merely a general subject relationship to the resource.

LCRI 9.7B, marked "LC Practice," deals with "Remote access electronic resources that are no longer available."

Because of OCLC's indexing needs and its electronic address checking software, however, we suggest leaving URIs in field 856 subfield $u and adding an appropriate subfield $z note under the following circumstances:

- URI no longer works at all, does not redirect to a more current URI.
- 856 4 $u [Dead URI] $z This electronic address not available when searched on [Date].
- URI redirects (either automatically or with a forwar-ding link) to a new URI.
- 856 4 $u [Redirected URI] $z This former electronic address redirects to current address when searched on [Date].

In both of these cases, change the 856 Second Indicator to blank.

Character	Hex Value	Note
Spacing Underscore	%5F	Because the spacing underscore may cause problems with MARC output users may prefer to continue entering it with the hex value %5F.
Spacing tilde	%7E	
Spacing grave	%60	
Spacing circumflex	%5E	
Vertical bar or pipe	%7C	Continue to use the hex value for this character.

In cases where multiple URIs may be appropriate, record them as follows:

- Record a PURL and its corresponding original URL (both of which resolve to the same resource) in separate subfields $u in the same 856 field.
- For most other instances of multiple URIs, record them in separate 856 fields.

When the following characters appear in URIs, you may now use the proper character or substitute the appropriate hex value.

GENERAL MATERIAL DESIGNATION

The General Material Designation (GMD) "[electronic resource]" will now be used for items that are coded as Type "m." Also use the GMD "[electronic resource]" for all records that would include the computer file 006 according to the OCLC guidelines, regardless of the Type Code.

INTEGRATING RESOURCES

According to AACR2, 2005 Update, an integrating resource is: "A bibliographic resource that is added to or changed by means of updates that do not remain discrete and are integrated into the whole. Integrating resources can be finite or continuing. Examples of integrating resources include updating loose-leafs and updating Web sites."

Beginning immediately, follow these guidelines for integrating resources:

- Use the Continuing Resources (formerly Serials) workform when creating records for textual integra-ting resources. Continue to use the 006 field for Continuing Resources (formerly Serials) to create 006 fields for non-textual integrating resources.
- Use Bibliographic Level code "i" (Integrating Resource) when coding a record for an integrating resource. DO NOT use Bibliographic Level code "s" (Serial) or "m" (Monograph) for an integrating resource.
- For an electronic textual integrating resource, the typical Continuing Resource fixed field will be coded as follows:

<table>
<tr><td>Type: a</td><td>ELvl: |</td><td>Srce: d</td><td>GPub: _</td><td>Ctrl: _</td><td>Lang: |||</td></tr>
<tr><td>BLvl: i</td><td>Form: s[1]</td><td>Conf: 0</td><td>Freq: _[2]</td><td>MRec: _</td><td>Ctry: |||</td></tr>
<tr><td>S/L: 2[3]</td><td>Orig: s</td><td>EntW: _</td><td>Regl: _[2]</td><td>Alph: a</td><td></td></tr>
<tr><td>Desc: |</td><td>SrTp: _[4]</td><td>Cont: ____</td><td>DtSt: c[5]</td><td>Dates: ||||,9999</td><td></td></tr>
</table>

- [1] *Form:* For electronic integrating resources, continue to use code "s" in Form.
- [2] *Freq and Regl:* If the integrating resource is truly "continuously updated" (for instance, a constantly updating database, a newspaper's Web site that gets updated as news occurs, etc.), use the Frequency Code "k," which means "the item is updated more frequently than daily;" in that case, the correct Regularity

code is likely to be "r" for Regular. More commonly, when the resource is updated less frequently than daily and none of the other Frequency codes apply, use "blank" for Frequency and "x" for Regularity.

- [3] *S/L:* In the continuing resources fixed field, use code "2" in Entry Convention (S/L, formerly Successive/Latest Entry) to indicate that the record was formulated using the revised rules for integrated entry.
- [4] *SrTp:* In the element SrTp (Type of Continuing Resource, formerly Type of Serial), use code "d" for updating databases, code "l" for updating loose-leafs, or code "w" for updating Web sites, as appropriate.
- [5] *DtSt:* For integrating resources that are currently published, use code "c" (rather than the former practice of code "m"). For integrating resources that have ceased publication, use code "d" (rather than the former practice of code "m").

- Continue to include a computer file 006 and a computer file 007 field in records for electronic integrating resources. For a textual electronic integrating resource, the typical computer file 006 and 007 fields will be coded as follows:

COM 006:	Type: m	Audn:	File: d	GPub:
COM 007:	c $b r $d c $e n			

URIs and LCRIs 9.7B and 21.3B for Remote Access Electronic Resources

Two Library of Congress Rule Interpretations, 9.7B and 21.3B, offer some guidance about how to deal with remote access electronic integrating resources and the disposition of the resource's Uniform Resource Identifier (URI). When the original URI is no longer accessible, but the resource (or a new iteration thereof) is now accessible at another URI, you may edit the existing record to reflect this. When the original URI is still active but now represents an entirely different resource, rather than a new iteration of the original resource, you may create a new record for the new electronic resource. In cases where you are unable to edit, or prefer not to edit the existing record, you are encouraged to report the necessary changes to OCLC.

SEPARATE RECORDS VERSUS SINGLE RECORD

Creating separate records for an item is preferable when both remote access electronic versions and tangible or direct access (including, but not limited to, print and other nonelectronic) versions exist. You may, however, find a single record approach is better for your local environment. OCLC recommends that you verify the impact of these options with your local system vendor and other partners prior to implementation. Use of the term "nonelectronic" in the options that follow is meant as shorthand for any tangible resource (including print, videocassette, videodisc, CD-ROM, etc.) and is not meant to exclude, for instance, tangible resources that may have electronic aspects. In that light, elements of the recommendations may need to be adjusted to accommodate such aspects (for example, inclusion of fields 006 and/or 007).

Option 1: Separate Records

Nonelectronic item:

- Select the workform based on the current definition of "Type" and the primary aspect of the item.
- Do not input fields 006 and 007 and do not code "Form of Item" (008/23, 008/29, 006/06, or 006/12, depending on bibliographic format) for the electronic versio
- Note the availability of the electronic version in field 530.
- *Example:* Available also on the Internet.
- Add a 700-730 added entry field for the electronic version when the main entry differs.
- Optionally, link to the electronic record with field 776.
- Optionally, provide the location of any remotely accessible version(s) in field(s) 856. Use second indicator "1" when the address is for a version of the resource other than the one described in the body of the entry, or "2" when the address is for an otherwise related resource.

Electronic Item:

- Select the workform based on the current definition of "Type" and the primary aspect of the item.
- Include field 006 for computer file, if Type is not "m."
- Include field 007 for computer file.
- Code "Form of Item" (008/23, 008/29, 006/06, or 006/12, as appropriate, depending on bibliographic format) for "electronic" (code "s").
- Note the availability of the nonelectronic version in field 530.
- *Example:* Also available in printed form.
- Add a 700-730 added entry field when main entry for the nonelectronic version differs.
- Optionally, link to the nonelectronic version using field 776.
- Provide the location of any remotely accessible version(s) in field(s) 856. Use second indicator "0" when the address is for the resource itself, "1" when the address is for a version of the resource other than the one described in the body of the entry, or "2" when the address is for an otherwise related resource.

Option 2: Single Record with a Reference to the Electronic Item

You may create a record for the nonelectronic version and add an annotation about the existence of and access to the electronic version. The nonelectronic version is the primary version and the electronic copy is secondary:

- Select the workform based on the current definition of "Type" and the primary aspect of the item.
- Do not input field 006 for the electronic version.
- Do not code "Form of Item"(008/23, 008/29, 006/06, or 006/12, depending on bibliographic format) for the electronic version.
- Optionally, include field 007.
- Note the availability of the electronic version in field 530.
- Add a 740 added entry when the title for the electronic version differs.
- Provide the location of any remotely accessible version in field 856. Use second indicator "1" when the address is for a version of the resource other than the one described in the body of the entry or "2" when the address is for an otherwise related resource.

Additional Separate Versus Single Record Considerations

If you are cataloguing an electronic item, you need not verify the physical existence of the nonelectronic version or whether it has been cataloged. Similarly, when you catalogue a nonelectronic item, you need not verify whether an electronic version exists.

In both cases, you need not apply these guidelines, and you may catalogue the item as if no other version exists. Apply the input convention in this document if you have verification that electronic and nonelectronic versions exist, and you want to record the existence of both.

In all cases, you may add references to electronic resources that are related to the item described in the body of the record when those references are thought to add value.

The CONSER Cataloguing Manual: Module 31—Remote Access Electronic Serials (Online Serials) permits a single record for a nonelectronic item to include information for the electronic version. OCLC's guidelines are currently compatible with CONSER's.

INTEGRATING RESOURCE OR MONOGRAPH VERSUS SERIAL

The decision to code an electronic resource as a monograph or as a serial is a decision made separately from the Type Code decision. Note that for electronic serials where Type is not "a" or "m", two 006 fields will be necessary, one for the electronic aspects and one for the serial aspects.

Apply the current AACR2 definitions of monograph and serial to electronic resources. Treat as serials (Bibliographic Level: s (or b)) only those continuing resources issued in a succession of discrete parts with no predetermined conclusion. The parts may constitute an issue, or in some cases, an individual article.

Applying the current AACR2R definitions may result in different manifestations receiving different cataloguing treatment. For example, a manifestation in print form, such as an annual directory, is cataloged as a serial whereas it is cataloged as an integrating resource when the directory takes on the form of an electronic file that is continuously updated. LC and CONSER adhere to current definitions, and OCLC recommends its users do the same.

Remotely accessed electronic resources of a dynamic nature that are currently excluded from serial treatment are:

- Databases (including directories, A&I services, etc.)
- Electronic discussion groups (*e.g.*, SERIALST)
- Electronic discussion group digests (*e.g.*, AUTOCAT digest)
- Gopher servers (*e.g.*, LC-MARVEL)
- Online public access catalogues (*e.g.*, OCLC, RLIN)
- Online services (*e.g.*, America Online)
- Web sites (*e.g.*, the CONSER home page)

These electronic resources should be cataloged as integrating resources or monographs, as appropriate.

Electronic Reproductions of Items Previously Published in Print Form

In May 2000, the Library of Congress issued a revised version of LC Rule Interpretation 1.11A.

The revision expands LC's "microform exception" to AACR2 to include remotely accessed electronic reproductions of works previously published in printed form (including electronic books). This practice applies only when the reproduction manifestation is represented by its own bibliographic record, separate from any record for the original.

In essence, LCRI 1.11A calls for users to:

- Transcribe the bibliographic data appropriate to the *original* work being reproduced in the following areas: title and statement of responsibility; edition; material (or type of publication) specific details; publication, distribution, etc.; physical description; series.
- If appropriate, give in the title and statement of responsibility area the General Material Designation that is applicable to the format of the reproduction (in the case of electronic reproductions, the GMD "[electronic resource]").
- Give in a single note (533 field) all other details relating to the reproduction and its publication/availability, including format of the reproduction, dates of publication and/or sequential designation of issues reproduced (for serials), place and name of the agency responsible for the reproduction, date of the reproduction, physical description of the reproduction if different from the original, series

statement of the reproduction (if applicable), notes relating to the reproduction (if applicable).

- Use a physical description fixed field (007) applicable to the reproduction, and for electronic reproductions, also supply information about the electronic location and access (856 field).

In addition, OCLC users should include the appropriate field 006 and code "Form of Item" for "electronic" (code "s") as outlined earlier in these guidelines. Optionally, OCLC users may also include a field 539, following field 533, containing data about the reproduction in coded form.

DEALING WITH EXISTING RECORDS

These guidelines, of course, do not resolve all problems. OCLC's Duplicate Detection and Resolution software, for example, cannot always distinguish one version from another.

Indexing and identifying a record as a computer file may not be possible if the local system does not index field 006 or field 007.

The cataloguing of these electronic resources remains very much in flux, as do the resources themselves. The rules for dealing with them remain a work in progress.

OCLC users are encouraged to submit to the Library of Congress Network Development and MARC Standards Office (ndmso@loc.gov) examples of any electronic resources about which there is ambiguity concerning the coding of Leader/06, CF 008/26, and/or CF 006/09, and any instances not covered by LC's "Guidelines."

OCLC any needed Type and/or BLvl code changes, as well as any other changes to existing WorldCat records, either by phone, paper, or electronically, as appropriate. OCLC would prefer that you not add duplicate records in these instances.

Minimal-Level Upgrade continues to allow changes of BLvl only within the same bibliographic format, except:

- In records with Type Codes "a" or "t," BLvl "a," "c," "d," or "m" can be changed to BLvl "i"
- In records with Type Code "a" and BLvl "b" or "s," the BLvl can be changed to BLvl "i"

WorldCat Database Enrichment currently allows Full Mode users and above to add field 006 and/or 007 to most records through lock and replace. OCLC recognizes that the conversion of existing records for electronic resources is a significant issue for many groups within the OCLC membership.

Through Minimal Level Upgrade, Database Enrichment, CONSER, and Enhance, many OCLC members have the ability to fix many of the records in question. OCLC encourages users to report other records that need to be converted, via any of the usual means.

DRAFT INTERIM GUIDELINES FOR CATALOGUING ELECTRONIC RESOURCES

BACKGROUND

The Library of Congress has become increasingly engaged in the world of those electronic resources requiring the use of a computer. In the early 1980s it began to assign International Standard Serial Numbers (ISSN) to directly accessed serial electronic resources and in 1988 to those that are online. In the early 1990's the Library, through the Cooperative Online Serials (CONSER) Programme, began to address the cataloguing of online serial resources, with an emphasis on those available on the Internet. It began to catalogue monographic computer files in the late 1980's.

In the early 1990's, the Library began the digitization of original materials from its special collections under the aegis of the American Memory programme. In 1996 an informal group of staff members with interests in issues relating to digitization, not only of original materials in special collections, but also including some book materials, met on an irregular basis to begin exploring issues of common interest.

While the group's initial concern was the cataloguing treatment of materials that LC was digitizing from its own collections, it also encountered issues that relate to the bibliographic control of material in special collections, particularly "special format" material whose mode of expression is other than that of language material (non-manuscript language material) or whose modes of expression are mixed (*i.e.*, collections of mixed material).

Even so, the issues are not solely the domain of these materials, as the group discovered with some of the collections of language materials (*e.g.*, various pamphlet collections; broadside collections). Cataloguing electronic reproductions of material held by the Library as well as cataloguing other electronic resources, whether electronic manifestations of new or already existing material, raises several issues.

One of the most important is the use of one record or two to describe closely related content. Thus a medium that spans both general and special cataloguing requires Library-wide application of a standard set of guidelines to ensure clarity in bibliographic records both for public catalogue users and for effective biblio-graphic control.

It has been the intent of the Cataloguing Policy and Support Office (CPSO) to develop conceptual guidelines for the cataloguing of electronic resources. That effort has been delayed for various reasons, and towards the end of 1996, stimulated by increased activities in the area of digitization, CPSO invited a small group of staff members to develop interim guidelines for cataloguing electronic resources. These guidelines are the result; they have been reviewed within LC by representatives of the units most directly concerned with cataloguing electronic manifestations, particularly by the staff members. Additional consultations were held with Copyright Office staff, and some changes were made to some of the terminology that had originally been proposed to accommodate the copyright perspective.

PURPOSE AND CHARACTER

The purpose is to establish an interim set of guidelines to be used for cataloguing electronic resources in the Library of Congress based on a common conceptual context and a common terminology.

The intent of the guidelines is to apply to resources of divergent character produced under varying circumstances and managed by different entities, a set of conventions for bibliographic control that will enable genera-lized, standard practice to the extent judged practicable in a diverse, dynamic environment.

It also endeavours to engage the electronic world on a broader scale by providing a conceptual framework for treating electronic resources. This framework is followed by the establishment and definition of concepts and terms appropriate to electronic resources in an attempt to ensure clear communication based on a common understanding.

The guidelines then include:

- Policies on when to use multiple records and when to use a single record;
- Conventions developed especially for the single-record technique;
- Directions for indicating the existence of other physical formats (530 field);
- Directions related to electronic location (856 field);
- Directions relating to collocating records (710 field) and linking them (76X-78X fields);
- Directions relating to identifying in MUMS those records related to a specific project (985 field; mandatory for American Memory projects).

The overall guidelines try to show how the cataloguing of all electronic resources fits together, but they do not cover the specifics of all resources. This table shows that the specific guidelines are more nearly oriented to electronic reproductions of materials held by the Library, for example, using a single-record approach for delineating these electronic manifes-tations. This emphasis is driven by the fact that the digitizing efforts of the Library of Congress and the need for their public representation as viable resources compel immediate attention.

In meeting the needs of the Library of Congress in this regard, it remains to be seen whether the guidelines developed for these LC materials will necessarily be applicable elsewhere. The one obvious lacuna in the current document is the absence of guidelines relating to the treatment of Internet resources—particularly with respect to which ones should be represented in the catalogue, under what circumstances, and in what detail. This is because the collection development guidelines for electronic resources are only now beginning to be formulated. Thus the issues related to cataloguing these materials have not been fully confronted.

One question of concern is the impact the nature of the medium itself will have. For tangible non-electronic materials, their very tangibility fixes the intellectual content. This tangibility is common across all items in a particular manifestation, thus allowing the description of one item to apply to all the others in the manifestation. Changes in physical characteristics are used to surmise that there are changes in content, which is the basis of creating a new bibliographic record.

With respect to cataloguing remotely accessed electronic resources, it will be interesting to see what the impact of the accessing mode will be, particularly, with regard to:

- The basis for determining that the content is "fixed," absent tangibility as a basis for doing this;
- The basis for determining that the content has changed, again, absent tangible characteristics for doing this.

On a more mundane level there are issues relating to:

- The disposition of information that is universal and that which is local;
- Determining who we are providing the information for (again universal/local);
- "Custody" (is it relevant?);
- Classification (should we attempt to classify?).

REASONS WHY THE GUIDELINES ARE INTERIM

The Guidelines are interim for the following reasons:

- Some of the copyright and collection development guidelines with respect to remotely accessed electronic resources are only now beginning to be formulated; the universe of material for which bibliographic control is to be applied will have a substantial impact on the resources available for this purpose and will in turn influence the nature of the conventions themselves (the larger the number of materials to be controlled the less labour intensive the conventions to control them can be);
- The dynamic nature of the environment of electronic resources is profoundly affecting the standards upon which current conventions of bibliographic control rest; it is necessary to monitor the changes that are developing in AACR2, in USMARC, and in such international activities as the ISBD (ER): International Standard Bibliographic Description for Electronic Resources and the IFLA study on the

Functional Requirements for Bibliographic Records, and make adjustments accordingly;

- Experiments applicable to particular kinds of resources (*e.g.*, serials and CONSER policies; the BEONLINE project for business and economic resources) are under way with evaluation of results and implications for policy guidelines still to be determined;
- System considerations at LC are in a state of flux, particularly with the impending procurement of an Integrated Library System; hypertext links are still not available in the traditional interfaces to MUMS and SCORPIO; once this feature is more widely available, perceptions of which resources should be represented in the catalogue and how data need to be depicted may change.

CONCEPTUAL FRAMEWORK

The Interim Guidelines establish a common context through the use of entities and concepts derived from an entity analysis technique and based on work done heretofore in LC as part of information modelling and in the more recent work that resulted in an IFLA study: Functional Requirements for Bibliographic Records: Final Report. The following entities/concepts, applicable to all forms of material, are taken directly from the aforementioned IFLA study in a condensed but usually directly quoted form. They are stated here because they provide a vocabulary that clarifies conceptually what is currently embodied in a bibliographic record.

- *Work:* A distinct intellectual or artistic creation; a work is an abstract entity
- *Expression:* The intellectual or artistic realization of a work in the form of alpha-numeric, musical, or choreographic notation, sound, image, object, movement, etc., or any combination of such forms; an expression is the specific intellectual or artistic form that a work takes each time it is "realised"; inasmuch as the form of expression is an inherent characteristic of the expression, any change in form (*e.g.*, from alpha-numeric notation to spoken word) results in a new expression; similarly, changes in the intellectual conventions or instruments that are employed to express a work (*e.g.*, translation from one language to another) result in the production of a new expression
- *Manifestation:* The physical embodiment of an expression of a work; as an entity, manifestation represents all the physical objects that bear the same characteristics, in respect to both intellectual content and physical form; when a work is realised, the resulting expression of the work may be physically embodied on or in a medium such as paper, audio tape, video tape, etc.; the physical embodiment constitutes a manifestation of the work; in some cases there may be

only a single physical exemplar produced of that manifestation of the work (*e.g.*, an author's manuscript, a tape recorded for an oral history archive, an original oil painting, etc.); in other cases there are multiple copies produced in order to facilitate public dissemination or distribution

- *Item:* A single exemplar of a manifestation; an item is a concrete entity; it is in many instances a single physical object (*e.g.*, a copy of a one-volume monograph, a single audio cassette, etc.); with respect to intellectual content and physical form, an item exemplifying a manifestation is normally the same as the manifestation itself; however, variations may occur from one item to another, even when the items exemplify the same manifestation, where those variations are the result of actions external to the intent of the producer of the manifestation (*e.g.*, damage occurring after the item was produced, binding performed by a library, etc.)

The entities shown in diagram "represent the different aspects of user interests in the products of intellectual or artistic endeavour. The entities defined as work (a distinct intellectual or artistic creation) and expression (the intellectual or artistic realization of a work) reflect intellectual or artistic content. The entities defined as manifestation (the physical embodiment of an expression of a work) and item (a single exemplar of a manifestation), on the other hand reflect physical form.

The relationships depicted in the diagram indicate that a work may be realised through one or more than one expression (hence the double arrow on the line that links work to expression). An expression, on the other hand, is the realization of one and only one work (hence the single arrow on the reverse direction of that line linking expression to work). An expression may be embodied in one or more than one manifestation; likewise a manifestation may embody one or more than one expression. A manifestation, in turn, may be exemplified by one or more than one item; but an item may exemplify one and only one manifestation.

BASIC CONCEPTS/TERMS

The Guidelines use the following basic concepts and terms with their associated definition to establish a consistent vocabulary, recognizing that there may not always be full agreement in particular cases. The basic concepts/terms are presented alphabetically for ease of reference.

Some apply at a general level, others are more nearly related to electronic resources themselves:

- *Accessing Mode:* A concept that characterizes the means of access to an electronic resource; it is applicable at the item level.
  - *Direct Access:* The term used to characterize access to an electronic resource resident in a carrier such as a computer disk

or a CD-ROM that a user physically inserts into a computer, typically a microcomputer.

- *Observation:* A tangible resource may also be accessed in an online mode as if remote (*e.g.*, networked CD-ROMS; data copied onto UNIX hosts).
  - *Remote Access:* The term used to characterize access to an electronic resource resident in a carrier that a user cannot physically handle, *i.e.*, a resource accessed, processed, executed, etc. remotely. Frequently this involves connection through a computer network. This type of access is often referred to as "online" access.

Adjunct see under Selected relationships:

- *Aggregates/Components:* Concepts pertinent to the make-up of a work. A work may be an integral unit or it may represent an aggregate of individual works (*e.g.*, a compilation), a set of individual monographs brought together by a common theme or topic (*e.g.*, a series), or a group of private papers organized by an archive as a single collection. A work may also represent an intellectually or artistically discrete component of a larger work, *e.g.*, an article in a journal, a monograph in a series.
- Entities at the aggregate or component level are seen as the same as entities at the integral unit level.
- *Compilation:* An electronic anthology whose constituent elements have been brought together and selected, coordinated, or arrnaged to form a new work.
- *Delineation:* A technique used in lieu of separately cataloguing a manifestation whereby detailed information about that manifestation is given in the bibliographic record for another manifestation; simply noting the existence of another manifestation does not constitute what is meant by delineation

Directly accessed electronic resource see under Physicality:

- *Electronic Conference:* A conference held in a virtual mode that takes place within the context of an interactive software environment running on the Internet. Headings for such conferences are treated the same as those for other conferences except headings for electronic conferences do not contain the name of the local place or other location in which the conference was held.
- *Electronic Discussion Group:* The term used to refer to a forum conducted electronically; these services, commonly called newsgroups and listservs, allow a computer user to post messages to, and read messages from, a group of people who have a common interest, usually by means of the Internet, a commercial online service, or

electronic mail. For cataloguing purposes, treat such a discussion group as a work entered under title (X30 series of tags).

- *Electronic Resource:* The term used to refer to a manifestation of a work encoded for manipulation by computer. The manifestation resides in a carrier accessed either directly or remotely. It is the term used in the revised ISBD (ER) and serves in lieu of other terms currently in use such as computer file or digital resource. Some electronic resources may require the use of a peripheral device attached to a computer (*e.g.* a CD-ROM player). Note that for these Guidelines this term does not include "electronic" resources that do not require the use of a computer, *e.g.*, music compact discs, videodiscs.

BASE GUIDELINES (GENERAL)

Use the following base guidelines in determining the cataloguing treatment of a particular electronic resource. In general, the cataloguing treatment applied depends upon important factors related to the creation of the electronic resource itself, most importantly whether the resource is a sole manifestation or one of multiple manifestations and the realization of the work as a matter of time, *i.e.*, whether it is judged to be a monograph or a serial.

CONTENT VERSUS CARRIER (ELECTRONIC RESOURCES)

How to characterize records for electronic resources in terms of their primary form of material (the issue of "content versus carrier") has been widely discussed. AACR2 is oriented towards basing cataloguing treatment on carrier. Until 1997 the definition of computer file in USMARC (Leader/06 code"m") also indicated that the record would be coded for carrier. However, as a result of a change approved by MARBI in June 1997, Update No. 3 to the USMARC Bibliographic Format revised the definition of code "m" to allow for computer files to be coded for their most significant aspect.

That definition now reads:

- Code m indicates that the content of the record is for the following classes of electronic resources: computer software (including programmes, games, fonts), numeric data, computer-oriented multimedia, online systems or services. For these classes of materials, if there is a significant aspect that causes it to fall into another Leader/ 06 category, code for that significant aspect (*e.g.* vector data that is cartographic is not coded as numeric but as cartographic). Other classes of electronic resources are coded for their most significant aspect (*e.g.* language material, graphic, cartographic material, sound, music, moving image). In case of doubt or if the most significant aspect cannot be determined, consider the item a computer file.

In conjunction with this change, field 007 for computer files is now mandatory in any record representing an item whose carrier is a computer file. Directly accessed electronic resources have been treated as computer files at LC as have most of those accessed remotely. Directly accessed electronic resources have been represented in the COMPUTER FILES file, the BOOKS file (those that accompany books), and, with format integration, in the SERIALS file.

With respect to cataloguing remotely accessed electronic resources, LC has been most active in cataloguing electronic serials/journals and electronic counterparts or subsets of tangible, original items or collections.

In most cases, the latter do not receive separate catalogue records; instead, they are delineated in records for the original items or collections. The special format divisions are interested in providing an integrated approach to the bibliographic records for the materials of interest to them. Currently, that is done through the disposition of physical files under MUMS, essentially by type of material. Under an ILS it will be a requirement to be able to approach the catalogue in a similar way as at present but it will probably be a logical disposition instead of a physical one.

In the future when the shift in approach from carrier to content is implemented at LC, fundamental changes in the current LC environment will be required. Those electronic resources judged to have a significant aspect other than that of a computer file would now be represented in the file appropriate to what is judged to be the significant aspect. For example, if the significant aspect of a monographic electronic resource is judged to be language material, that resource would be represented in the Books file, not the Computer Files file (use of the GMD "[computer file]" will continue). As of the current writing, not all the details of the impact of this change have been worked out, but it is assumed that staff in the Computer Files/Microforms Team will continue to catalogue those general monographic electronic resources not pertaining to the materials of interest to the special format divisions. However, they will do so by working in the file judged appropriate to the resource being cataloged.

It is further assumed that special format divisions will continue to focus on cataloguing (except for Music, RBSCD) and servicing material acquired for the collections in their custody. The change in approach that emphasizes content will, mean that electronic resources will now be represented throughout the files that constitute the catalogue, not just in the Computer Files file. An issue of potential significant impact relates to those computer-related electronic resources acquired by the special format divisions for their collections.

As of this writing, it is not clear how some of these materials will be treated with respect to:

- Who will catalogue these materials and
- What cataloguing treatment they will receive.

It is assumed that those judged to be cartographic materials will continue to be cataloged by staff in the Geography and Map Division (G&M); those judged to be serials will be cataloged in the Serial Record Division (SRD)). The treatment of other monographic materials is less clear. For example, will a directly accessed electronic resource manifes-ted in multiple copies whose significant aspect is judged to be moving image be cataloged in MBRS under the AMIM rules and, if circumstances warrant, added to the record for another manifestation? This would be in lieu of being cataloged according to the general rules of AACR2 as a manifestation receiving a separate record by staff either in MBRS or in SMCD. The Library of Congress will develop/change workflow and cataloguing policies related to "content vs. carrier" issues and will make them available to the larger cataloguing community.

MONOGRAPH OR SERIAL

Apply the current AACR2 definitions of monograph and serial to electronic resources. Treat digitized texts, individual Web sites, and indeterminate works not issued in separate parts, particularly databases, as monographs. Treat as serials indeterminate works issued in separate, designated parts. The parts may constitute an issue, or in some cases, an individual article.

Applying the current definitions may result in different manifestations receiving different cataloguing treatment. For example, a manifestation in print form, such as an annual directory, is cataloged as a serial whereas it is cataloged as a monograph when the directory takes on the form of an electronic file that is continuously updated. This practice may change, but for the present LC and CONSER adhere to current definitions.

Remotely accessed electronic resources of a dynamic nature that are currently excluded from serial treatment are:

- Databases (including directories, A&I services, etc.)
- Electronic discussion groups (*e.g.*, SERIALST)
- Electronic discussion group digests (*e.g.*, AUTOCAT digest)
- Gopher servers (*e.g.*, LC-MARVEL)
- Online public access catalogues (*e.g.*, OCLC, RLIN)
- Online services (*e.g.*, America Online)
- Web sites (*e.g.*, the CONSER home page)

SINGLE MANIFESTATION

An electronic resource that exists solely in a single manifestation, *e.g.*, a publication that exists solely online, by definition is represented by a single bibliographic record in the same manner as other non-electronic resources that exist in a single manifestation. Currently, those judged to be monographs are cataloged as computer files by the Computer Files/Microforms Team of the Special Materials Cataloguing Division (SMCD) or as cartographic materials by staff in the Geography and Map Division (G&M) or, if judged to be accompanying material, by the general cataloguing divisions.

Those judged to be serials are cataloged in the Serial Record Division (SRD). Both monographs and serials are cataloged according to AACR2R, LCRIs, DCM, LCSH, SCM, LCC, USMARC, and supplementary documentation appropriate to each category of material.

MULTIPLE MANIFESTATIONS

An electronic resource that is another manifestation of a work is likely to be one of the following:

- A manifestation that is a counterpart or subset of a published resource (tangible or otherwise, usually directly accessed) or an adjunct to it;
- A directly accessed manifestation that is:
  - A counterpart or subset of a tangible resource (either at the collection level or item level or both);
  - A reproduction in electronic form done by or for the Library of Congress of a resource held by the Library;
- A remotely accessed manifestation that is
  - A counterpart or subset of a tangible resource (either at the collection level or item level or both);
  - A reproduction in electronic form done by or for the Library of Congress of a resource (including material that may have been published) held by the Library.

Materials in categories a) and b) are usually cataloged by staff in the Computer Files/Microforms Team, SMCD (computer files), or in G&M (cartographic materials) or in SRD, depending upon whether the resource is judged to be a monograph or a serial. Materials in category c) are usually delineated by staff in the special format division that has custody of the tangible, non-electronic resource.

Note that a manifestation of conventionally published materials, including directly accessed electronic resources, usually consists of multiple copies. Unique collections usually occur in a single instance, although electronic manifestations of the original collection may be mirrored or copied and therefore exist at several storage locations.

The data elements contained in the USMARC biblio-graphic format are predicated on data elements common to all the copies of a manifestation. Those applicable to a particular copy are generally treated as "local" or as holdings information.

This concept is less appropriate to a unique tangible resource such as an archival collection, although this does not preclude the concept of "copy specific" as applied to a particular item in a collection when the manifestation of the item itself consists of multiple copies.

Single/Multiple Records for Multiple Manifestations (Electronic Resources)

Criteria for Determining Single/Multiple Record Approach

Acquisitions/Initial Bibliographic Control (IBC) Criterion

Determine the processing state of the electronic resource from the perspective of acquisitions or the need for IBC data. The degree of detail required for the management of initial and subsequent acquisitions actions may influence the employment of a single or multiple record approach as may the workflow steps required subsequent to the acquisitions process.

Citation Criterion

A user must be able to get to the manifestation cited in the record the user is observing.

When a single bibliographic record includes one or more citations to multiple manifestations, each citation the user is observing must state clearly and succinctly the content of the manifestation(s) cited:

- For the directly accessed, the format of the manifestation more than likely requires a separate record to fulfil the citation criterion;
- For the remotely accessed, a separate record is less likely to be needed to fulfil the citation criterion unless the content among multiple manifestations varies substantially.

INTERLIBRARY LOAN (ILL) CRITERION

The receiver of a request must know which manifestation is being requested and the initiator of a request must know the manifes-tation(s) available for loan:

- For multiple directly accessed manifestations, multiple bibliographic records make it more clear which manifestation is being requested;
- Employment of a single bibliographic record that represents both tangible and remotely accessed manifestations is unlikely to cause confusion with respect to the manifestation available for loan, since it is unlikely someone would request the loan of a remotely accessed resource;
- When a single bibliographic record represents both a tangible manifestation (electronic or otherwise) and a remotely accessed one and the Library "holds" only the latter, it is more likely to cause confusion with respect to the manifestation held and whether it s likely to be available for loan.

Bibliographic Details Criterion

When there is more than one manifestation, the significant bibliographic details of each need to be recorded to identify and to access each. When using a single record that includes one or more delineations, it is necessary to find ways to indicate the significant bibliographic details of all the manifestations, not just those for the primary one. In the past the Library of Congress has attempted to provide catalogue records not only for use in the catalogues of the Library of Congress but also of use in the catalogues of other libraries. For economic reasons, the present Guidelines now provide for the use of a single record to represent more than one manifestation in the cases. This necessarily focuses on the needs of the Library of Congress but may pose difficulties on other libraries that may wish to represent such resources in their catalogues.

Multiple Manifestations in a Single Record (Electronic Resources)

Two techniques are available for indicating the existence of an electronic manifestation in a record for another manifestation. Both are in lieu of LC's cataloguing the remotely accessed resource separately.

Delineate Another Manifestation

When using a single record to describe a tangible resource and also to delineate an electronic manifestation, consider the information provided in the delineation of the electronic resource as being in lieu of a separate catalogue record. Use the 530 field (Other Physical Form Available Note) to focus all the information about the electronic resource in one place.

Organize the delineation to include at least:

- An introductory phrase indicating the additional availability of an electronic manifestation;
- The name or title of the electronic manifestation if it varies from that of a tangible counterpart or subset;
- Information about the content of the electronic manifestation when it varies from that of the original, *e.g.*, a subset of the original or additional material;
- General information about access, particularly any restrictions on access or information about availability.

If a finding aid in electronic form is involved and it is the kind that incorporates actual material from the collection such that the finding aid itself becomes a remotely accessed electronic manifestation of the content of the collection or a subset of it, describe this special condition in the delineation.

The data making up a particular delineation are not prone to a structured presentation; therefore, the flexibility of the 530 field was chosen for delineation over the more structured 533 field. Also use of the 530 field avoids any implication that the original is not held, an implication often associated with the use of field 533. When the electronic manifestation bears a title different from that of the tangible resource, provide uncontrolled title access through the title that differs. Do these by means of a 740 field with indicator values set to 0#? This is an exception to the general LC policy of providing title access through a controlled form (730).

Note the Existence of Another Manifestation

The cataloguing rules have long provided for indicating the existence of another manifestation in a note (field 530), usually in a very brief statement. With respect to serials, CONSER's Interim Guidelines for Online Versions allow CONSER institutions either to create separate records or to note the existence of an remotely accessed electronic manifestation on the record for the print (or other) serial. Practically speaking, this policy is quite similar to delineating; however, there is a difference in the intent.

The CONSER guidelines aim to retain the integrity of the print (or other) record in a shared database in which separate records for the remotely accessed electronic manifestation might exist or be created later. Thus, field 007 is not given in such records and 530 notes tend to be less detailed than those given in records for LC's special collections. Field 740 may also be given when the title of the remotely accessed electronic manifestation differs from that of the original. LC applies the CONSER single record option only for one-to-one reproduc-tions of serials and in other cases creates separate records.

Multiple Presentations of the Same Electronic Resource

If an electronic resource is available in multiple presen-tations that may be generated from different underlying digital representations, *e.g.*, images in TIFF or JPEG format, it is not necessary to acknowledge the condition.

Electronic Resources in Bibliographical References

With respect to bibliography notes, interpret the term "bibliographical references" to include all kinds of resources, including electronic resources; do not give any special treatment to, or provide special mention of, the latter.

**Electronic Manifesatation–original in Non–
Electronic From–specific Guidelines**

General

This is the condition in which an electronic resource is the digitized counterpart to, subset of, or an adjunct to, a tangible manifestation of a work, and the decision has been made to represent the electronic manifestation in the catalogue. Determine whether it is preferable to do this by a single-or multiple-record approach (the single-record approach requires a record for the original, tangible manifestation; one may already exist or it may need to be created). For remotely accessed manifestations of tangible LC materials, a general reference to the Library of Congress Web site is sufficient, since the specific location is always given in an 856 field.

For uniformity of presentation, use the terminology illustrated in the following examples to the extent practicable:

- 530 ## $a Available also through the Library of Congress Web site under title: America's first look into the camera: daguerreotype portraits and views... This finding aid in electronic form, with repro-ductions, captions, and subject indexing for each image, was produced in 1995 for the National Digital Library Programme, American Memory collections.
- 530 ## $a Available also through the Library of Congress Web site under title: Colour photographs from the FSA and OWI, ca. 1938-1944. This finding aid in electronic form contains reproductions with full caption information and subject indexing for each image.
- 530 ## $a Available also through the Library of Congress Web site under title: Documents from the Continental Congress and the Constitutional Convention 1774-1789. At least one facsimile image of each broadside is presented along with a narrative introduction.
- 530 ## $a Available also as part of a microfilm with title: Continental Congress and Constitutional convention Collections. Washington, D.C.: Library of Congress Photoduplication Service. 1 microfilm reel; 35 mm.
- 530 ## $a Available also through the Library of Congress Web site in two forms: as facsimile page images and as full text in SGML.
- 530 ## $a Available also through the Library of Congress Web site as a raster image.
- 538 (System Details Note)

CONCLUSIONS

We conclude that, although more popular than the card catalogue, the actual effectiveness of online catalogue is lower than has been assumed. Where a searcher's terms coincide with the system's terms and when the searcher has a specific, definable target in mind, all may be well. But when these conditions do not hold, all is not well. First and second generation catalogues are quite well defined.

What of the third generation? It should add the following:

- Provide an entry vocabulary capability to lead from users' terms to the system's terms
- Prompt the user at any time in a situationally sensitive manner
- Have a well developed tool-kit for retrieved set analysis
- Support 'nearest neighbour' searching–Find more like this one!–and, perhaps through 'zoom' commands, allow the searcher to browse across the database using any one or more attributes of a record
- Offer document ranking or a mechanism for converting any retrieved set into small, ranked subsets

More generally, the future catalogue should blend harmo-niously with other retrieval tools, with the sources to which it provides access, and with the user's personal working environment. Using it should, in itself, be a learning experience. How this functionality will be provided is less clear, but there are numerous options to be explored. In the preparation of this review we concentrated on identified problems in the use of the online catalogue and on actual proposals for its improvement.

At the same time it became increasingly clear that deeper, more fundamental developments were afoot:

- In the last few years the online catalogue situation has been dominated by the effort of adoption and imple-mentation. There has been gradual movement from first to second generation catalogues despite the substantially greater storage and computing resources required and numerous smaller refinements. These have typically included options to search by call number and limiting searches by date of publication, by language, and/or by library in a union catalogue. In brief, progress has been more a matter of widespread adoption of existing functionality than of advancing the state of the art. But if the state-of-the-art does not appear to have advanced much in the past several years, there are reasons to expect major changes in the future.
- Although it has always been accepted that the catalogue is the key to the library, it has, in many ways, been determined by the needs of cataloguing and technical services. However, since cataloguing was in practice limited to the edition of the monograph and the title of the periodical, the extent of bibliographic access was in reality quite limited. This situation is changing radically. Other database files are being mounted alongside the catalogue and, increasingly, links are being made from the records in these bibliographies to the library's holding records. This can be seen either as a redefinition of the catalogue or as a return to an earlier era when analytical entries could be afforded. Either way, a significant and popular enhancement of bibliographic access results. Another of the major new growth areas for library catalogues is the linking of the catalogue record to the address of full-text in electronic form, allowing, in principle, a smoother transition from record to text than with paper documents. Further, as all forms of media are increasingly stored online in digital form, the distinctions between the media become less significant, promising an increasingly unified approach to multiple media. In addition, as ever increasing numbers of electronic journals, books and texts become available, online catalogues will take on many of the functions of document delivery by enabling the user to inspect, to download, or to request document delivery - all from the catalogue

terminal. But as more and more of these resources become available, how will they be indexed? A conventional catalogue record may enable one to identify and locate a text, but is of little benefit thereafter in finding material within the text. As the role of libraries expand to include access to many of the resources provided by the online environment, many new forms of information are falling within the domain of the online catalogue, for example, non-bibliographic records of community information and referral and *'campus-wide information services'* (CWIS). These expanded frontiers bring new challenges. These additional resources, which may have little or no human indexing, bring with them a whole new set of problems for both users and the catalogues. Some significant extension in our view of the catalogue and of cataloguing practice would appear inevitable following such convergence. Libraries and other organizations that manage large amounts of information have a great need for increased capacity to deal with the steadily increasing flow of electronic information from a wide variety of sources. Yet this increase is also contributing to the rapid growth in the number, size and complexity of databases. Much of the original search and display software was not designed for such large size and complexity.

- Catalogues are becoming less isolated. Librarians and library users are reaching beyond the online catalogue and venturing out onto the Internet. Comparison of catalogues has become much easier now that a few hundred online catalogues are accessible over the Internet and 'pass-through' connections are making access to multiple online catalogues routinely available to library users. Electronic bulletin boards such as PACS-L greatly enhance the possibilities for discussion and for the rapid dissemination of information and facilitating discussion.
- After years dominated by implementation, experience in using the systems provides a basis for considering what enhancements are needed. Tools are increasingly available for more evidence-based analysis. In particular, the analysis of transaction logs provides a diagnostic tool not available with card catalogues. The literature has, hitherto, often been impressionistic. It need not stay that way. In effect, we have a new window on the user.
- Experimental prototypes are increasingly feasible. The increasing power of low-cost work-stations, decreasing mass storage costs, and the growing availability of large sets of records for experimental purposes makes online catalogue experimentation possible for many more people than before. Technology permits greater flexibility and standardized network protocols are making access to a wide variety of information resources increasingly feasible.

We are now at an exciting juncture. There has been a change in the way that online catalogues are perceived. The initial concern was to connect the online catalogue to the library's technical services system. Now there is interest in relating the online catalogue to online resources everywhere.

On-line catalogues are now evolving into much more than automated card catalogues for a single library's collection. They are changing how library users interact with the library services. If these interpretations are correct, then examination of the difficulties currently encountered in online catalogues and of proposals for improvement become very timely as the online catalogue shifts from being the end-product of technical services to being the framework for bibliographic access.

8

Developing Digital Libraries for Global Children

INTRODUCTION

The International Children's Digital Library (ICDL) was initially created by an interdisciplinary research team at the University of Maryland in cooperation with the Internet Archive.

Members of the team include computer scientists, librarians, educational technologists, classroom teachers, graphic designers, and graduate students from the University of Maryland's (UMD) College of Information Studies (CLIS) and the UMD Human-Computer Interaction Lab (HCIL), a leader in children's interface design.

The mission of the International Children's Digital Library Foundation (ICDL Foundation) is to support the world's children in becoming effective members of the global community - who exhibit tolerance and respect for diverse cultures, languages and ideas by making the best in children's literature available online free of charge.

ICDL: FOUNDATION

- *Collection*: To create a collection of more than 10,000 books in at least 100 languages that is freely available to children, teachers, librarians, parents, and scholars throughout the world via the Internet. The materials included in the collection reflect similarities and differences in cultures, societies, interests, lifestyles, and priorities of peoples around the world. The collection's focus is on identifying materials that help children to understand the world around them and the global society in which they live.
- *Education*: To develop a greater understanding of the relationship between children's access to a digital collection of multicultural materials and children's attitudes towards books, libraries, reading, technology, and other countries and their cultures.

- *Technology*: To collaborate with children as design partners in the development of computer interface technologies that support children in searching, browsing, reading, and sharing books in electronic form.
- *Business*: To provide a platform for operational excellence that insures the Library grows in strict accordance with it strategic priorities and in a manner that leverages its outstanding human and intellectual resources to achieve the Library's mission of reaching as many children as possible with the best of children's literature.

CONTEXT OF EVALUATION

Digital libraries are complex social, institutional and technical systems. No evaluation can possibly address all of these aspects together. Thus, different approaches have been used for different evaluation goals.

Context includes selection of a goal, framework, viewpoint or level(s), basic approach or perspective of evaluation. There are different types of approaches of digital library evaluation on the basis of different aspects. No single approach can exhaustively evaluate the all aspects of any digital library. Here we try to incorporate most of the approaches as possible.

The approaches are:

- *System-centered approach*: Most prevalent. Involves study of some aspect of performance. Includes assessing effectiveness and/or efficiency of some feature or some specific design or some technological component. Applied in a number of studies with results that may inform specific choices in design or operations.
- *Human-centered approach*: Also widely applied. Involves study of behaviour in respect to given information needs, such as information seeking, browsing, searching including performance appraisal of given tasks, either predetermined or observed in natural settings. Used in a number of studies that illuminated human behaviour, requirements, needs, or difficulties encountered. Provides implications for design, but indirectly rather than directly.
- *Usability-centered approach*: Involves assessment of different features, particularly in respect to portals, by users. It is a bridge between systems- and human-centered approaches. Used in several studies with mixed, or self-evident results.
- *Ethnographic approach*: Involves study of life-ways, culture and customs in a digital library environment. Also involves study of impact of a digital library on a given community. Applied successfully in a few studies, with illuminating results, particularly as to impact.
- *Anthropological approach*: Involves study of different stakeholders or communities and their cultures in relation to a given digital library. Applied in one study with interesting results illuminating barriers between stakeholder communities.

- *Sociological approach*: Involves assessment of situated action or user communities in social setting of a digital library. Applied in one study with disappointing results.
- *Economic approach*: Involves study of costs, cost benefits, economic values and impacts. Strangely, it was applied at the outset of digital library history (*e.g.*, project PEAK) but now the approach is not really present at all.

CRITERIA FOR EVALUATION

Criteria reflecting performance as related to selected objectives. They include:

- What parameters of performance were concentrate on?
- What dimension or characteristic were evaluate?
  Criteria refer to chosen standard(s) to judge things by. Criteria are then used to develop measures.
- The importance of criteria follows from this truism: there can be no evaluation without explicitly or implicitly having some criterion or criteria first.Since, 1950's evaluation of IR systems uses relevance as the basic criterion for evaluation. Libraries use a variety of (more or less) standardised criteria for evaluation of components, such as a collection, or services, such as reference. Digital library efforts have not as yet developed anything similar as to evaluation criteria. A summary of most often used criteria follows.

USABILITY

Usability has been used widely in digital library evaluation, but there is no uniform definition of what does it cover in digital library context. Usability is a very general criterion that covers a lot of ground and includes many specific criteria – it is a meta term This was pretty much the umbrella under which usability was used in digital library evaluation. Here is a list of specific usability criteria applied in various studies:

- Content (of a portal or site):
  - Accessibly, availability
  - Clarity (as presented)
  - Complexity (organisation, structure)
  - Informativeness
  - Transparency
  - Understanding, effort to understand
  - Adequacy
  - Coverage, overlap,
  - Quality, accuracy
  - Validity, reliability
  - Authority

- *Process*: Carrying out tasks such as search, navigate, browse, find, evaluate or obtain a resource, etc.
  - learnability to carry out
  - Effort/time to carry out
  - Convenience, ease of use
  - Lostness (confusion)
  - Support for carrying out
  - Completion (achievement of task)
  - Interpretation difficulty
  - Sureness in results
  - Error rate
- Format:
  - Attractiveness
  - Sustaining efforts
  - Consistency
  - Representation of labels (how well are concepts Represented?)
  - communicativeness of messages
- Overall assessment:
  - Satisfaction
  - Success
  - Relevance, usefulness of results
  - Impact, value
  - Quality of experience
  - Barriers, irritability
  - Preferences
  - Learning

SYSTEMS FEATURES

As digital libraries are systems, many traditional systems evaluation criteria were used.

Some pertain to performance of technology others to performance of given processes or algorithms using technology.

- Technology performance:
  - Response time
  - Processing time,
  - Speed
  - Capacity
  - Load
- Process/algorithm performance:
  - Relevance (of obtained results)
  - Clustering
  - Similarity
  - Functionality

  - Flexibility
  - Comparison with human performance
  - Error rate
  - Optimisation
  - Logical decisions
  - Path length
  - Click throughs
  - Retrieval time
- Overall system:
  - Maintainability
  - Scalability
  - Interoperability
  - Sharability
  - Costs

USAGE

A number of studies concentrated on use of a digital library, considering this as evaluation.

Usage in itself is a criterion involving studies of:

- Usage patterns
- Use of materials
- Usage statistics
- Who uses what, when
- For what reasons/decisions

ETHNOGRAPHIC AND OTHER CRITERIA

Several ethnographic and anthropological studies used criteria derived from those fields. Among others, these involve determination of conceptions and misconceptions in and between different groups, their practices and environments, their culture, their language and frames of reference, priorities, learning, impacts and similar aspects that provide comparative evaluation in a broader context of a digital library..

ICDL: EVALUATION METHOD

The range of methods used in digital library evaluations is wide. It would be hard to find a scholarly evaluation method that was not used. It involves: What measures and measuring instruments were used? What samples were used? What procedures were used for data collection? What procedures were used for data analysis? In the present study involves mainly limited user study and systematic study of web site of ICDL with respect to Intel Pentium PCs with MS Windows having 14", 17" and 19" monitors.

Actually methodology includes:

- Surveys, including direct questionnaires and online surveys
- Structured interviews

- Focus groups
- Observations
- Task accomplishment
- Think aloud
- Case studies
- Transaction log analyses
- Experimentation
- Records analysis
- Usage analysis
- Documents, meeting, communication analysis (anthropology)
- Economic analysis

DATA COLLECTION

As the scope is very much little as per time span for evaluation and other constraints, only user survey and web site study were used for data collection.

ICDL: ANALYSIS AND EVALUATION

AUTHORITY

The ICDL was initially created by an interdisciplinary research team at the University of Maryland in cooperation with the Internet Archive. Members of the team include computer scientists, librarians, educational technologists, classroom teachers, graphic designers, and graduate students from the University of Maryland's (UMD) College of Information Studies (CLIS) and the UMD Human-Computer Interaction Lab (HCIL), a leader in children's interface design.

The ICDL is now the principal activity of the independent not-for-profit ICDL Foundation, which continues to work closely with the University of Maryland by providing generous support for ICDL related research in the Human Computer Interaction Laboratory and the College of Information Studies. (The ICDL is a five year project funded primarily by the National Science Foundation (NSF) and the Institute for Museum and Library Services (IMLS) for creating a digital library of international children's books.

This five-year research project, created in collaboration with the Internet Archive and conducted by the University of Maryland, has five primary goals):

- To create a collection of more than 10,000 books in at least 100 languages that is freely available to children, teachers, librarians, parents, and scholars throughout the world via the Internet;
- To collaborate with children as design partners in the development of computer interface technologies that support children in searching, browsing, reading, and sharing books in electronic form;
- to better understand the concepts of rights management and "fair use" in a digital age;

- To evaluate the impact that access to digital materials may have on collection development and programming practices in school and public libraries;
- To develop a greater understanding of the relationship between children's access to a digital collection of multicultural materials and children's attitudes towards books, libraries, reading, technology, and other countries and cultures.

An initial prototype of the ICDL was introduced at a celebration at the Library of Congress in Washington, DC, in November 2002. At that time, the collection consisted of 181 books, which were provided by national libraries and other government agencies, public library systems, collaborating publishers, and individual authors and illustrators. Approximately half of the titles were within copyright protection and half were freely available in the public domain.

The materials selected for the prototype generally were in compliance with the selection criteria established for the collection by the National Advisory Board of Librarians; however, efforts were made to acquire and digitise as diverse a collection as possible to ensure that the functions of the ICDL interface could be effectively tested. Now International Children's Digital Library Foundation manages ICDL. From very beginning ICDL was developed and powered by well-reputed institutions. The ICDL Foundation has famous and scholar personalities in Foundation Directors and Board of Advisors.

AUTHENTI CITY

The information in the web site are very much authentic because the metadata regarding each item/book are explicitly stated with each and every book. Again authority and authenticity are correlated to each other.

COLLECTION/RESOURCES

The collection in the ICDL is comprised of different children books written in different languages. All books consisting of the scanned pages arranged serially. At the end of the initial research period, it is anticipated that the collection of the ICDL will consist of approximately 10,000 materials in at least 100 languages.

Materials within the collection are made available through the Library over the Internet to all users without charge. The project does not support downloading, copying or printing of any materials in the collection.

The materials selected for inclusion in the ICDL are those that:

- Support the understanding of similarities and differences among and within countries, peoples, and cultures;
- Promote tolerance and acceptance;
- Are considered relevant to children in today's world;
- Have a high degree of appeal for children of an age between 3 and 13;

- Meet professionally accepted quality standards in terms of content, format, and presentation; and,
- Can be presented effectively in a digital format.

Relevance

Librarians, teachers, authors, illustrators, publishers, and children from all over the world suggest books that they think should be considered for our collection. Each book must be carefully evaluated before it can be added to the Library. In accordance with the goal of the ICDL, all information are relevant. Again as per the audience is concerned, the books included in the library are of basically children books. The metadata associated with the item are reasonable and relevant.

Formats

The formats of the books in the ICDL are of scanned image.

The digitised formats are obtained through:

- *Choosing books*: The ultimate selection of the books to be scanned.
- *Scanning books*: Books have to be scanned and saved TIFF image format into our database in order to get the book pages into our computers. Scanners take very detailed pictures of pages and save the images in a way that the computers of ICDL can recognise. Some of the books that are scanned for the ICDL are cut up and sucked into a scanner one page at a time to be automatically scanned. Other books are scanned one page at a time without destroying the books. Some of the really old books in the collection have to be repaired before they are scanned because the scanning process could cause them to fall apart. Sometimes the people who donate books scan them for ICDL. Other times the people who work at the ICDL scan them. Sometimes ICDL pay another company to scan books for the library. The technical specification including formats, naming convention and guidelines for scanning are enumerated below:
  - Technical Specifications:
    a. *File Format:* Uncompressed TIFF
    b. *Pixel depth*: 24 bit colour
    c. *Spatial resolution*: 300 dpi
    d. *Example*: Caralic-0001.tif (11.5 MB)
  - Naming Convention:
    a. Filenames should use the format <id>-####.tif where:
       i. <id>

Guidelines

- Scanning of the book cover to cover, including blank pages. Scan 0001 is assumed to be the front cover. If all pages are scanned, there should be an even number of scans. All scans should represent a single page, even if an image spans multiple pages.

- Cropping of the scan to the edge of the page. Clear direction is given to make all scans, including the cover page, the same size and dimensions (*i.e.*, number of pixels), or as close to the same size as possible.
- Scanning of pages with rotated images as they appear in the book.
- Provision of address for contact ICDL authority at icdl-rights@cs.umd.edu if senders have any questions.

Library Materials Selection

Selection Criteria for the ICDL

Materials selected for inclusion in the ICDL collection during the first five years of the project must support the research goals of the project and must be appropriate for one or both of the primary audiences identified as users of the Library.

The materials in the International Children's Digital Library, which are intended primarily to be used by children, parents, teachers, and school and public librarians, should:

- Support the understanding of similarities and differences among and within countries, peoples, and cultures;
- Promote tolerance and acceptance;
- Contribute to children's understanding of the diversity of the global society;
- Have a high degree of appeal for children of an age between 3 and 13;
- Meet professionally accepted quality standards in terms of content, format, and presentation;
- Be considered relevant to children in today's world;
- Be appropriate for the age levels of the intended audience for the collection;
- Be presented in their entirety and not adapted or abridged from their original published form; however, works originally published as abridgements or adaptations of other works may be included in the collection; and
- Be presented effectively in a digital format.
- Expand the scope and variety of cultures represented in the collection;
- Have achieved historical significance;
- Represent exemplary artistic, historic, and literary qualities, such as award winners; or
- Contribute to the project's research priorities.

Acquisitions Process

Materials included in the collection may be:

- Freely available in the public domain;
- Contributed by a National Library or another national agency that holds the rights to the materials;
- Acquired by the ICDL under a contractual agreement with the creator(s) or publisher(s) of the work or with another entity that has legal authority for its intellectual property rights; or
- Collaboratively acquired by the ICDL and other private or public special collections through a contractual agreement with the rights holders

Reconsideration of Materials

Objections to materials included in the collection will be considered by the ICDL National Advisory Board of Librarians and/or the International Advisory Board.

The Board(s) will use the established selection criteria in determining whether the item is appropriate for the collection. The recommendation of the Board(s) will be given to the Director of Collection Development for the Library. The final decision concerning the retention or withdrawal of a work will be made by the Director of Collection Development.

USER INTERFACE

All web sites particularly a digital library is only as good as its interface. The interface is the entry point into the library. The user interface is the aggregate of means by which people (the users) interact with a particular machine, device, computer programme or other complex tool (the system). The user interface provides means of: Input - allowing the users to control the system, Output - allowing the system to inform. The junction between a user and a computer programme.

User interface design important for several reasons.

- First of all the more intuitive the user interface the easier it is to use, and the easier it is to use and the less expensive to use it.
- The better the user interface the easier it is to train people to use it, reducing your training costs.
- The better your user interface the less help people will need to use it, reducing your support costs.
- The better your user interface the more your users will like to use it, increasing their satisfaction with the work that you have done.

The ICDL uses Graphical User Interface (GUI) that takes advantage of the computer's graphics capabilities to make the programme easier to use.

In ICDL, as maximum users are of 3-13 years age group, the GUI is appropriate.

The ICDL interface uses most of the basic components of GUI such as:

- *Pointing device*: The mouse that enables users to select objects on the display screen.
- *Icons*: Small pictures that represent commands, files, or windows. By moving the pointer to the icon and pressing a mouse button, users can execute a command or convert the icon into a window.
- *Desktop*: The area on the display screen where icons are grouped is often referred to as the desktop because the icons are intended to represent real objects on a real desktop. The ICDL interface is comprising of well-grouped desktop.
- *Windows*: In ICDL interface no such frames are used by dividing the screen into different areas where in each window user can run different programmes. But there is the possibility of opening separate window for certain purpose.
- *Menus*: Most graphical user interfaces let the users to execute commands by selecting a choice from a menu. The ICDL uses different menus and drop-down sub-menus in each menu for various information. The animated presentations of menus create a attracting and elegant effect.

Presentation

Overall presentation of web site is quite satisfactory in ICDL. It includes:

- *Information flow*: Information flow throughout the web site is very much impressive.
- *Navigation*: One can search or browse the required information directly by using different attributes that are relevant for the children. Different types of book reader are there for presenting the pages of the book.
- Again the options like next page, zoom in, zoom out etc are present for smooth navigation.
- *Visuals and icons*: Meaningful icons and graphics are used that create a pleasant flavour to the eye.
- *About texts*: Texts are legible and nicely looking.
- *Working with colour*: Colours used for the different components are really attractive and eye appealing mainly for the children.
- *Screen design and layout*: The ICDL uses tables for accommodating various elements of the web page.

Consistencey

Consistency must be acquired in many fields like visual appearance, control, and functionality, etc., for increasing the recall of the users. It includes:

- Different functions keys always have the same effects throughout the site.
- Prompt and help messages appear in the same way and the same place throughout
- Different colours used in the web site always have the same meaning
- Consistent use of headings
- Consistent use of terminologies and abbreviations throughout
- The main menus appeared on the top portion of the home page is absent in the other subsequent pages.

Organisation

The organisation of the information and different components of the web pages are very important for the users. The proper organisation may lead easy navigation of the relevant information the user needed.

It includes:

- Relative positions of different information in the page are nicely organised.
- Right linking of relevant information
- Well positioning of functional keys
- Inclusions of all relevant information in the small space mainly in case of advance search.
- Getting of information by minimal mouse clicking
- Systematic organisation of information so that users get the information they need by minimum scrolling of pages

Interactiveness

It includes dynamic nature of pages where web page cans response to the users. It is very much effective a informative web site like digital library. The ICDL has provisions of interactivity. In the searching mode, the Boolean search is very much interactive to the user's search query.

Attractiveness

It includes overall getup of the site.

It may comprising of:

- Use of proper colours in accordance with the children's liking and choice
- Use of different graphics instead of texts.
- Use of colorful cartoon-like icons
- In location search there is the provision of graphical search by using world map which is very attractive to the children

User Friendliness

User friendliness is the ultimate aims of user interface. The design should be synchronise with the user's needs and behaviours. The ICDL web site is very user friendly. The target audience, *i.e.,* children of different geographical and linguistic regions of the world, can easily find their relevant information through easy navigational tools.

There are various provisions of browsing and searching of books. In case of Boolean search, the search phrase formulation is shown in the page explicitly (e.g. Main collection AND Ten to thirteen AND Pink covers AND hobbies and crafts = 1 Books). In every searching and browsing mode there is the provision of language of the book, which is very much user friendly as per the children of diverse linguistic regions are concerned. Again country wise books are also useful for the wide range of children.

USE, USAGE AND USABILITY

The usage and usability of digital library is gaining the focal point of study. Actually the use of any digital object is the ultimate objective of any web site or digital library. Therefore the information must be uniform, consistent and well-organised, so that one can retrieve the relevant information by using navigational tools. The ICDL can be accessed through the commercial search engine like Yahoo, Google, etc.

The following search data are shown:

- Google search engine:
  - Search by the term 'ICDL' fetched 775000 listing in 0.12 seconds.
  - Search by 'international children's digital library' lists 3520000 sites in 0.11 seconds
  - Search by exact phrase "international children's digital library" through advanced search fetched 96800 listing in 0.14 seconds
- Yahoo Search Engine:
  - Search by the term 'ICDL' fetched 775000 listing in 0.12 seconds.
  - Search by 'international children's digital library' lists 3810000 sites in 0.02 seconds
  - Search by exact phrase "international children's digital library" through advanced search fetched 63500 listing in 0.31 seconds
- Use and users' statistics:
  - The ICDL has been visited by over a million unique visitors since, the launch in November, 2002.
  - Google is the number one Web site directing Internet users to the ICDL, followed by Farsibooksonline and Yahoo.
  - The users come from 166 different countries, most frequently from:
    a. United States (50%)
    b. South Africa (15%)
    c. China (7%)
    d. United Kingdom (6%)

e. Canada (5%)
f. Iran, Islamic Republic of (4%)
g. Taiwan (4%)
h. Philippines (4%)
i. Australia (3%)
j. Egypt (2%)

- *Top books visited*: Our book preview pages have been visited over 650,000 times.
- *Book reader*: Our standard book reader is chosen most of the time to read books in the ICDL. The book readers receive the following use:a.Standard reader (52%) b.Adobe reader (23%) c.Comic reader (15%) d.Spiral reader (9%) e.Plus reader (1%)
- *Registered users*: On May 25, 2005, we launched a new interface that allows library users to log in with a user name and password. Currently, registered users can choose their preferred search interface and what language the library appears in. Kids can also choose a monster to guard their password. In the future, users will be able to personalise their search results, save favorite books on a bookshelf, and return to the last page they were reading. Here are some facts about our registered users:
  a. 1082 adults, 508 children -1031 females, 560 males,Preferred languages (of the nine languages the library is currently available in):
     i. English (72%)
     ii. Spanish (11%)
     iii. Chinese (5%)
     iv. Persian (4%)
     v. Arabic (4%)
     vi. Filipino (1%)
     vii. French (1%)
     viii. German (1%)
     ix. Hebrew (1%)
  b. Adults can choose their preferred search interface, and they choose Simple Search 73% of the time, followed by Advanced (24%), and Location (3%).
- Connectivity: The connection speed of our users breaks down to 17% dial-up, 40% high-speed, and 43% unknown.

From the data we can conclude that the library is used by varieties of users in all respect. We can say that the usability of ICDL is good as the aims of the Foundation is concerned. But still there are some scope of attaining the degree of usage and usability of the library.

Different usage and usability criteria used in ICDL and gaps if any are enumerated below.

- Graphics,
- Text,
- Content/Information
- Updates
- Layout/Space
- Presentation of information: It concerns the implications of using colours, fonts and display styles to present information. The colours used in the ICDL pages are very much eye soothing and also attractive. The display styles for pages in the book are very lucrative in the spiral reader.
- Categorisation of Information
- Navigation,
- Colour,
- Visual Appearance,
- Advertisements/Pop-ups/Animation,
- *Downloading Time*: It includes factors in designing that impacts speed of downloading. As all pages of books in the library are of scanned images, it takes some amount of time to be downloaded.

SECURITY/PRIVACY

Security/privacy is the vital issue for any digital library. The ICDL states "Feel secure using the ICDL knowing that we protect the privacy of our members, especially children".

The International Children's Digital Library (ICDL) is committed to protecting the safety and privacy of the users, especially children. The ICDL does not require anyone to provide any personal information to use the site and no one is excluded from the site for not providing personal information. The ICDL does allow users to create an optional profile that provides access to extra features such as selecting a preferred reading language.

If a user chooses to create a profile, ICDL ask them to provide the following personal but not personally-identifiable information (only a user name and password, etc., are required):

- User name
- Password
- Age
- Gender
- Preferred reading language

users who register may choose to use their e-mail address as their user name. This information will only be used for two purposes. First, it allows the ICDL to send users a new password if they forget their old one. Second, adult users who register with their e-mail address may also opt to be on our mailing list to receive announcements about the ICDL

COST EFFECTIVENESS

As information are only accessed through network, the cost effectiveness is the vital issue when evaluating a digital library. The books can be accessed in ICDL without paying any money; it is absolutely free of cost.

SERVICES: REAL LIFE SITUATION

Services are comprised of searching and browsing of relevant information using the various tools provided in the web site. This is the ultimate objective of any digital library.

The search statistics may help to develop better interface. Between May 25, 2005 and August 31, 2005, ICDL looked at what the library users were searching for. This data helped to improve the search interfaces and understood what library users are looking for in a digital library and accordingly new interface was designed on March 22, 2006. Users overwhelming prefer the Simple search interface. The usage of the various search interfaces breaks down to the following:

- Simple search (71%)
- Advanced search (15%)
- Text or keyword search (10%)
- Location search (3%)
- Author search (1%).

Availability

Most of the books included in the ICDL are always available through the searching and browsing tools. Actually I tried for 100 books and no such false link is there.

As the total collection is not verified I prefer to use the term 'most of the books'.

Searchability

Searchability basically includes effectiveness in searching and browsing so as to get required pages of the books. At first it is better to enumerate the provisions of searching and browsing in the ICDL site.

Searching

Simple Search

Various search facilities are there in the simple search. The menus/icons are arranged in four sides of the page. The provisions are: Location search In location search there are two versions.

- Graphical version using globe having world map and provision for turning the globe by clicking the arrow provided for the purpose. This is effective for little children who just learning the locations in the world map.
- Text version by using names of continents and countries.

Advanced Search

Advance search is composed of using various criteria for single search. Actually it is Boolean search using only AND operator.

The criteria are:

- Keywords
- Language
- Audience: Age, collection, etc.
- Appearance: Cover colour, format, length, shape, etc.
- Content: Continents, character, countries, time period
- Type: Feeling, rating, etc.
- Subject: Culture, history, science and nature, animals, etc.

The beauty of advance search is "unified search using more than one criteria used in the simple search at a time". The stating of search formulation statement is another effective feature in the advance search. The statement (e.g. Main collection AND Ten to thirteen AND Pink covers AND Hobbies and crafts= 1 Books) may increase the confidence of the users.

Keyword Search

As the pages of the books are of scanned image in TIFF format and no provision of using OCR technology, full text search is not possible. It only includes the meta-information about the books.

Directions:

- Typing the keywords into the search box
- Selecting the language user is searching in from the pull down menu
- Clicking the Search button to search for books with matching information

Browsing

Browsing of books will be done through four ways mentioned below:

- Recently added books
- Award-winning books
- Full book list
- Author and illustrator list

The browsing through Author and Illustrator list are effective but there are the oddness:

- No such indication element for author and illustrator; names are alphabetically arranged according to the surnames but no rendering of names are there which create confusion to some extent.

Referral

The ICDL provides referral service by mentioning link through which one can get the books. When we select any book, the metadata are listed in the right side to the cover/title image of the book. At the end of metadata, there are the provisions of links stating the addresses of the organisations from which one can purchase the same.

Links

The links in the web site are very much systematic and relevant. Not so false link is there in the page so far as my verification is concerned.. The links in the 'announcement' in the home page is not retrieved.

After selecting a book to be retrieved there is the provision of link to the similar books available in the ICDL. No such external links are there for similar books the ICDL has. The links among the different pages are explicitly shown in the Sitemap menu.

POLICY

The policy of any digital library like ICDL, includes the written guidelines for attaining consistency and effectiveness in the web pages. The policy in the present study is comprised of collection development, copyright, privacy and link.

Collection Development Policy

Examination of the criteria used to select books that are appropriate for the ICDL collection. All works will be presented in their entirety and will not be adapted or abridged from their original published form; however, works originally published as abridgements or adaptations of other works may be included in the collection.

Materials included in the collection may be:

- Currently available in print and within copyright;
- Out of print but within the copyright protection of the country in which they were
- Published; or
- Freely available in the public domain.

Copyright Policy

Find out how ICDL protect the interests of rights holders while sharing their books with audiences throughout the world. The International Children's Digital Library respects the intellectual property rights and other proprietary rights of others.

The ICDL has negotiated rights to include the books in the collection. These rights do not allow downloading, printing, or further distribution of the books in ICDL by the users. To obtain permission to download, print or distribute the books in ICDL, the user must be contacted to the rights holders directly. The ICDL software does not support printing, emailing or saving of material accessible through the ICDL If any user believes that his copyright has been violated by material available through the ICDL, there is clear statement on behave of the ICDL Copyright Agent with the following information:

- Identification of the copyrighted work that user claim has been infringed;
- An exact description of where the material about which user complain is located within the ICDL collection;
- Users address, telephone number, and e-mail address;
- A statement by user that he has a good-faith belief that the disputed use is not authorised by the copyright owner, its agent, or the law;
- A statement by user, made under penalty of perjury, that the information in users notice is accurate and that the users are the owner of the copyright interest involved or are authorised to act on behalf of that owner;

Privacy Policy

ICDL is always trying to protect the privacy of the users/members, especially children. The privacy is maintained particularly for the personal information of the users. More provisions are already analysed in the Security/privacy section.

Links Policy

Links appearing on the ICDL web site must conform to the selection criteria for the books included in the collection.

The sites linked should expand, enhance, and support books included in the collection.

Sites linked to the ICDL must:1.Have a high degree of appeal for children from ages 3-13; 2.Support the understanding and use of books in the collection; 3.Be appropriate for the age levels of the intended audience for the collection; 4.Include content that is relevant and of interest to children ages 3-13; 5.Support the understanding of similarities and difference among and within countries, peoples, and cultures; 6.Contribute to children's understanding of the diversity of the global society; and, 7..Meet professionally accepted quality standards in terms of content, format, and presentation.

LEGAL ASPECTS

Some books are very old and others are just like those that user might find in school or public library. Most of the old books are out of copyright. This means that nobody owns these books so ICDL Foundation can put them on the ICDL without getting permission from anybody.

For the newer books, the authority must get permission from the people or the company that owns the words and the pictures in the books. All of the books in the ICDL must meet the collection development standards. These standards are the rules that use to choose which books can go into the ICDL. The Advisory Board of Librarians and International Advisory Board created the rules for the purpose. Some of the legal aspects are included in the section 'Copyright policy'.

CONSTRAINS

- No main menus in the same fashion in the pages other than home page.
- No links in few places
- The ICDL software does not support printing, emailing or saving of material accessible through the ICDL
- No born digital objects are included in the ICDL
- External hyperlinks are few
- Some contradictory data exit
- The scanned pages need to remove noise
- No provisions of audio that are interesting to the intended audience
- No provision of machine translation

RECOMMENDATIONS

The ICDL has its strong objectives and planned policy. According to the aims and objectives of ICDL Foundation, the web site of International Children's Digital Library is very impressive in all respect.

Still some recommendations are given for the overall development of the ICDL.

- Some good animations may be inserted to the menus/icons to add the extra flavour
- Besides books, some non-book material like audio, video, animation, etc., may be included to instigate appetite of the children
- The scope will be given for inclusion of born digital books
- Digital noise in the scanned images have to be removed for better viewing the pages
- Some external links for similar information may be sited to the web page

CONCLUSION

In conclusions, as per the aims and objectives are taking into consideration, the ICDL is unparallel. They strictly follow the pre-defined policy. The ICDL always promote cross-cultural development among children, and therefore it intentionally not use the machine translation.

But it mentions some volunteer translator for the same. Within a short period of time ICDL has flourished rapidly in wellorganised way. It maintains the list having date wise addition of books in the collection. The ICDL is very transparent in its each policy and function.

Bibliography

A.K. Gupta: *Digital Library and Education*, Pearl Books, Delhi, 2012. Ajay K. Srivastav: *Digital Library Environment and Networking*, Sree Publication, Delhi, 2006.

Ajit Singh: *Information Technology and Library Sciences*, Ancient Publication, Delhi, 2011.

Amjad Ali: *Information Technology and Libraries*, Ess Ess Publication, Delhi, 2004.

Ann Peterson Bishop, Nancy A Van House and Barbara P Buttenfield: *Digital Library Use : Social Practice in Design and Evaluation*, Ane Books Pvt. Ltd., Delhi, 2005.

Cheriyan Mathew: *Current Trends in Library Services*, Cyber Tech Publications, New Delhi, 2011.

G.K. Sampath Kumar: *Digital Library Automation Planning Designing and Development*, Akhand Publication, Delhi, 2012.

G.K. Singh: *Principles of Digital Library Development*, Shree Publication, Delhi, 2004.

J. Sridevi and Vijay Laxshmi: *Model of Digital Library*, Shree Publication, Delhi, 2004.

K. Nazeer Badhusha: *Digital Library Architecture*, Ane Books Pvt. Ltd., Delhi, 2008.

K. Rajasekaran, R. Raman Nair and K.M. Nafala: *Digital Library Basics: A Practical Manual (With Software CD Inside)*, Ess Ess Publication, Delhi, 2010.

K. Veeranjaneyulu, Rabindra K. Mahapatra and P. Visakhi: *Library* Services in the Knowledge Web (Collection of Papers in Honour *of Dr. Stanley Madan Kumar)*, New India Publishing Agency, Delhi, 2012.

Kusum Verma: *Digital Library and Information Developments*, Vista International Publication House, Delhi, 2008.

Kusum Verma: *Digital Library Preservation Strategies*, Akansha Publication, Delhi, 2005.

Kusum Verma: *Metadata and Digital Library Systems*, Akansha Publication, Delhi, 2004.

M. Suriya, L.N. Uma Devi, R. Vijay Arumugam, V. Ganesh and V. Parthasarathy: *ICT and Library Services*, APH Publication, Delhi, 2011.

Mahendra Nath: *Handbook of Library Services*, Pointer Publication, New Delhi, 2001.

Mange Ram and Ram Chander: *Recent Trends in Library Services*, Vayu Education of

India, Delhi, 2011.

Omesh Aadhavan: *Development of Digital Library*, Oxford Book Company, Delhi, 2010.

Omesh Aadhavan: *Management of Digital Library*, Oxford Book Company, Delhi, 2010.

Pramod Kumar Singh: *Digitised Methods of Library Services*, Shree Publication, Delhi, 2004.

Purushotham Tiwari: *Digital Library*, APH Publication, Delhi, 2014.

Purushotham Tiwari: *Information Technology and Library Evolution*, APH Publication, Delhi, 2012.

R C Ganguly: *Transformation of Library Services*, Isha Books, Delhi, 2007.

R.C. Chakravarthy and P.R.S. Murthy: *Information Technology and Library Science*, Pacific Books International, Delhi, 2012.

R.C. Chakravarthy and P.R.S. Murthy: *Information Technology and Rural Development*, Pacific Books International, Delhi, 2012.

R.C. Mishra: *Information Technology and Poverty Reduction in South Asia*, Authors Press, Delhi, 2003.

R.K. Singh: *Basic Facts of Digital Library*, Shree Publication, Delhi, 2004.

R.K. Tailor: *Information Technology for Management*, RBSA Publication, Jaipur, 2010.

Raghunath Pandey and M.N. Velayudhan Pillai: *Digital Library : Trends and Prospects*, Jnanada Prakashan, Delhi, 2011.

Raghunath Pandey and M.N. Velayudhan Pillai: *Modern Library Services*, Jnanada Prakashan, Delhi, 2011.

Rashmi Upadhyay: *Digital Library Management*, Alfa Publication, Delhi, 2011.

S.C. Dwivedi: *Digital Library (2 Vols-Set)*, Shree Publication, Delhi, 2005.

Sandhya Aggarwal and R.D. Mehla: *Library Services : Challenges and Solutions in Digital Era*, Ess Ess Publications, Delhi, 2012.

Savita Mittal: *Digital Library Resources*, Ess Ess Publication, Delhi, 2005.

Tariq Ashraf: *Library Services in Electronic Environment : Changes Challenges Issues and Strategies*, Kaveri Publication, Delhi, 2004.

V.K. Iyenger: *Digital Library Use : Librarian's Guide to Internet*, Arise Publication, Delhi, 2011.

V.K. Jain: *Information Technology for Digital Library Management and Automation*, Atlantic Publication, Delhi, 2009.

V.M. Mohanraj: *Library Services for Children*, Ess Ess Publication, Delhi, 2004.

Vasu Deva: *Information Technology and Marketing Management*, Commonwealth Publication, Delhi, 2003.

Index